"I am an at-home Mum. When I met Karyn, I had absolutely no experience running an online business. She happily gave up a great deal of her time walking me through making my new dream a reality. She has a great wealth of knowledge and experience. Karyn is super approachable. I always feel 100% comfortable about contacting her whenever I need help. With Karyn's support, I have been able to not only launch the business but give it a very personal, unique, and creative flair. Using the tools Karyn showed me, I have grown a loyal customer base that is extremely engaged on my social media page. Because of Karyn's coaching, what could have been an expensive gamble has become a highly successful online business. This brought thousands of dollars to my family during the Melbourne lockdown."

—Rae Schwartz

Founder of Tupper-rae, Direct Seller

"Karyn is a born leader and works immensely hard. I have never witnessed such grit and dedication; she chooses to do whatever it takes to get her work done. The CEO of our company entrusted her with the task of launching and growing our company in Australia after having been with us for just a couple of weeks. Our CEO, a highly successful businessman, has personally met with Karyn to plan his vision for immense growth within Australia. Karyn is a true inspiration; she is talented and honest, and I am so proud that I have the privilege of working with her and calling her my friend."

—Julie Ludwig Kelly

Founder of Julie Kelly, Entrepreneur, Mentor & Coach

"Karyn is a leader and entrepreneur making an impact. She supports and trains those who want to build a business using digital marketing. If you are looking for a mentor, I highly recommend her."

—Chef Katrina Van Oudhousden

Founder of Marketing Ingredients LLC,

Speaker & Business Marketing Mentor

BOUNDLESS SUCCESS

with **KARYN MAHONEY**

ALSO FEATURING
OTHER TOP AUTHORS

© 2021 Success Publishing

Success Publishing, LLC
P.O. Box 703536
Dallas, Texas 75370 USA

questions@mattmorris.com

All rights reserved. No part of this book may be reproduced, stored in a retrieval system, or transmitted in any form or by any means - electronic or mechanical, photocopy, recording, or any other - except for brief quotations in printed reviews, without the prior permission of the publisher. Although the author(s) and publisher have made every effort to ensure the accuracy and completeness of information contained in this book, we assume no responsibility for errors, inaccuracies, omissions, or any inconsistency herein.

Table of Contents

1. Solving The Rubik's Cube Of Network Marketing 9
   By Karyn Mahoney

2. From Bound To Boundless 17
   By Matt Morris

3. Scared Shitless 25
   By Steve Moreland

4. Dream, Struggle, Victory 33
   By David He

5. From Struggle To Magic 39
   By Aina Brandholm

6. Why Not You? 47
   By Allan Main

7. Finding Your Purpose 55
   By Amanda Meyer

8. Becoming A Leader While Hiding In Plain Sight 61
   By Anita Renee Blue

9. Up From Stinky Thinking 69
   By Cecelia Williams

10. When Passion Becomes Purpose 75
    By Dolly van Zaane

11. The Day I Took Control Of My Emotions 81
    By Frederik van Rensburg

12. The Journey 87
    By Gregory Stack

13. The Gold In Consistency 93
    By Hadassah Were

14. Tapestry 101
    By James A. Railey

15. What's Missing In Leadership? 107
    By John N. Harris, Jr.

16. The Refining Process 113
    By Karen Westerman

17. Perspective Unlimited 119
    By Kristie Jensen

18. Fight To The Finish 125
    By Keith and Lakeisha McKnight

19. The Vacation Principle 133
    By Lee Murch

20. Taking Full Responsibility For My Piece Of The
    American Dream 141
    By Leslie K Williams

21. The Power Of Choices 147
    By Lynda Nabayiinda Were

22. So What? Who Cares? 157
    By Mary Etta Dockery

23. Success As A Choice 163
    By Moetini Tihoni

24. Successful Thinking 171
    By Paul Prinsloo

25. The Power Of Authenticity 177
    By Priscilla Olson

26. Change Your Thoughts And Change Your Life 183
    By Rick Dorr

27. From One Acorn A Thousand Forests Are Born 189
    By Ry Fry

28. Letting The Cat Out Of The Bag 197
    By Sandy Lowe

29. When Adversity Came Knocking, It Was Game On This Time! . . 203
    By Steven Stemberger

30. Awakening 211
    By Winston Broderick

31. There Is Light At The End Of Every Tunnel 217
    By Yeliz Nuray

32. The Person You Fight To Become 223
    By Inez Kuz

CHAPTER 1

Solving The Rubik's Cube Of Network Marketing

By Karyn Mahoney

Ever feel like you are trapped in a Rubik's cube while trying to work out how to get through this journey of network marketing? That's how I felt for twenty plus years. It's a puzzle other people seem to be able to work out but not me.

I have joined many opportunities; some I've done well at and others not so well. I even became a manager and had a small team under me. My biggest achievement was being the No.1 New Manager for the year 2016 in my distributorship. I still hold the record for most sales in one week for a New Manager—$14K plus.

So, I worked out that not being successful must come down to me, but ...

Did I even have the desire, motivation, or determination to get there?

After paying thousands of dollars over the years for mentors and coaches, why isn't success happening for me?

I read self-development books; I do all the training. Still, it wasn't working. I couldn't figure out why I wasn't a success yet!

The words "mindset" or "find your Why" drives me nuts: I don't have kids, so I don't really have that "why" parents seem to have. Yeah, I want the nice house and not having to worry about where the money is coming from to pay the bills. But I don't want to slave for someone else at a 9 to 5 job.

Mindset. Find your WHY. Blah! If it were that easy, wouldn't everyone be successful?

I joined a few other opportunities, each time thinking, "this will be the one, I know it!"

Then 2020 happened; my trip to Bali got canceled. That was okay—I could go without a holiday—but I could not stop thinking about my beautiful Bali family—Gday, my driver, his wife Arick (my Bali sister), and their kids—how they would survive with no work? How would they feed their kids? How would they pay the rent? I didn't sleep well because I knew that if they were struggling, then many others were too.

My best friend was also struggling to buy nappies for her little girl, toilet paper, wipes, and many other essentials she needed for her family. I recently made the decision to move interstate, so I was not there to help. I sent my best friend a voucher for an online store, so she could get what she needed.

I also took a collection up between family and friends to send Gday and Arick money to help them feed their family and loved ones, but that would not keep them going. And how many other families were and are still suffering?

Arick was about to have a baby, and they were so grateful for the money.

A few months later, their newborn baby ended up in hospital with a lung infection. That was scary, as Bali's hospitals and services are not as well-equipped as those here in Australia. Plus, I knew the cost would cripple the family, who struggled as it was.

Then Arick called me in tears; I could hear the fear in her voice. Not just for her baby but for her whole family. She told me they had already sold the car (Gday's pride and joy) and all the jewelry they owned. I could not sit and do nothing. Again, I did a collection drive and raised more money, so at least they could give the hospital some money and feed the family.

I cried myself to sleep that night, feeling so helpless. How could I help from here in Australia? How could I make a difference to people who are in need—I mean real need.

Then it hit me—I suddenly had my WHY!

After all these years, I now knew what my mentors and coaches meant when they talked about finding your WHY.

I want to create a legacy based on helping those in need and can't help themselves.

Something else I always wanted to do since having my own team in my direct sales business is to help entrepreneurs put into action what they learn. I had this vision of people from different companies all working together, sharing knowledge. I have a saying, "Knowledge Shared Is Power," which means helping each other out and learning from each other.

Something a lot of people do is attend training after training and look busy; it makes them feel like they are taking action. But are they really?

Now that I had my Why, suddenly, my mindset came along for the ride.

Mindset and your Why are everything; just keep looking until you find them. All the knowledge you gain in the meantime will come in handy, I can assure you. I am now enjoying my journey and not finding it so frustrating. Yes, there are still ups and downs, but the difference is that now I know I can get through them and that most successful people have been through them too.

It is a tough journey but worth it in the end.

Only those willing to work at the Rubik's cube will solve it. If you keep putting it aside, saying I can't do it, it's too hard, then it will be. Never give up, keep trying, keep learning. Once I work something out, I just want to show others how to do it.

It doesn't matter what others think, especially your family and friends. They love you so much they are fearful for you. People fear change—in themselves and others. They are fearful you will fail, but failing is required in this industry, several times if possible. It will make you more knowledgeable, more determined, and into someone to whom others can go when they feel like giving up, to show them it can be done.

Don't fear change, embrace it—fail forward!

When I got over worrying about how others perceive me, I got over my fear, started taking action, and began seeing results.

Taking action eliminates fear!

Surround yourself with like-minded people, those who understand your craziness and passion for achieving. Surround yourself with people who bring out the best in you and learn lessons from those who have already achieved what you want.

No coach is teaching anything new; success lies in how they put the information across and how you relate to it. Find coaches and mentors with whom you can relate. Keep looking until you find that coach and community that will support you one hundred percent.

The biggest change in my mindset was when I found the right mentors and community to support me.

Another piece to the Rubik's cube I needed to solve was acknowledging that people DO need to hear my story, my lesson, my WHY. Imagine if it helped them write their first book, make their first sale, or their first million!

Everything I experienced in my life gave me the strength to keep going when it got hard. Over the past twenty years, one of the hardest things was coming to terms with my partner committing suicide

Then came a bad breakup with another long-term partner that caused me much anxiety. Ten years of a near-perfect relationship, and then he changed dramatically. Then, there were two years of suffering, with him bordering on getting physically abusive and me realizing he was on ICE. I finally decided to leave. I packed a suitcase and stayed with one of my old bosses I was still close to. I didn't want my partner to harass my friends.

The hardest thing was: it was MY house, not his, but I had to leave!

Barry did start to harass my friends—going to my best friend's house and threatening her partner, whom he didn't even know. He went to another friend's house and harassed her tenant, as she had just moved interstate. He even found a list of names and addresses from a baby shower I had thrown for a friend and had gone to nearly every house on the list to find me. One of them called the police on him, and he was charged. But that did not stop him.

One day, not long after I left to go to work, I felt as though a car was following me but dismissed it as nothing more than an idiot driver. I went to pull into a park at the shops, and before I had a chance to get out of the car, I realized it was Barry. I took off quickly, but he followed me and tried to run me off the road. I was so scared. I called the police and told them I was being followed by an ex and was too scared to stop. They told me to put my hazard lights on and keep flashing my lights and honking my horn until I got to the police station. When I got there, I raced out of my car—Barry was right on my tail—and bolted into the police station. The police grabbed me and took me straight out the back and dealt with Barry screaming and yelling at me over the counter.

They did not charge him. Instead, they just let him go. I went back to my boss's house, but by now, Barry had found out where I was and was threatening them too. I thanked my boss and her husband, got in my car, and drove all night to my home state, back to my mum's.

I left MY house, my job, my friends, my life. I left with just a suitcase, and it was hell for the next year or so to get him out of MY house and out of my life. He would call me constantly—I don't know how many numbers I blocked or how many times I changed my number, but he always found a way to get it.

He would call my mum at her work daily, to the point she called me and said, "I can't handle this, Karyn." Uh, Mum, what do you think he is doing to me? I could not be held responsible for his actions, as I had left him.

So, after I finally got him out of my life, I was still left with depression and added anxiety.

The trauma of it all was so bad that I had to stop working as a debt collector and take some time out to heal.

I moved in with my aunt as her caregiver and started another direct selling business—I think my fourth or fifth by that time. And I was running a cleaning business at the same time. I did well for a time, but it didn't seem to be working out as with everything in my life. I was never consistent; I was never able to get that motivation.

Then my aunt suddenly died. I was devastated; she had been my rock. How would I ever get over her loss?

I thought it was the depression and anxiety holding me back for so long, but that's the kind of thing we tell ourselves to explain our lack of success. During some soul searching after my aunt died, I realized I have a fear of failure, but, worse, I also had a fear of <u>success</u>. I would succeed a little, then fall right back because it scared me to think that I might actually have to pull my finger out and take action. I didn't know what to do next—how to scale my business or even if I wanted to.

After so much frustration and hating the cold climate where I was living, I made the choice to move again. I got my aunt's unit ready for sale and sold it on the first open day. I moved to Queensland, the sunshine state.

I have now been here on my little island for nine months, and I am loving life. I am finally reaping the rewards of never giving up and learning the skills needed to succeed.

I finally have worked out some of that Rubik's Cube and can't wait to solve more.

BIOGRAPHY

Karyn Mahoney is an Aussiepreneur Action Coach and a founder of YEP—Young Entrepreneur Project. Karyn is passionate about helping others achieve their dreams. She has been involved in network marketing and direct selling for over twenty years. Karyn achieved No. 1 New Manager in sales for Australia and New Zealand in 2016 and still holds the record for most sold in one week in her distributorship—more than $14K. Karyn also ran a successful AIRBNB Cleaning business on the Mornington Peninsula,

Victoria, Australia. Karyn's vision is to bring knowledge and training with massive action guidance to Aussie business owners, so they can also be successful Aussiepreneurs. Karyn also loves dogs and has fostered many over the years, which her own dog, Koda, loves to help out with. Karyn also helps out raising funds and volunteering for the community and kids on the small Island in Queensland, Australia, where she lives as a caregiver for her uncle.

Contact Karyn Mahoney via https://linktr.ee/KarynMahoney

CHAPTER 2

From Bound To Boundless

By Matt Morris

As a speaker and coach for the past 20 years, I've been blessed to help several thousand people become full-time entrepreneurs with hundreds in the six-figure range and over 50 documented million-dollar earners.

It's also rewarded me with a lifestyle that I never would have imagined as a boy. If you would have told me I'd be a millionaire at twenty-nine, earn eight figures in my thirties and generate several billion in sales, all while adventuring to over 80 countries by my early 40's; I wouldn't have believed you.

I also never imagined I'd be blessed with a career that fills me up with such immense levels of fulfillment and significance, knowing that I've been able to assist so many others in achieving what most would consider "boundless" levels of success.

The question I'm asked all the time is . . . How?

In asking that question, most people are looking for the tactics and strategies. And I'll admit, early in my coaching days, I focused my mentorship almost solely on teaching the how-tos.

Unfortunately, that made me a pretty lousy coach.

I'd give them the tactics that allowed me to become a superstar salesperson, run a multi-million dollar company, or speak powerfully from stage.

My students would apply the how-tos and come back frustrated with mediocre improvements at best.

What I failed to realize in my early coaching days is a quote from the late Brian Klemmer that says, "If how-tos were enough, we'd all be rich, skinny, and happy."

As we explore the secrets to experiencing boundless levels of success, we must first examine what keeps us bound to our current situation.

Hint: It's NOT a lack of tactics and strategies.

With a quick google search, you can find hundreds of YouTube videos and blog posts that will teach you the strategies to having six-pack abs. The reason most don't have that six-pack isn't that they don't know the how-tos.

When it comes to making your goals a reality, whether that be to have a sexy body, to become a top sales leader in your company, to start your own business, or any other worthwhile dream, the ONLY thing holding you back from achieving that goal is your mental programming.

The challenge most face in achieving a grand visionary future for themselves is the fact that it runs so completely contrary to their current vision, or identity, that's running them now.

Your current identity is made up of the beliefs you currently hold to be true about yourself. It's essentially how you genuinely see yourself.

Your personal identity subconsciously influences every decision and action you make (or don't make), thus influencing the level of success you're able to achieve.

If your personal identity is that of someone who is out of shape or overweight, you may go on streaks where you eat right and exercise vigorously, but you tend to always shift right back into your old ways. Irresistible cravings, lethargy, sleeping in, etc., are somehow always overpowering your desire to be fit.

Why is that the case?

You'll want to write this down.

The Law of Commitment and Consistency

The law of commitment and consistency says that we will remain committed to remaining consistent with who we genuinely believe we are.

That being true, we must understand that in order to change our results, we have to change the beliefs we have about ourselves.

Let's take a deep dive into beliefs.

Take a look at the middle three letters of the word "beliefs," and what word do you see?

LIE

Consider for a moment that the story (the beliefs) you've been telling yourself about who you are as a person are simply lies you've made up.

Stories you may have accepted as "fact" like you're:

- Shy
- Self-conscious
- Lack self-confidence
- Not a morning person
- Afraid of public speaking
- Not a good communicator
- Not as smart as the others

Would it be empowering to know that any of the negative beliefs above, along with countless others, are nothing more than lies you created subconsciously through a belief-building process you went through and didn't even know you were going through it?

What makes me so certain these "character traits" are lies? Because I had all of those beliefs about myself that I once accepted as fact.

Today, if you told me I was any of those things, I would laugh in your face because it would be completely absurd in my mind to accept any of those as true.

If you're willing to take a journey with me, I'll show you how I literally rewrote my entire identity from a broke, scarcity-filled, self-conscious young man into a confident and powerful multi-millionaire.

I'm here to tell you that whatever limiting beliefs you've created for yourself are absolute and total crap. I'm proof of it and many of those I've mentored for the past 20 years are proof of it.

I don't know what lies about yourself you've accepted as fact, but I know beyond a shadow of a doubt that, at your core, you are not a bad communicator, you are not unworthy of finding love, you are not a failure, you are not destined to always struggle, or any other negative belief.

Whatever they might be, you have the power to change those disempowering beliefs that serve only to limit the amount of success and personal fulfillment you experience.

If your current beliefs are what determine your success, the big question becomes how do you change your beliefs to create the results you want?

Before we answer that question, you first need to understand what shapes your beliefs in the first place. What has caused you to hold the beliefs that you do? Understanding where they came from will help you change them.

The belief building process you went through to come up with the beliefs you currently hold to be true have been shaped by three main factors:

1. Experiences
2. External programming
3. Internal programming

Experiences:

Every experience you've ever been through has been forever deposited and stored somewhere in your subconscious mind.

Maybe you were teased as a kid in school because you stuttered, and now you believe you're a poor communicator. Maybe, you were laughed at in class as a kid for giving the wrong answer, and you took on a belief that you're not as smart as the other kids. Maybe you made a few horrible business choices when you were first starting out, and now you think you're lousy in business.

Whether you've realized it before now or not, those deposits were the first major factor that gave you the foundation of your identity.

Here's the way it works . . .

An event happens and then you make up a story (a belief) about what that event means.

Most of us tend to create a negative meaning based on what we perceive to be a negative experience. We create a victim story – I'm not loved because my parent abused me or left me. I'm a terrible business person because I failed for five years. People are not trustworthy because my business partner stole from me (all personal stories I made up at one point).

Think about some examples from your past. Can you think of some examples of events where you created a negative belief?

Real power comes from understanding that nothing has meaning until we give it meaning.

Events are neutral. It's the story we make up from the event that holds all the power. Rather than the victim story you may have been running in your mind, how can you create a new and empowering meaning based on that experience?

Understand – you have the power to choose. Victim or Victor. Which will it be?

External Programming:

Whether you want to believe this or not, you've been programmed.

Your parents programmed you as a child to believe certain things about yourself, other people, money, religion, and many other things.

The school system, your friends, the media, television, and other factors have programmed you to believe many of the things you do today.

Some of this programming has likely been healthy and gotten you to where you are and built you into the person you are today. Unfortunately, we also all have some less than empowering beliefs, and associated fears, that we've adopted as well from that external programing.

By the time you were two years old, you heard the word no thousands of times more than you heard the word yes. It's no wonder so many people, when presented with an opportunity to start a business or take on a challenge, are paralyzed with fear and are hesitant to take action.

At some point in your life, you've most likely faced a moment where someone said something negative to you or doubted your ability, without even meaning to. For a lot of people, that first comes from their parents and family members.

The things that people say to you, whether they intentionally mean harm or not, can profoundly shape who you are—*but only if you let it*. You obviously can't go back into the past and change the negative things you've heard, but you can make the decision right now to no longer let those things define you.

You can recognize that what someone says about you has no basis in reality unless you *choose* to believe it. It's a choice. A choice you can start making right now, today, to say **no more**.

Internal Programming:

More than your experiences and more than the voices of the people around you, the greatest and most powerful way your beliefs are shaped is from your internal programming. Thankfully, it's also the mechanism you have the most control over.

Every word that comes out of your mouth and every thought that comes out of your mind serves as a programming tool. Those thoughts and words get entered into your subconscious mind and then work to create your habitual routines and mental thought patterns.

Psychologists who study brain science agree that your subconscious mind is infinitely more powerful than your conscious mind. The subconscious is the driving force behind your belief system and your identity.

The subconscious mind has a goal that can serve you negatively or positively. That goal is to keep you in line with your identity. Remember the law of commitment and consistency?

If, based on your regular programming, you tell yourself you're broke, you're tired, and you suck as an entrepreneur, your subconscious mind figures out a way to keep you consistent with that programming.

If, however, you continually tell yourself you're wealthy, you're energized, and you're an amazing entrepreneur, your subconscious mind begins doing everything in its power to create *that* reality.

Here's the best way to understand it.

Whatever you say about yourself makes it more true.

If you say, *"I'm an idiot,"* you become more of an idiot. If you say, *"I'm a genius,"* you become more of a genius.

Your consistent programming creates your identity.

Here's the trick; your subconscious mind does not know the difference between the truth and a lie. It simply does its best to carry out exactly what you've programmed it to believe.

So when you say, "I'm sexy, I'm confident, I'm a millionaire," your conscious mind might be telling you you're full of it, but your subconscious mind, which is where the true power lies, will take that as a command and start working out a way for you to be all of those things.

The key to reprogramming your subconscious and change your deep-seeded beliefs is to change your deposits. You do this by constantly filling your subconscious mind with empowering, uplifting, and motivating thoughts and words.

If you continually profess what you don't want, or focus on the things you don't have or aren't, then you actually attract more of that negativity and continue to reinforce more of that personal identity. ***What you focus on expands***.

BIOGRAPHY

Author of the international bestseller, *The Unemployed Millionaire*, Matt Morris began his career as a serial entrepreneur aged eighteen. Since then, he has generated over $1.5 billion through his sales organizations, with a total of over one million customers worldwide. As a self-made millionaire and one of the top internet and network marketing experts, he's been featured on international radio and television and spoken from platforms to audiences in over twenty-five countries around the world. And now, as the founder of Success Publishing, he co-authors with leading experts from every walk of life.

Contact Matt Morris via http://www.MattMorris.com

CHAPTER 3

Scared Shitless

By Steve Moreland

How do you keep from tossing in the towel at age thirty-five because a twenty-five-year prison sentence for crimes you did not commit is just a bridge too far?

As I read G. K. Chesterton's book *Orthodoxy* one night inside that icy, cement cell, it felt like a ray of hope had pierced the dark maze that often felt like a grave.

> "Courage is almost a contradiction in terms. Valor means a strong desire to live, taking the form of a readiness to die. 'He that will lose his life, the same shall save it' is not a piece of mysticism for saints and heroes. It is a piece of everyday advice for sailors and mountaineers. It might be printed in an Alpine guide or a drill book. The paradox is the whole principle of courage, even of quite earthly or quite brutal courage. A man cut off by the sea may save his life if he will risk it on the precipice. He can only get away from death by continually stepping within an inch of it. A soldier surrounded by enemies, if he is to cut his way out, needs to combine a strong desire

for living with a strange carelessness about dying. He must not merely cling to life, for then he will be a coward, and will not escape. He must not merely wait for death, for then he will be a suicide, and will not escape. ***He must seek his life in a spirit of furious indifference to it; he must desire life like water and yet drink death like wine.***"

I was trained to believe the test of a man is what it takes to stop him. Grit is what it's called in Texas. It's brutal. And it's not about anything other than performance, because no one cares to hear your weak, sniveling excuses. So, you grow up learning how to numb the pain of the sun burning the back of your neck and from suffocating in the 110-degree, breezeless terrain. You get used to the burnt grass, the scrub pines, the desolate landscapes, and the intolerant demands for excellence from a decorated war hero called Dad.

The first time I came home beat up at age twelve by three fourteen-year-olds, I expected some sympathy. But boy, was I mistaken! I revered his service to our country as a Marine, whose last mission to destroy an embedded bunker on the DMZ in Vietnam in 1968 resulted in half the recon team KIA (killed in action) and the other half WIA (wounded in action). Valor, in the face of overwhelming force, had caused his thousand-yard stare that freaked out most people. But to me, he was Dad.

After explaining how I'd been jumped by three bigger boys, he began demonstrating techniques to snap their necks or break their spines. In utter disbelief, I argued that I could not murder them. And then his emotionless response caused my heart to sink, when he replied, "Okay, then, if you come home beaten up again, I'll beat you worse."

Talk about jumping from the frying pan and into the fire! My heart stopped. I had gone to him for help. But instead, I was sure my days on earth were numbered because I cried to the wrong Marine. And yet, the next time Jeff Hayes came after me, I reacted with a level of force that terrified me. It wasn't pretty. It wasn't Bruce Lee level awesome. It came out of sheer terror. What some call scared shitless! And to my amazement, it worked.

In life, you're first given the test, later the lesson.

Life has rarely made sense to me. You'd think we'd get an instruction manual explaining how to solve life's challenges. Instead, we often get advice from "armchair quarterbacks" who hide from any real risk because they've never learned how to perform the common (duties) under uncommon conditions. They give you tons of "ideas" that are as worthless as those theories blathered by our business professors, who have never spent a single day performing in the real world.

He'd sadly pronounced at an early age that I didn't have a lick of athletic talent, so I was ordered to make first-squad by out-practicing everyone else. I worked extra hard until the coach felt guilty for not letting me play—raw discipline fueled by being scared shitless not to measure up to Dad's expectations.

Years later, I found myself fighting in martial art tournaments for the thrill and outrunning state troopers on my Kawasaki Ninja motorcycle at over 100 MPH to supply that "fix" of scared shitlessness. Later, it was fighting in parking lots against half of the offensive line of some goat-roping town out in the sticks nearby or joy-riding in stolen cars. Recklessness had become my drug of choice.

Then, as fate would have it, I accidentally won academic scholarships and Dad forbade me to enlist in his beloved Marine Corps. His "change of orders" was to get a degree from those professors with little to no experience, and return to the Corps and lead as an officer instead of battle-proven Gunnery Sergeant. So, what did I do but blow up my scholarships with my disrespectful comments to the dean of business, when he refused my challenge to compare his tax return to mine. You see, in 1986, I'd reported over $40,000 from my part-time grass mowing business, when I wasn't working out, playing point guard on the squad, or traveling with the TaeKwonDo team. So, after my BCD (Marine lingo for a "bad conduct discharge") from my scholarships, I sought out a new challenge to redeem myself in the eyes of the Marine I feared I could never equal in acts of valor.

I ran headfirst into corporate America after watching the movie *Wall Street*. Though I outperformed the guys with the degrees (that I secretly envied), my addiction demanded more. So I became a workaholic. And when the pedigreed boys laughed me out of their Monday morning sales meetings for my atypical marketing ideas, I didn't curl up in a fetal position like most folks would. I got angry, crazy-mad with revenge. I showed up earlier, stayed later, worked all weekend. I then added to my regimen the discipline of listening to personal mindset development cassette tapes. One after another, while speeding all over Dallas until that wasn't enough. So I went to sleep with more subliminal tapes playing in the background—scared shitless that my lack of natural talent would prove me unworthy by comparison. I was determined to train my mind to think better, react faster, and perform with less apprehension of risks. To win, or die trying ... if that's what it took!

And it worked! I'd traded in my dream of becoming a lifer as a gunnery sergeant in the U.S. Marine Corps, like Clint Eastwood's character in *Heartbreak Ridge,* to become Bud Fox in the 1985 film *Wall Street.* I ranked as the top producer in several Fortune 500 companies before I was twenty-five, started my own brokerage agency for a Canadian insurance juggernaut shortly thereafter, and fearlessly catapulted myself into the shark-infested waters of offshore private banking and venture capital investing, all before age thirty. I was prouder of my titles than my eight-figure net worth: director of offshore operations for my mentor's hedge fund based in Turks and Caicos, president of a fifty-eight-office trust and accounting firm based in Utah, and co-principal in a pre-IPO SaaS technology company in California.

And then the phone call came the day after returning home from our international shareholder's event in Vegas. The voice rambled on about the Feds raiding our offices, freezing all our accounts, and the founder being held in his house at gunpoint.

Since I was under the assumption that we'd been attacked without any justification and because I was being groomed to take over the reigns of the company in the next ten years, technically, I was now in command. So, everyone was waiting for my decisions amidst the absolute chaos.

Finally, war had found me. I was going to get my chance to prove my worth. And I performed with ice in my veins.

I defended our operation to prevent further wrongdoing by what I believed to be just another Jeff Hays bully coming to kick my ass. Within twenty-four hours, I had secured our offshore holdings that hadn't been discovered, relocated our command and control to a foreign country, and caused several thousand investors to literally disappear from the open internet and onto an encrypted server based in Ireland. In Dad's lingo, I'd successfully hardened communications, reinforced HQ, and secured our resources.

And boy, did I piss off the wrong gang of bullies!

By July 2002, I was inside a ten-week federal money-laundering and investment fraud trial. The prior fourteen months from federal detention in Seattle was a blur of filing motions against the U.S. attorneys, though I'd never been to law school. And by September, I was taking the stand to fight the senior prosecutor, *mano a mano*. Many of the other co-defendants had lied because they were scared shitless and had taken plea bargains to reduce their prison sentences to under five years. I refused, purely out of principle, even ignoring a direct order from Dad to break our family honor code and take the ten-year plea bargain deal.

> "A man is never more than a man than when he embraces an adventure beyond his control, or when he walks into a battle he isn't sure of winning."—John Eldridge

In the middle of such extreme risk, there's no such thing as fearlessness: There's feeling the fear and acting the right way regardless. So I learned that real performance is just continuing to engage, even when you're scared shitless. It's finding that space called faith. Not faith in the Creator but faith in your ability to endure levels of agony that would cause the hearts of most to seize up.

In Will Smith's movie *After Earth*, he plays the character of a valiant general attempting to guide his son on a perilous mission. His son had already failed Ranger school, but now their lives depended on him doing the impossible.

"Fear is not real. The only place that fear can exist is in our thoughts of the future. It is a product of our imagination, causing us to fear things that do not at present, and may not, ever exist. That is near insanity. Do not misunderstand me, danger is very real. But fear is a choice."

I lost at trial! Yet I continued my mission, fighting another year from detention, only to secure a seemingly minor win of a 292-month sentence instead of the life sentence in federal prison that the gang of bullies requested from the judge. When I walked onto my first yard in Beaumont, Texas, in October 2003, I was nicknamed "the yacht man" because of my once-upon-a-time wealth. It would eventually become "Sergeant Slaughter."

Amid the daily struggle against life's scum and with zero reinforcements, I secured three consecutive wins in the circuit appellate courts, more than any other white-collar, first-time, non-violent offender in history. But the real trophy was reversing my own case in the United States Supreme Court in 2009. And while fighting these near-impossible obstacles, the mother of my children turned on me during an ugly divorce and attempted to take away my rights as a father and erase me from the lives of my two children. Her father warned her, "Dumb mistake, Steve doesn't surrender!"

For 5,544 days, I marched across hell. The demons walking the halls at night relentlessly whispered that I was a fool, insane, exhibiting conduct unbecoming of a father and husband. And maybe they were right. Perhaps I should have acted like a coward and broken our family's honor code by lying about doing something I did not. Perhaps I should have set the example for my children by giving lip service to my creed but breaking weak when life got ugly. That's what most others would have done . . . and then justified their cowardice with lame excuses.

From experience, not theory, I can tell you there are no perfect solutions to impossible scenarios. So I'll share with you how I reasoned why I was being tortured. I penned an essay in 2007 entitled *A Perfect Imperfection* and published it on my blog from prison. My blog is called Tsyo Matte, samurai lingo for "Be Strong!" (https://tsuyomatte.wordpress.com/).

Therefore we must ask ourselves what makes our heroes heroic? Are they perfect? Hardly. What makes a hero so heroic isn't that he's perfect, but that he is imperfect. A hero is a person who overcomes his own limitations, transcends his weaknesses, and stands his ground when most retreat to excuses. He becomes, in effect, a perfect imperfection, just as a perfect storm achieves its terrifying strength through a perfect combination of imperfect—that is to say, disorderly—elements. Valor can only be found in these most imperfect of places, confusing places, that leave behind clues of "how" the few performed, and more importantly, "why." These characteristics conceal themselves; they hide within enigmas and paradoxes—buried inside legends, lore, and myths. And the cardinal paradox cloaking itself within the imperfect chaos of battle is a pure and relentless allegiance to a sacred cause, a meaning so perfect, the warrior "performs the ordinary under extraordinary conditions."

In that lonely trek across my desert challenge, life became really simple. I came to understand that the test of one's caliber is what it takes to stop you. In those endless days and darkest nights, I found a few lines from the book *Endurance: Shackleton's Incredible Voyage* that transformed the hopelessness into meaningfulness. After seventeen months stranded on the Antarctic ice shelf, twenty-eight survivors made it back to civilization. While reading their journal entries, I noticed that, in some ways, they had come to know themselves better in that lonely world of ice and emptiness. They had achieved at least a limited kind of contentment. One unique entry spoke volumes. ***"We'd been tested . . . and found not wanting."*** It went on to describe how they felt that special kind of pride of a person who, in a foolish moment, accepts an impossible dare—then pulls it off to perfection.

This secret that I've shared with you can carry you through life's impossible missions. It begins with a commitment to principle, to a code, that dishonoring scares you shitless. The agony that you'll suffer during your commitment must torture your soul less than standing in front of the ultimate tribunal to account for your conduct under duress.

But beyond that commitment to purpose and principle, you must possess something called passion. In my case, that passion was the fatherly love for my children. In my mind, again and again, two films replayed. One, my children standing over my headstone that they'd chosen, "Here lies an average man, like everyone else." And the other, just one word. "Worthy."

Passion fueled this father's trek across hell. It was about being scared shitless to account to my children that I'd cowered to the bully called fate and dishonored them by my fear. This fueled me to rise just one more time and trust the Creator that only through being scared shitless can we be *tested . . . and found not wanting*.

BIOGRAPHY

As a human that has intimately danced with tragedy, injustice, and anguish, Steve lives to inspire the few destined to impact the many. He's director of performance for Success Publishing where he coaches authors inside his best friend's Mastermind group to "embrace the suck" by expressing courageous vulnerability in telling their Stories.

Mission: To deliberately cause affirmative outcomes that would not have occurred otherwise
Slogan: *Chance favors the prepared*
Mantra: No one left behind

Connect with Steve via LinkTree: https://linktr.ee/steve_moreland

CHAPTER 4

Dream, Struggle, Victory

By David He

Overture: one evening of August 2016 in Melbourne, Australia: I was standing in front of Mom's house, and she handed me a pile of neatly stacked cash. I was forty-two, my debts had finally caught up with me—and that hurts when it bites you. Mom calmly said: "Son, this is all I have, the very last bit of my retirement money." My eyes grew wet, and my heart felt like a knife had just gone through it: Not because I had just borrowed every cent that my mom had, not because I had ruined my restaurant business, not even because I couldn't afford to buy my daughter a twenty-three dollar Barbie doll; they were nothing compared the look in Mom's eyes. It hurt so much because there was not even a sign of disappointment in her eyes. It was as though I had just borrowed her car and would return it the next day.

Act 1: The Dream

My story started in the year 1986 in China, and the first day for me at the Shanghai Dance Academy. It was two degrees outside, and I was standing inside a dance studio at one of the best ballet schools in China. There were twenty-seven kids in the room, all handpicked out of 30,000 from all across

China. But if I said I had shared the same dream as Billy Elliot back then, I'd be lying to you.

In China, my generation is known as the "last generation of the cultural revolution." Growing up, we had no idea that such a thing as television even existed. My father was a professor at a university, and my mother worked in a factory near Shanghai. As a child, many of us don't dare to dream that one day we might become, say, a scientist or an astronaut. We were poor, and when you are accepted into a fully-funded government boarding school, you went there, whether you wanted to or not.

Growing up, we were forced to do what our families wanted us to do, and getting accepted into one of those special government schools was one of them. It was like a ticket to dreamland. Maybe I got lucky, or perhaps sometimes the dream chooses you? Sometimes, when people push their dreams onto you, often for loving reasons, it becomes your "thing"—but it is never your dream. Dance was never a dream for me, but, for the next four years, I was forced to get up at six in the morning and do ten full hours of ballet training, six days a week. It was nothing but pain, with no dream of mine involved at all. I'm sorry if that disappoints you and you're wondering why the hell you're reading a story about a dream without a dream.

In February 1990, my dad told us that he feared we would never be able to leave China if we waited any longer. He decided we were going to Australia so that he could continue his Ph.D. studies there. We had just over $1000 to take with us out of China—everything we had. We had heard that the best ballet school, the Australian Ballet School, was based in Melbourne, but the school wasn't free for international students. So, my mom decided to do extra work sewing to earn enough to pay the school fees for me. Her wage was $2.30 per hour at an Asian cloth factory.

The Australian Ballet School is the best dance school in Australia. Back in the 1990s, the school had no academic classes, just full days of dance training spread over three years. Although my dream was to become a great dancer and join a professional company, like the Australian Ballet Company, my fear of speaking English and worries about how I appeared to others soon became too much for me to cope with. Before long, I hated even going to school; I'd pretend to go, but instead, I would wander the streets all day. This was while my mom was working for $2.30 an hour to pay my school fees. For an impressionable kid from China, the Australian convenience shops quickly became a little too convenient. I realize now that the only effort I was putting in was putting stuff straight into my pocket! It was all too easy. Then, one day, my parents had to pick me up from the police station. I saw the tears in my mother's eyes, the kind of tears that stay in your eyes for a long time. That was a pivotal moment for me. I kept that memory of Mum's tears in my head, and it became my motivation for getting back on track. Two years later, my dream had still not come true; I didn't get accepted into the Australian Ballet Company. So, I decided to travel around the world and audition with other dance companies. I soon settled down in Hong Kong, where I spent eight years of my dance career. In 1997, I got my very first leading role on stage, with many more to follow. It seemed as though my dance dream had finally come true. But that was not quite the case.

Act 2: The Struggle

Dec 2001: Oh, if only I hadn't broken my ankle on stage! I was so close to my dream, but it was just out of reach. I still remember the pain, not the pain in my leg but of having to sit on the sidelines and watch others taking over the leading roles that would have been mine. Even after a year of rest, my foot injury didn't allow me to get back into my previous shape. Everything I knew was leaving fast, and the fear got to me big time; fear of the stage, fear of stepping back into the studio, fear of losing everything and, once more, having nothing. It all affected me badly. I stopped going to the studio and started wandering the streets again. The difference this time was that the city was the one they say "never sleeps"—Hong Kong. I turned to alcohol and anything I could get my hands on, to help me forget my troubles, forget the embarrassment, forget my family, and forget my friends. I would go to bars and hang out there until dawn, night after night, week after week. Finally, I lost my job. One day, the company asked me politely to resign. Soon, I had spent all my savings on the substances that helped me forget. But I believe that all things happen for a reason and the dots will always connect when you look back. One night I was drinking as usual and I met Karen. She was together and I was all over the place. I still don't know why she agreed to go out with me, as I had nothing to offer. After I had used up all my savings, I had only one choice—to go back to Australia to live with my parents again. Karen said, "Yes, let's start over again in Australia."

In August 2007, after a thirteen-year absence, I finally returned to Melbourne. I couldn't stop asking myself one question: "IS THIS IT?" Is this going to be there for the rest of my life? I decided then that I would buy myself a dream— a business franchise. Karen and I borrowed money from my mom and dad and bought into a local café. Things seemed to get back on track, and for the next four years, we did well.

By 2013, I felt so good that I wanted to show my friends that I had made it. This time, I decided to "go big," so I borrowed half a million dollars from a bank, sold the old café, remortgaged our house, put in everything we had, and bought a bigger restaurant. Looking back, I can see it was all to bolster my ego. No one in the family agreed with my decision, but the need to prove my success to people was overwhelming. I quickly learned that trying to fulfill the dream of proving yourself to others never works. Over the next three years, the restaurant business went from bad to worse. My sixty hours a week increased to one hundred.

Each day, I woke up at five in the morning and worked until closing time at ten-thirty. I couldn't see any light at the end of the tunnel. Soon, suppliers and debt collectors were repeatedly ringing every day, but I became afraid to answer any calls. I started to feel a numbness in my head. I was only seeing my kids for a few hours each week. I couldn't afford to hire anyone or pay anyone to fix anything, including the restaurant toilet. One day, the staff told me the toilet was blocked, but I couldn't afford to hire a plumber. The solution seemed simple—do it myself! That didn't go too well. When I say I got shit all over my hands, I mean that literally! I remember that moment when I stood in front of the mirror in the toilet, looking at my reflection. I was in so much pain inside that I felt numb. I was crying, but no tears came. I asked God what he wanted from me. Was it too much to ask almighty God just to let me pay the rent and feed my kids? I was numb for a long time, and every night my only wish was not to wake up again in the morning.

Back to 2016, that night at my mom's doorstep; she handed me the cash for the last time. Over the past three years, she had given me all her savings. Selfishly, I had drained all her retirement money, money that she started earning at a rate of just $2.30 per hour twenty-five years ago. That night, I walked back to my car and just screamed and screamed. I slapped myself hard in the face so that I could feel the pain again. I begged God to show me a sign, something, anything. I promised Him that if he granted me one last thing, I would do whatever it took to get myself back on track.

Act 3: The Victory

Well, maybe the Big Guy up there heard me this time.

One day in November 2016, I was wandering aimlessly in a shopping center, when a stranger tapped on my shoulder. I don't know if he saw the desperation in my eyes, but he asked me if I was willing to open my mind and accept an opportunity. I had never done it, but I knew he was talking about network marketing. I told him I would take anything that came. I had nothing to lose, so I had nothing to fear. For the next three years, I woke up every morning to revisit the day when I had stood in front of the mirror in the restaurant toilet and that look in my mom's eyes. I wanted to remember those two things, although it hurt a lot every time I thought about them. But that got me through each day, not even countless rejections from people, friends and strangers can hurt me anymore. Remembering those two incidents were like my breakfast energy bar; they gave me a kick in the head when I was afraid that someone might laugh at me or reject me. It never once crossed my mind that I would make a success of network marketing.

But I had made a big change in my thinking. I decided to make that change by choosing to use my struggles to challenge my status quo. I decided never to look back and feel sorry for myself but instead to revisit my pain every day to fuel my desire not to achieve a dream but to make my own victory!

Today, I'm proud to say that I have achieved one of the top ranks in my company, a rank that only a handful of people ever made. I have enjoyed every minute of it, and now my dream is to help others to realize their dreams. Many of them have been through similar struggles, and my job is to help them see the light at the end of the tunnel. Not everyone knows what their dream is, but we all feel our struggles. They are the reason to propel us forward, not the dream itself. Too many people mistake their dream for their destination. I like to think the dream is like Cinderella—it will disappear at midnight! It is only through our struggles that we find our courage and are awarded the crystal slipper of victory. Ultimately, the victory will lead us back to our dream, where everything begins. Life is like a giant circle. When life pushes us to our knees, and we feel as though we're taking our last breath, that is the moment life has prepared us for. The moment when we unleash that last bit of strength toward becoming who we are meant to be. I wish that all of you take that breath and become the people you want to become.

BIOGRAPHY

David He is a creative performing artist with an entrepreneurial mindset, whose career spans the extremities of artistic excellence to business acumen. After graduating from the Australian Ballet School, He has performed on many international stages for over 20 years. He held the position of Principal Dancer. He merges arts and entrepreneurship with different philosophies, knowledge, methods, goals, and thinking. He gets a great deal of pleasure from identifying, mentoring, and sparking his passion for realizing their power to dream and succeed, which has become the core motivation for all his excellent work. He currently resides in Melbourne, Australia, with his wife and two children.

You can connect with David at https://www.facebook.com/tinybigpurpose/

CHAPTER 5

From Struggle To Magic

By Aina Brandholm

If someone had told me years ago that I would become the successful person I am today, I would never have believed them.

It was a summer day back in 2013 when I looked at myself in the mirror and didn't recognize myself. I was shaking and scared to death. And now, I'm going to tell you how it all began.

My family, including me, my parents, and my little sister, lived in a small town in the south of Spain, where I grew up. I was very insecure when I was younger. I went through a lot of pain, experienced a lot of anger, depression, and unhappiness. But I always had big dreams. I dreamed mostly of becoming a professional dancer and someone with authority and influence. But back then, I felt alone, and I was afraid of what people thought of me. This was maybe because I was raised to believe that you must pretend that everything in life is good and perfect. I lived in a beautiful mansion, but I never had an abundance of the right sort of support in my life.

My mom was a singer and an artist before she met my dad. She gave up her dream when my sister and I were born so she could take care of us. My dad was a captain in a shipping company and quite successful, but he was away working for half of the year, so I didn't get to spend much time with him, which is why my mom couldn't continue with her career.

Throughout my childhood, I saw that my parents were unhappy. There was a lot of yelling and screaming at each other, which created what I think of as a big hole in my heart because of which I lacked self-love, kindness, and compassion. I was also bullied in school, and that made me feel even more insecure about myself. I continually felt I was not good enough. A lot of kids go through bullying. If you have kids, please talk to them daily, and let them know that they have your support. Tell them how wonderful they are, how beautiful and talented they are, because that will help build a positive self-image.

Being bullied really hurt. And what do people who are hurt often do? They can respond with either flight or fight. I chose to fight. I was always in trouble in school, with the students and teachers. I was kicked out of the classroom many times because of my behavior. I took on the rebel role. But as I got older, I realized I couldn't continue with that attitude because it would ultimately take me nowhere. Later on in life, the pain I felt inside led me to search for communities and groups of people who had experienced similar things, with whom I could share my pain.

But I didn't choose the people I surrounded myself with very wisely; by the age of thirteen, I was already drinking alcohol, and my life soon became a mess. Then, aged fifteen, I started attending a dance school, and I believe this is what kept me alive and gave me some inner drive to succeed. But at sixteen, I stopped going to school. Instead, I started partying and drinking more and more alcohol until I finally became addicted to alcohol and drugs. I was an addict for many years. Then, suddenly, my life took a 360-degree turn.

That was the moment when I looked at myself in the mirror and couldn't recognize myself. I asked myself: Who am I? Where did all my dreams go?

I decided then that I hated the way I lived my life, and I was so afraid of staying stuck in it that I realized there was only one thing left to do: CHANGE.

My family decided to move to Sweden, and I took the DECISION to change my life. My passion for dancing helped me move forward and find the ambition I needed to grow. I started investing my time and money into dance; I danced between four to five hours every day for five years. To pay for my dance classes, I took waitressing jobs. It wasn't fun, but I knew I had to do it.

But my struggle against my former lifestyle didn't finish back in Spain; my subconscious mind kept pulling me back to the same old habits; procrastination, partying, and just spending money like water. Aged twenty-four, I was introduced to a home-based business—and I loved it. I had known nothing about the possibilities of becoming financially independent. All I wanted to do was dance, travel around the world, and help others do the same. It was there that I saw the possibilities for me. I suddenly saw the light. I saw there was something big waiting for me, and that put the sparkle back in my eyes.

So, what happened after going into business for myself? Was it something magical, or something more real to do with me?

Well, after some ups and downs, within a few months of launching my first business, I did pretty well. But inside, I was still feeling miserable. I was still carrying around the earlier feelings of sadness and anger, but the deep desire inside me to achieve my dream always drove me to try to keep moving forward, no matter what. After spending six years living in the amazing, but cold country of Sweden, I decided to move back to Spain to build my organization, imagining that things would be better there, that escaping would solve my problems. I was so wrong. Once I had moved to Spain, I found I still felt the same way inside.

Now I'm going to tell you how it felt to have to work in a job I hated and being so broke I had to eat nothing but rice and bread for weeks. You see, when I first returned to Spain, I had to take the first job opportunity on offer, which was as a telemarketer in the sales department of an electricity company.

Imagine answering the phone every day and having to talk to people who are angry, who yell at you and insult you. I had to do that every day, calling between three- to five hundred people a week. Despite that, in my mind, I had the goal of getting good at it—I wanted to be the best in the office. I started making three to five sales every day, and I became the top seller in my first month of working there. Every day, my name was in the top three of those with the most sales. But I had to ask myself what it was all for. I hated it. I didn't believe in the product, and, eventually, I thought, what am I doing here? Why am I doing this? Why is nothing changing for the better? Why are things still the same in my head, and why am I still broke, both financially and mentally?

After two months in Spain, I discovered I was pregnant. That was the turning point in my life. I panicked. I had an anxiety attack. I didn't know what to do with my life, and I was scared. Back to Sweden I went, back home to my Mom and sister, hoping to feel protected and secure. The pain was still inside me, so, with a broken heart, I decided not to have the baby. Some people will probably frown at my decision, but it made no sense to me to bring a baby into the world with a mom who was depressed, broke, anxious, and without any love for herself. I sincerely believed that to love the baby, I first had to learn to love myself. That was the point when I decided to change. I wanted to become the best version of myself—happy, healthy, wealthy, confident, and to be able to provide the best value and quality of life possible for my future family and build a legacy for future generations.

Discipline and creating the right habits made me into the person I am today. As soon as I had made my decision to change, I gave up smoking, drinking, drugs—all my former bad habits. Now people ask me how I did it. They say that they also want to quit but can't. Truthfully, in my book, it's not about whether you can or can't; it's about the pain you relate to what you are doing. If the pain is big enough, you will stop that bad habit. I learned this from one of my mentors, Tony Robbins. In his book *Awaken the Giant Within*, he writes that people will do more to avoid pain than to gain pleasure. I was in such deep pain, I looked at myself in the mirror and cried every day. I didn't want to live that way any longer. I wanted to *be* more, to *do* more with my life. I had the conviction that I was created to do big things, as I believe we all are.

The "magic" happened when I started becoming obsessively focused on my personal growth. I threw myself into reading self-help books, attending seminars, listening to audios, writing down goals, affirmations, doing daily exercise, daily meditation, and yoga. I changed to a completely healthy lifestyle and put extra time and effort into my business.

Isn't life exciting? Imagine life without its ups and downs—wouldn't it be kind of boring? We need all the struggles to achieve the magic of change. I can tell you that, when I look back over my past actions and connect the dots, I can see why things happened as they did, and I can understand them better. But the past is the past; there comes a point where we have to stop criticizing ourselves for what we did or didn't do or could have done. We have to stop looking at our lives as though they are something beyond our own control. Sure, we can't control the external things that happen to us, but we can control the internal, so why don't we quit looking backward, start moving forward, and take action to ensure we make the best of our lives and ourselves?

To finish this chapter, I'm going to tell you three things that helped me move from struggling to the magic of positive change, which I know will help you to do that as well:

1. **Work out what your life goals are.** Write them down and look at them daily; repetition is vital. It will reprogram your subconscious mind, so you can start attracting whatever it is you want, personally and professionally. However, it's crucial to first work out what your goals are. To do that, you need to listen to your inner voice and intuition; don't listen to what the exterior world is telling you.

2. **Change your environment**, your friends, what you watch on TV. Look to associate with people who you admire and then follow their steps. Always try to learn from the best. Doing that means that you, too, will become the best possible version of yourself. Read daily, listen to audios, podcasts, invest in seminars. (Tip: lots of this stuff is available for free on YouTube, but remember to always be careful about who you listen to there. It's essential to do your research first and check their results. It's unwise to automatically believe everyone because there's a lot of bullshit out there too!)

3. **Take action!** Stop saying you're going to do things and go and actually do them.

If they make you feel uncomfortable, do them anyway because that's the only way to learn. But it isn't enough to take action if you have no real belief in what you're doing. It's essential to believe in what you do, believe in your dreams, and imagine yourself achieving your goals. Use the tools available to you that can help you, such as meditation and affirmations.

I've always been very passionate about everything. There's a saying; How you do anything is how you do everything. But, in my case, what fueled my dreams was the deep passion I have for dancing. I know that's what helped me stay alive, move forward, and become more confident. Of course, I wasn't that good at it in the beginning. If I look back at my old dancing videos, I can see I sucked. But we have to suck first to be great! I didn't become a professional dancer just by thinking about it: I worked my way up. I trained like crazy for years, worked for free, paid for all my training and courses to become better, and I'm still doing that. I went from being an insecure dancer to a teacher, mentor, and inspiration for many dancers who also had insecurity problems.

Imagine: One day you're a girl from a small city in Spain, with no formal education, a high school dropout, with no influence, no experience in sales or marketing. Then, the next day, you wake up, and you're living your dream dancing in a professional dance academy, traveling around the world, impacting lives for the good. Today, I have become an author, an entrepreneur and a professional dancer. I am continually working towards my goals, building a legacy, and creating something bigger than myself, helping those in need, giving, and serving others.

Never give up on your dreams because they are yours, and no one can take them from you, only you.

BIOGRAPHY

Aina Brandholm is known for her discipline and courage. She started her journey as a dancer, and now she helps people feel more confident and secure about themselves through different body movement techniques. She has been teaching, performing, and traveling around the world for the last five years. Aina is also an entrepreneur with strong leadership and communication skills. She is currently training and teaching teams in multiple countries within her network marketing business. Her mission is to empower women worldwide and build schools in poorer countries, where kids can learn creative subjects such as dancing, music, art, mind-body-soul connection, and how to program their subconscious mind that can build a healthy self-image. She is currently living her dream in Denmark and is active in education in one of the world's most prestigious dance schools.

Aina's contact details are available at https://linktr.ee/ainabrandholm

CHAPTER 6

Why Not You?

By Allan Main

No matter what others might think of you or the lies told about you that you've come to believe are true, I can assure you that you have just as much right as anybody to pursue a longed-for goal and live a blessed life.

Based on my experiences, here are some of the ways you can achieve just that.

Choose Your Friends Based on Your Dreams, Not Your Fears

Childhood was a cruel joke on me: I often cried from feelings of loneliness and rejection. I felt like the loneliest kid in school growing up, always walking around by myself. I tried to join conversations with the cool kids, but they would often be mean to me. The pretty girls made fun of me, and even kids I thought were my friends would get together to push me around and throw punches. The constant rejection made for a painful existence, and I would stay away from anyone in whom I detected any meanness. Stuttering in conversations and avoiding eye contact, too nervous to engage with people, I was socially beaten down and kept in my place. That treatment was more effective than a tiny rope that holds the strong elephant in place, defeated by its programming. When you walk the halls every day, just hoping that something will change, you begin to believe many untrue things about yourself. The result was that I was failing a lot of my classes.

As a child, I couldn't understand why I should be assigned such a lowly position in society. Okay, I was awkward in sports, but I loved to play. Eventually, running from trouble made me fast, so running became a passion, and I developed a dream of becoming an Olympian. Speed became my identity and, at last, I earned respect from some of the jocks, but I was still ridiculed by most. With aspirations of becoming a scientist, I read books on astronomy and geology, but I began to lose hope in those dreams. I remember deciding, "To hell with the cool kids! If they won't accept me, then I'll make my own kind of cool." I finally became part of a group of friends who were fun-loving troublemakers. We ran around with long hair and the logos of our favorite metal bands emblazoned across our shirts. Like most teens, it seemed that I knew better when I was younger. For instance, I had been arrested a few times for shoplifting, running from cops at night for sport, and my friends and I knew all the shortcuts in town. I'd reached the point where I'd traded my Olympic dreams for cigarettes and stuttering for smoking weed.

Develop Your Passions

Learning to play the guitar opened a whole new world for me: I began to learn about myself and what I was capable of. I went for some of the most demanding metal songs to play, as I thought this would be my escape to relevance. I wasn't known for being a great guitarist, but I studied it to a degree that surprised me. I had developed a new passion in life—and I was hungry for more.

Choose to Focus on the Positive

When my friends started to hang out with a Satanist, I became curious about God. My eighteenth birthday felt like a very low place. Surely, I thought, I'm not supposed to be feeling so alone all over again. I was finally free from police custody but still on probation for stealing a bottle of Jack

Daniel's. I had no place of my own, no car, not even a decent guitar. I felt like a lonely drifter, and nothing I had accomplished up to that point felt as though it mattered much.

As I grew older, my spirit of optimism grew. I was enjoying more liberty and freedom. I graduated from continuation school and even started attending a community college to learn the trade of electrician, following in my dad's footsteps.

Choose a Supportive Life Partner

I was forced to grow up when my girlfriend announced she was pregnant. Stepping into the rest of my life, I became a young father. I had to quit college because of my girlfriend's jealousy of the imaginary women I was supposedly meeting in school, or anywhere. She was insecure, and everything was a fight. I was made to feel horrible for going to work or wanting to buy tools while training to be a carpenter. She wanted me to stay home with her and get stoned. This behavior meant that we were evicted from every apartment we rented, and I had to start over many times. Often, I had to do this by myself, as she tried to replace me with someone more understanding of her partying habits and cheating, even though we now had three children together.

Embrace Setbacks as Gifts in Disguise

Around this time, unaware that there was an outstanding warrant on me for a previous mistake, I was arrested and spent a life-changing week in jail. A copy of the New Testament was left on my bed, and God had my attention during the whole time I was waiting for my trial. Throughout that week, I found the answers to many of my questions about life in those pages. I came out with a whole new curiosity for spiritual things, and I entered back into daily life with a growing feeling of a new purpose for myself and my family.

Do What You Love for a Living

Fulfilling my new sense of purpose continued with building houses where we lived in Paradise, California. My introduction to carpentry was carrying an entire house's worth of lumber for the framers to build while becoming a framer myself. The work meant enduring many hot summers and freezing winters. It was hard but rewarding work. I felt that being a tradesman was the real, tangible value that I needed in my life. I enjoyed the respect I got, as well as my much-improved prospects for the future. I felt I was finally becoming a good man, with friends to rely on. Even with family life being very difficult, I was finding ways to bless people very rewarding.

Share Your Knowledge

We ended up moving to Lake Tahoe, waiting tables to support my kids, with my Mom helping out by providing daycare after the family fell apart. I was busy and trying to stay positive, but after three years, the work and the lifestyle just wasn't fun anymore. I had begun to allow myself to be mistreated by the customers. I saw a customer scowling at me one day. It was just a few times too many. "I don't have to take that disrespect coming from you," said the voice in my head. That moment was an epiphany that gave me a new license to stand up for myself. One positive thing I did get out of that time was overcoming the challenge of learning how to run a busy dining room from memory during my last two years as a waiter. I found that bragging about it was not as exciting as telling people they could learn it as well. I had found another way to bless people.

Triumph and Tragedy

Construction was calling me back. I knew that working with wood and nails gave me more feelings of satisfaction and inner grit. I deliberately made myself a useful man to have on site. I arrived early and took all the overtime I could get. In addition, I was working out and getting skilled with my tools. In the warmer months, I took my kids with my coworkers on hiking trips, where we would go rafting, rock climbing, and camping. Times like that made being a poor single father feel not so bad. My kids were my life, and I was determined we were going to make it, no matter what.

Throughout these years, their mother was in their lives on and off. I think it was good that she got to see them after two years of not being in their lives. Two days after that first meeting, our first-born, Alisha, died in a snowboarding accident. I was distraught, and one of the main things that were most upsetting to me was that I had not been able to give her, or her siblings, a better childhood. Although there were lots of good times that we are very thankful for, it's true to say that much of it was rough. It was a surprise to me that losing a child did not destroy me in the way I thought it would. Maybe that was because of the strength my faith gave me, as, at that time, we had been attending the Calvary Chapel three times a week. Another factor affecting my grief may have been leaving the hospital alone, seeing the newspaper headlines about the devastation caused by the great tsunami that killed over 200,000 people.

And God Bought Eve to Adam

Despite everything, I knew I had to keep going somehow. My spirit of optimism would not quit. I kept growing in my work skills and self-worth. Before long, I met Kelly online. Our dates were often spent at church, playing guitar in the park, or on a hiking trail around Lake Tahoe. A year later, we got married, and I began helping her with her CCW business (weapons safety training & certification). This forced me to put aside the last of my shyness, learn about guns, and learn how to talk guns to retired military and law enforcement alpha males. I found it helped that I could also talk about love for God and country with them. At the same time, Kelly and I also were getting into network marketing, but we had little success. However, the training we got fed my spirit of optimism; it showed me ways to win at life that I had never learned in school or elsewhere. We took Kelly's business from a few small classes in Reno to traveling to parts of northern California and Nevada to promote and grow our venture. Working as a team, we made "Armed and Safe" the most referred CCW class in Northern Nevada, and people loved to come from California to get their Nevada permit. I became passionate about helping people learn how to be safe and accurate with their pistols. Our hard work paid off, and we found ourselves in a financial position where we could finally build our own home—something I'd always dreamed of. Kelly and I worked tirelessly, with help from my dad, my son, and a few friends—and I'm proud to say we did it free of debt.

Perfect Match

Throughout these years, Kelly has been not only my wife but also my girlfriend and the best friend I've ever had. This life has become an adventure for us, stretching from the Oregon Coast to Zion NP, from Yellowstone to Yosemite, from island hopping in Hawaii to scuba diving in Belize. Life is fulfilling, and I no longer feel the need to "belong" as I did when I was younger. Nowadays, I'm accepted everywhere I go, and I have a wife whom people love to meet. I'm so proud of Kelly; everyone she encounters finds her one of the friendliest and most welcoming person they've ever met. She is behind me in everything I ought to do, not everything I want to do, and I've learned to take her advice as I have from a few others.

Fulfillment Adventure

Looking back, life could certainly have been better for the younger me, but I would not trade who I am today for any of it. Of course, there are many things I would have done differently—like tried to work harder, longer, and smarter. But the last ten years of life seem to me to have been worth all the struggle that finally got me to where I am now. Along the way, I've learned to live in the sunshine of God's blessings, and I'm eager for the next chapter. I firmly believe that life is a buffet of opportunities gained through struggle. I took on easy challenges as though they were hard, so I could conquer hard challenges as though they were easy. I believed there was value in doing the hard things. I began with stacking skills to achieve goals because that's all I could do. Opening doors that suggested good outcomes were often key to reaching new levels of achievement, and achievement feels good. Believing in myself meant that I could not give up on myself, that I would have to conquer adversity to finally triumph. Every day that I make the world meet me on my terms is my victory over those who tried to dictate my place and convince me that the good life wasn't for me: I've shown them that it is. So, in the long run, I wonder if maybe it was better that it wasn't so good back then. Through the struggles, I've acquired an appreciation for every victory I've had and every accomplishment. The process starts with believing that you're worthy and that the good life is for you. I firmly believe that everyone can find their best life possible, so why NOT you!

BIOGRAPHY

As a child, Allan Main was shunned by schoolmates and townspeople, but through hard work and optimism, he has found a fulfilled life. With persistence, Allan found how a relentless pursuit of demanding his dignity from the world and claiming his right to pursue his happiness can turn any life around. Hitting rock bottom more times than he can remember, Allan has also become acutely aware of simple changes people can make to discover for themselves a brand-new level of freedom. Allan Main and his wife Kelly have brought her concealed weapons training business from the ash heap to local favorite throughout Northern Nevada and Northern California. Overcoming a childhood stutter, Allan has since spoken to large churches for Gideon's International and participates in teaching gun safety classes. He believes that every summit is a false summit, as it should be because the journey should never end.

Connect Allan via Linktree: https://linktr.ee/allan_main

CHAPTER 7

Finding Your Purpose

By Amanda Meyer

I believe that there are three types of people. The first are the ones who go through life with a level of certainty, knowing their life's purpose and who they were destined to be; the second type spend the majority of their lives searching for their life's purpose and who they are destined to be; the third type are those who struggle throughout their lives, merely existing and without any desire to discover who they are destined to be.

I remember having that A-Ha moment at nine years of age and living in Florida. I recall it being a beautiful summer's evening. I looked up to the stars above and dreamed of becoming an astronaut. But there was an obstacle: I knew that one needed great intelligence to accomplish something like that, but I was a C student at best. I had battled with reading comprehension throughout my entire school-life. In some ways, I was fortunate that my parents never pressured me to aim at going to college. The only thing I really had was the desire to travel. As we lived so close to Miami, I decided to try to break into the modeling industry. For that, I didn't have to be "book smart," and I thought it would pay me enough to travel and see the world.

I was a typical teenager—I thought I knew everything, so the summer before my senior year, I decided to move out of my parent's house and get my own place. That meant I had to choose where I was going to live and how I was going to complete my last year of education. I was determined to figure out how to accomplish that, when the restaurant owners where I was working at the time invited me to live rent-free with them in their two-bedroom apartment. But there were two conditions: the first was that I complete my senior year and graduate on time; the second was that I had to be clean and tidy and buy my own groceries.

But after a few months of living with them, I thought it best to find work elsewhere. The $4.25 an hour they were paying me to be a hostess was no longer enough to live on, especially now that I was "on my own." I needed more than just an hourly wage and was lucky enough to find a waitressing job at a sports bar in the next town. I had to hustle for every dollar, but I knew that the harder I worked, the more money I would make. Then came a night when one of the bartenders didn't show up for their shift. This was my opportunity; "Amanda, we need you behind the bar!" the manager yelled at me. Well, bartending paid better than waitressing, but I'd never done it before. I didn't know then what I soon learned; in the words of Richard Branson, "If somebody offers you an amazing opportunity, but you are not sure if you can do it, say yes—then learn how to do it later."

My schedule at this point was bartending until 2 a.m., getting home by 3:30 a.m., and then getting up for school at 6:30 a.m. I was sleep-deprived and pretty much slept through my entire senior year. I did only the bare minimum necessary to graduate. By that time, I was beyond mentally and physically exhausted, but I was determined to graduate on time because I had given my word to the people who had given me a shot and a free place to live. I thought I owed it to myself, as well. What would it have said about my integrity if I hadn't followed through with what I had said I was going to do? It would have been crazy to quit just at the point when, after eleven years of what I considered the agonizing pain of attending school, I was about to graduate—which I did in the spring of 1995. Having, at last, managed to achieve what I set out to do, I felt a huge sense of accomplishment. However, now that I was an adult in the real world, I began questioning what my purpose in life was.

I was twenty-four when I married my first husband, gave up on my dreams of traveling the world, and moved to Texas. At twenty-six, I gave birth to our son, Logan. I found myself in a tumultuous and unhealthy marriage, where we did nothing but argue. We were great parents to Logan, but we were not great together, so we called it quits on our marriage. I felt a huge sense of failure, being a single parent aged twenty-seven. I had no college degree, was bartending until 4 a.m., pawning my child off on anyone who would watch him while I worked, because I had no support system, as my family lived on the East Coast. My life had no direction. I felt lost, defeated, and broken. I felt that I needed some time to re-evaluate my life and set myself some goals, but instead, I jumped into another marriage one year later.

At the start of my second marriage, my husband was good to me, and, even more importantly, he was good to my son. He was in the military, so my son and I made the move to Georgia to be with him. At twenty-nine, I went through a heartbreaking miscarriage, but, one year later, I gave birth to our beautiful daughter, Mackenzie. Being a new mom again was exhausting, but I finally decided to re-enter education and study for a teaching degree. Parenting two phenomenal kids, being a military spouse, working as a bartender, and going to school certainly put a strain on our marriage. Somewhere along the way, we stopped respecting one another. I certainly didn't want another divorce, but I eventually found out that my spouse had been cheating on me for over a year. I found myself in another failed marriage. I knew I had to figure out how I was going to survive life sucker-punching me once again, but how was I going to juggle being a single parent, working, and continuing my education all at the same time? I learned that when your back is up against the wall, you go into fight or flight mode.

I realized that I could accomplish anything with drive, determination, and a clear plan of action. I refused to fail or feel like a failure ever again. I ended my first semester of school with three A's, and, for the first time in my entire thirty-two years, I felt smart. All I had needed was a little bit of belief in myself that I was capable of achieving my dreams, and I firmly believe that with belief in ourselves, we can all become who we want to become.

Over the next few years, the kids and I moved to South Carolina, where I completed my degree and graduated—with honors. During that time, I met the love of my life. With two failed marriages on my track record, I felt a bit undeserving of any chance at happiness, but he restored my faith in marriage on many levels. Finally, things seemed to be going my way: I was married to a wonderful man. I fell in love with his three older children, and our two families became one. I started my teaching career at the school my children attended, and I was finally feeling as though everything was coming together at last. Then, three years into teaching, I found myself working sixty-hour weeks while being bullied by the administration. I was burned out, and I did not like myself anymore, as a parent or wife; I realized that something had to change. I knew if I didn't *do* something different, I wouldn't *have* anything different. Around this time, a friend introduced me to network marketing. It was not something I thought I would end up doing, especially after working so hard to get my degree, but I decided to step out of my comfort zone. Through personal growth and development, vision, and the desire to help others, I was able to retire from the teaching profession twenty-five years early and pursue the life I know I was destined to live. I needed to immerse myself in a culture of personal growth and development. I realized my purpose in life was to be an educator, but not just in a classroom setting. I don't believe it's quitting to walk away from something that isn't serving you well, whether it be a failing relationship or a career you have put your blood, sweat, and tears into. To do so is being smart enough to know when someone or something is preventing you from growing and fulfilling your life's purpose.

By the time 2019 came around, I truly felt I had it all: the perfect family, a positive set of friends, money from my passion, and not a paycheck. I was finally traveling the world for a living as I had always dreamed of doing. But it's frightening how quickly life can humble you. My husband and I were in Netherlands, enjoying the sights and time together until, one evening, I was awakened by a phone call. It was every parent's worst nightmare: my son, Logan, who was sixteen at the time, was on the train tracks wanting to end his life. Everything suddenly screeched to a halt. There I was, sitting halfway across the world, feeling helpless and completely devastated. Guilt at my failure as a parent immediately consumed my entire being. Where had I gone wrong? What could I have done differently? A thousand and one questions and thoughts fluttered through my head, all paralyzing my body but leading to one simple answer . . . nothing.

Looking back now, I feel that a part of me died that day, but what I have come to realize through my tragedy is that people who decide to take their own lives don't really want to end it all, they just lose their purpose. Somewhere, somehow, my son felt as if he had no purpose in life. Since losing Logan, I have made it my life's mission to help others find their purpose in life. I had to discover mine all over again, and now I hope to inspire readers across the globe to step out of their comfort zone and into the life they were designed and destined to live. The choices we make in life lead us down the path that we are supposed to be on. It is similar to the butterfly effect: if you change one minor detail in your life, it will change everything in your past and your future, so that wherever you find yourself at any point in life, it's where you are supposed to be. I live with no regrets, and I am proud to say that I am still happily married to the love of my life for eleven years and we enjoy a healthy relationship. Together, we are learning to navigate life's ups and downs and heal as a family. My purpose in life is to travel the world and change lives. I had no idea that it would take the sum of all my failures and triumphs to figure that out. My son did not die in vain. He may have felt as if he had no purpose, but maybe, it was only meant for him to have sixteen loving years of existence to make his imprint on the world.

Whatever life throws at you, you have to keep your feet moving—because it's not just about finding your purpose, it's about learning and enjoying the journey of growth along the way.

BIOGRAPHY

Amanda Meyer is a military spouse, mother of five children, and a fitness competitor. With a bachelor's degree in Elementary Education, Amanda has taught writing to a wide range of age groups. Amanda has become a transformational leader within the network marketing industry, helping others achieve their goals and dreams. After losing her sixteen-year-old son to suicide in 2019, Amanda's life mission has been to travel around the world, helping others discover their purpose in life. As a national motivational speaker, Amanda teaches and inspires others to achieve success by stepping out of their comfort zone and into a life they were designed to live.

Amanda Meyer's contact details are available at https://linktr.ee/amandameyer2020

CHAPTER 8

Becoming A Leader While Hiding In Plain Sight

By Anita Renee Blue

All my life, I wanted to be *someone* special. I wanted to be a part of something special. But I had a secret . . .

I excelled in sports as the Captain of my basketball, softball, and track teams. I acted as squad leader in the Junior ROTC program during my high school years. Yet, I still felt I lived in the shadows. You see, I had a secret.

I come from a small town in central Louisiana. As the eldest of four children to a single mother who worked two jobs to support us, I took on responsibilities beyond my age. I grew up regularly attending church, went to Sunday School every week, sang in the choir, and was a junior usher. Church was a HUGH part of my life. But I had a secret.

My secret was that I was a victim of molestation and I was a lesbian. Now, back in the '70s and '80s, being gay or lesbian was truly frowned upon. Growing up, I knew I was different. I had stronger feelings for girls than I did for boys. But because of the stigma, I would act as if everything was normal. My mother was a very strong woman and my HERO but me talking to her at that time was not an option.

The night of my high school graduation, one of the most dramatic events happened. I was now 18, and I wanted to be me, my true self—no more secrets. I did not go to my prom because I did not feel comfortable pretending anymore. My girlfriend and I decided to celebrate together at the local gay club. So, we are in the club dancing, happy, and having a great time when we turned around and noticed several of our classmates in the club as well. We grabbed each other's hand and ran to hide behind the curtain on the stage. Sheer panic was what I felt! We looked at each other and whispered, "what do we do?"

And in that moment of fear, I found the courage from somewhere. And in that defining moment, we decided we no longer would live in this fear. Together, we stepped from behind that curtain, hand in hand, and confirmed what they had been whispering about for years. We were together, as a couple. And in that moment of truth, I felt that I was someone special and part of something incredible.

In a word. I felt Liberated.

Life moved on. My basketball scholarship to a Junior College took me to Ellisville, Mississippi, but she stayed in Louisiana to attend college. Life and the distance would not let the relationship last, so we ended it. In my desire to do right in the eyes of God and make my mother happy, I dated a football player at college. That ended up with me getting pregnant. And I felt so out of touch with myself and reality. I went home for the summer, suffered a miscarriage, and lost the baby. It was sad but a sigh of relief because I did not want to be a statistic. You know the one: another young, teenage mother. I had placed myself in a vulnerable situation and paid the ultimate price, trying to hide my secret.

I did not go back to Mississippi. Instead, I went to New Orleans to live with my aunt and go to college there. This is where I started to come into myself. I wanted my own car, and my mother was unable to buy me one. So, I had to figure out how to get the money for myself. It was 1986, and I decided to join the Air National Guard. This started my thirty-four-year military career.

Off I went to Lackland Air Force Base for basic training. I was chosen, once again, to be a squad leader. And honestly, I was terrified. You would never know it because I was a shy person. But I persevered and made it through. What a great feeling of accomplishment. I became the first person in my family to serve. Now mind you, I had no idea I would serve in the military as my career. I could not even imagine 34 years straight. I only joined to buy my car. And I did. It was a used yellow Mazda GLC, 5-speed, hatchback. You could not tell me anything about my new car. In my mind, this was my first major goal that I had ever achieved. Zig Ziglar helped me understand my first great lesson, "What you get by achieving your goals is not as important as *what you become* by achieving your goals." I was becoming a stronger leader and did not even realize it.

My next adventure took me to Anchorage, Alaska, in the dead of winter in January 1988. Yes, it was for love, no doubt, but that is another story. But remember, I am from Louisiana, so being around and driving in snow was a whole new world for me. So, take a guess what my first job would be. A courier for the Anchorage Times, working in the advertisement department driving around town in the snow delivering ad copy. But that did not last long. I started working for Alyeska Pipeline Company in the mailroom. And by the time I left the company five years later, I was working in human resources for the benefits department as the Savings and Investment Consultant, giving out loans to the employees. Talk about moving on UP! The company provided tremendous help to me to overcome my fear of public speaking by offering Toastmaster classes during lunch. I registered for the classes to overcome that fear!

At this time, I also went through a breakup with my girlfriend, a great time of confusion about my sexuality, and in that confusion, I became pregnant once more and had a beautiful baby girl.

This entire time I still served in the Air National Guard. And I kept my secret. No one in the guard, at work, or church knew about it. You must understand, I was in the military when you could be discharged just for being a lesbian! It was later that it evolved to "don't ask, don't tell." Then, you could serve and be lesbian and even get married. So, I was forced to keep my secret. I lived every day, hiding and denying myself my real truth, for many painful years.

Yet, as life would have it, I have been blessed with many opportunities to serve in leadership positions. And what I am going to share with you now is how I grew to become a leader. But first, it is important to understand what leadership means to me.

As I mentioned, I am the oldest of four, served as a squad leader in my Junior ROTC, and played as Captain in many sports in high school. This is what I call my foundations of leadership. I was young and already exhibiting leadership characteristics. With each leadership position, I have risen to the occasion and grown because of the responsibilities demanded of me in that role.

> "The most dangerous leadership myth is that leaders are born - that there is a genetic factor to leadership. This myth asserts that people simply either have certain charismatic qualities or not. That's nonsense; in fact, the opposite is true. Leaders are made rather than born."—Warren G. Bennis

Leadership is the art of flexibility. It is being able to adjust and communicate in different ways, specific to each person within your sphere. You must exhibit enough self-awareness to know what is going on around you and, at the same time, yield the best response from each person. This demands patience, empathy, and compassion.

And now, with thirty-four-years in the military as the basis of my experience, the following characteristics are what I feel to be the critical qualities of acting as a good leader:

Commitment
Clarity
Courage
Passion
Humility

The ability to act decisively reflects **Commitment**. When serving the Guard in Alaska, I was promoted to the rank of Staff Sergeant or E5. I was responsible for the storeroom in the dining facility. Now before this promotion, I wasn't the best Airman. I was late for duty and often called in sick or was simply not in attendance. But once I was placed in this leadership role, I knew confidence had been entrusted in me. And the feeling of that responsibility demanded that I had to be present and on time. I had to step up! I had to commit to becoming that better version of myself. A leader! And this evolution started with this first promotion. Thinking back on this key event, I recall what Ralph Ellison wrote, *"It takes a deep commitment to change and even deeper commitment to grow."*

When a leader has **Clarity**, it allows others to digest their goals and decide whether they will support the leader's cause. In the leadership role as a military member, I was trained to give detailed instructions so that my subordinates were clear about my expectations. And this clarity then assisted them in growing into their leadership roles. I gave and received feedback just for that purpose. It has been my experience that very few people know what they want, much less know how to get there. So, they gravitate to those who have vision, a clear picture that can be shared in the minds of those around them. Jim Rohn wrote that clarity leads to great achievement. *"Take advantage of every opportunity to practice your communication skills so that when important occasions arise, you will have the gift, the style, the sharpness, the clarity, and the emotions to affect other people."*

Demonstrating **Courage** as a leader is a BIG key. No, it is more than that. Demonstrating courage is absolutely critical. I have been in the military in three different states: Louisiana, Alaska, and Texas. I started out as a very shy person in life. But I had to become bold and practice acting courageously to be courageous. Moving through the ranks while facing adverse risk as a black, lesbian female meant always hiding in thought. It meant not being able to truly express myself. It meant living with a secret that could instantly end my career. And in the end, this courage helped me to fulfill my role as a good leader. You must remind yourself that your time is limited. You cannot waste a moment living with the results of other people's thinking. Refuse to allow the noise of the opinion of others to drown out your inner voice. And like Steve Jobs reminds us, *"have the courage to follow your heart and intuition."*

My **Passion** has always been shown in my love for people. How they are treated is rooted in my own experience of having to keep my secret and never truly having a voice. For thirteen years, I served as an Equal Opportunity Craftsman in the military. There I was able to train on Diversity, Inclusion, and Cultural Awareness. This role meant fighting for people in areas of sexual harassment as well as discrimination based on race, color, sex, gender, and national origin. And during my training for this career, I was sexually harassed. And I had to report it. He harassed the wrong person. And after a long fight, sexual orientation has been added to the protected classes for military members. And this gives me *hope* like the words of Maya Angelou, *"My mission in life is not merely to survive, but to thrive; and to do so with some passion, some compassion, some humor, and some style."*

And last but certainly not the least, I feel that to be a good leader, **Humility** is a MUST. It can be hard to admit your weakness or vulnerability, but a good leader will demonstrate it when required. Confidence is an attractive trait. And there is simply nothing like a humble character for creating a lovable persona. A good leader can *admit when they are wrong* and *take criticism as an opportunity for growth*. Michelle Obama's perspective inspires me every day, *"We learned about gratitude and humility - that so many people had a hand in our success, from the teachers who inspired us to the janitors who kept our school clean . . . and we were taught to value everyone's contribution and treat everyone with respect."*

Each of these characteristics have brought me to where I am today. And they will continue to carry me forward on my path to being one of the most outstanding leaders. And as a great leader, I aspire to become one of the greatest entrepreneurs in history. Leaders engage. They try different paths, like many of the business opportunities that have allowed me to grow tremendously. Each was like a stepping stone, making me stronger for the next one.

Knowing that I did my best in my mind just does not work for me. Instead, I look at each event as a chance to grow and pay attention to timing. Hindsight is 20/20, they say. And I believe that to be true in my case. You must stay the course! And whatever you try to accomplish, even if it does not turn out as you expect it, remember that we are all destined for something great in our lives. We just have to believe, keep the faith in ourselves, and fight through each challenge to find our own meaning of Victory and Success.

BIOGRAPHY

Anita Renee Blue is a thirty-four-year air force veteran, mother, wife, businesswoman, and an active member of her community. She has held many leadership positions in the military and as a civilian, adding to her extensive life experience in this arena. She desires to continue to be a servant leader to people throughout the world. She is highly motivated by seeing others achieving their goals and dreams through their commitment, courage, clarity, passion, and humility. Challenges will come, but she believes that whoever stays the course will eventually win the race of this thing called Life, with love in their hearts and joy in their souls.

Anita Renee Blue can be contacted via https://linktr.ee/AnitaBlue

CHAPTER 9

Up From Stinky Thinking

By Cecelia Williams

The thought of writing this book has floated through my mind for many years. Friends and acquaintances with whom I shared this story believe that others can benefit from my journey. I hold this to be true.

If you are someone who has lived through a traumatic childhood, struggled with moments of depression, suffered from feelings of low self-esteem and low self-worth, feel that you are not living up to your potential, feel unhappy with your life, and think that you will never live out your dreams, know that this chapter was written with you in mind.

What is Stinky Thinking?

As defined by the English Dictionary, stinky thinking is the belief that you will fail, that bad things will happen to you, or that you are not a particularly good person. Your behavior is positively or negatively influenced by whatever your mind believes. What we choose to think or do has a significant impact on our emotions.

I find it liberating to know that we have within us the ability to increase our happiness by thinking thoughts of empowerment and by taking actions that will fuel happiness. By questioning our mood and temperament, we can lead ourselves to live happier lives instead of blaming people or circumstances. Remember that your thoughts can place you in heaven or hell because each thought creates an emotion.

Armed with the definition of stinky thinking, let us determine whether you may or may not be a person who engages in stinky thinking. Simply stated, you become a stinky thinker when your thoughts are negative. Your thoughts, more likely than not, are based on your childhood experiences. Perhaps your caregivers did not make you feel safe, loved, or protected. More likely than not, you may have felt abandoned or experienced some other form of trauma. You can be the opposite of a stinky thinker by thinking thoughts of empowerment. Empowering thoughts are when: you feel happy and good about who you are; you believe that you can accomplish anything you set your mind to, and you are living your dream life.

I was a stinky thinker, and this is the story of how I transformed into an influential positive thinker. I began living out four biblical verses: Proverbs 3:1-4; Philippians 4:8; Matthew 22:37; and 2 Corinthians 5:7.

Before I began to live by these four scripture verses, I was a survivor: someone who endures their childhood trauma. Then after much work, I became a thriver: someone who overcomes their trauma. Today I am living my dream as an accomplished author and an inspirational speaker who is creating a generational legacy! You, too, can become a thriver, provided you are willing to put in the work. I attended support groups wherein we closed each session by stating in unison: "It only works if you come back and put in the work!" An extremely powerful statement. To heal, you must do the work.

As someone reading this book, you should expect to begin a life of triumph and success—especially if you are a believer. I have fallen many times, and the four verses above of scripture have helped me get back up on my feet.

Four tenets governed my journey of living out a life of transformation. These tenets coincide with the aforementioned scriptural verses: LOVE (unconditional); FAITH (without which it is impossible to please God);

BELIEF (knowing God has my back); and UNDERSANDING/TRUST (not leaning on my own).

I was born in Houston, Texas, under the care of two wounded souls. At the time of my birth, my father became a recovering alcoholic: he vowed never to drink again. Soon after my sister was born (a year and three months later), he became an ordained minister. At the age of four, my mother dropped my sister and me off at her husband's mother's house in Dallas. There, I was molested by my step-grandfather. My father came and took us back to Houston. My sister and I lived with him until he re-married (after he and my birth-mother got divorced).

My father loved my sister and me but had abusive mannerisms. At the age of 16, I ran away from home. I ran away to my grandmother's house, where I first began noticing how God protected and provided for me. This was on account of the fact that I walked to my grandmother's house, which was about 10 miles away, after 10 pm on Halloween night. I believed that God protected me. 'He had me,' I often told myself when I encountered dangerous situations such as meeting abusive, possessive men who thought of killing me if I left them or threatened to kill me for not wanting to be with them.

In my 18th year, I began dating a young man, about six years my senior, who was not abusive and convinced me to ask my parents if I could come back home. One night (after consummating our relationship), he drove me to my parents' house. When we arrived at the house, we discovered that my father and stepmother had separated. When I asked my father if I could move back home, he agreed. My boyfriend was delighted; also, I thought this was better for me. However, to my dismay, I left the next day because I was violated that night. I was back on the streets, but this time, being on the streets resulted in my being declared a juvenile delinquent and a ward of the court. To my surprise, my sister and I were awarded the same institution. Later, to my consternation, I was transferred to a home for unwed mothers—yes, I was impregnated by that family member the night I left my father's house.

During my stay at the Home for Unwed Mothers, I had a traumatic emotional breakdown. It happened during a telephone conversation I had with my caseworker when she told me that I had given birth to my brother—what horror and disbelief! I broke down because, until that moment, I refused to believe my father impregnated me; I felt assured my boyfriend was the father. This is when I put into practice two of my four tenets: FAITH and BELIEF. Right after the call with my caseworker, I began screaming and sobbing hysterically. I rocked back and forth on my bed, repeating over and over: 'God would not put more on me than I could bear.' I felt myself falling into a dark chasm. I must have cried and rocked back and forth for at least two hours, repeating that one phrase. But guess what? That phrase by itself would not have kept me sane had I not believed it with the totality of my heart. FAITH and BELIEF go hand in hand. When you find yourself in those kinds of circumstances, I say believe with all your heart and soul that God is there for you. He will not forsake you, no matter what the situation is. Walk by faith and not sight while holding on to your belief in Him.

My caseworker convinced me to give my baby up for adoption, but I later tried to renege on that agreement as I was confused at the time. I continued to do whatever I could to get my baby back, but to no avail. In retrospect, I'm grateful that I let it go because it gave me peace. 'Lean not to your own understanding,' I convinced myself that it was not to be.

Upon leaving the Home for Unwed Mothers, my sister and I were again reunited in a foster home since we had nowhere else to go; our parents had been declared "unfit." Our caseworker, who believed in us, used her influence and found us a foster mother who was willing to take in two teenage girls! Look at God, still protecting and providing. You must look for God's handiwork in such situations.

While living in my foster home, I enrolled in a Licensed Vocational Nursing (LVN) school. A year or so after beginning LVN school, I met another non-abusive man, whom I later married. This was my first husband, with whom I had my first boy. I did not complete LVN school mainly because I dropped out at the beginning of my pregnancy due to becoming extremely nauseous upon entering the hospital. After taking time off, I decided that being an LVN was not the best profession for me because I had no confidence in myself when it came to calculating and administering medications. I felt that I had neither self-worth nor self-esteem. I had been told that I would be like my no-good mother. Those words repeatedly rang in my head; the result was that I did not believe in myself.

After working a few low paying jobs, I decided that I would look for a job that would pay me the same amount as a college graduate—I applied to the United States Post Office. I was hired and remained there for ten years. During that time, I divorced my first husband and married my second.

I tell people that my second husband was an angel sent from heaven, even though he was an alcoholic and verbally, emotionally, and physically abusive. That relationship propelled me into a path of self-discovery. By attending Al-Anon meetings, I learned that I was existing, not living; I was sleep-walking, not creating; I was living unconsciously rather than making conscious decisions about my life. I was told that I unhappily remained in the marriage because the abuse I was receiving from my husband was familiar to me—eye-opener, right? Well, let me tell you, this sent me right into a tailspin that motivated me to start working on myself. I read many self-help books like *Healing the Child Within*, *Erroneous Zones*, *Creative Visualization*, *The Power of Positive Thinking*, and *Cybernetics*. I attended support groups for adult survivors of child abuse, adult survivors of incest, and people who were co-dependent. I prayed, spoke daily affirmations, and began believing in myself and knowing that I deserved a healthier life.

All those books, and many others I did not mention, were a tremendous help. Although I think of myself as Christian, the book *Three Magic Words* by US Andersen became my new Bible. I released negative thoughts by completing the 30-day mental diet prescribed in the book and daily affirming and positive thoughts. The diet suggested that you entertain only positive thoughts for 30 days. If you had a negative thought, no matter where you were in the diet, you had to begin over again until you reached the goal of having solely positive thoughts for 30 days. This exercise was extremely powerful and life-changing for me (I hope you will consider doing it as well). I had at least three do-overs before achieving the goal. Reading this book and completing the affirmations, along with the aforementioned scripture verses, got me to thriving in life instead of merely surviving, and here I am today. I am now living and creating my best life. No longer am I living unconsciously. I currently live a life of triumphant successes, creating a generational legacy. And I want the same for you.

Keep in mind these words from a great mentor of mine, Dr. Wayne Dyer (may he rest in peace): You can look back on your life and either feel sorry for yourself or treat it as a gift. Either something is an obstacle to your growth or an opportunity to grow; you make the choice.

EXERCISE: *Write something you believe and have total faith in or a situation that occurred wherein you demonstrated these two tenets. Now write a situation in which you used one or the other.*

BIOGRAPHY

Cecelia Williams is an overcomer of childhood traumatic experiences. As an esthetician with over 20 years of experience, she wrote many articles on skincare. Holding a master's in professional counseling and being a certified life coach, she counsels and coaches on overcoming and thriving to live a happy, healthy, and productive life. She is an ardent volunteer and a passionate advocate for the National Alliance on Mental Illness (NAMI), Greater Houston affiliate. She is a member of Positive Psychology.com, Adult Survivors of Child Abuse (ASCA), and Emotions Anonymous. Currently, Cecelia speaks, coaches, and advocates for emotional and mental wellness to help people understand that they can create their lives one way or another by consciously thinking or unconsciously living, knowing that the quality of their thoughts creates the quality of their life.

Cecelia Williams' contact details are available at https://linktr.ee/ceceliawilliams

CHAPTER 10

When Passion Becomes Purpose

By Dolly van Zaane

"I'm not going to an all-girls school," was my defiant reply, shaking my head to make my decision clear to my parents and the teacher who had suggested this option. I was sixteen years old and in my last year of high school. To further my education, I had to move to another school. One was an all-girls' school, and the other had higher standards and was a co-ed.

The teacher said I wouldn't be able to cope at the co-ed school, as my arithmetic was below average. But he had a point. In all my ten years of education, I had been below average when it came to numbers. I was fine with other subjects such as geography, languages, or history, but numbers and I just didn't get along. Moving to a higher-level school where I would need to do math maybe wasn't such a good idea, as it would set me up to fail.

"What do you want to do?" my mother asked. "Animals . . . I want to work with animals." No one had any idea where that came from, as we never even had a dog or a cat. I was a ferocious reader and, with my 1.50 guilder pocket money, I regularly bought paperbacks from a small bookshop, "'t Sluisje," to where I would go on my bicycle and search the shelves for anything that attracted my attention, including books about horses, dogs, trees, birds, and even Albert Schweitzer. I was also a familiar figure in our local library.

To their credit, my parents listened—for which I will be forever grateful. Mum produced the Amsterdam phonebook and looked for dog kennels and riding schools to call. While the kennels she called didn't answer the phone, the riding school did, and my fate was sealed. Fifty-three years later, the horse industry has been my life, my passion. I've learned so much from working with horses: about life and about committing to a dream. Horses give unconditional love. They don't judge. They don't care about your bad hair day or what language you speak.

The horses have given me purpose. Breeding is a long-term game, and you need to have a vision of what you want to achieve, not just for the current season, but for the following five, ten, or twenty years.

Being around horses has helped me through the lowest of the lows in my life. They have helped me more than any therapist ever could, although I've never been to one. I always say that horses are good for the soul.

From the first day I walked into the stable of that riding school in Amsterdam as a naive sixteen-year-old, I felt that this was what I was meant to do. Looking back, I now believe that my unconventional life stemmed from my parents allowing me to choose my own destiny by letting me do what I really wanted to, not what society thought I should do. It instilled in me the belief that I could achieve whatever I set my mind to.

In 1969, when I was eighteen, my dad died of a massive stroke. That morning, I had kissed him goodbye as I did every morning; and by lunchtime, he was gone. Losing him was so sudden and unexpected that it deeply affected my mum, my brother, and me. My mother went adrift and behaved uncharacteristically. My brother turned to alcohol. I was left feeling lost and alone.

Dad's death was followed by a restless period. I worked different jobs: from an office clerk in Amsterdam to a waitress in Switzerland, learning to educate horses to the saddle in South Africa, and being employed as assistant stud manager at a large showjumping stud in Belgium.

During that period, I also got married at the age of twenty-one, but then divorced after two years. Later, I met another kind man, and he agreed with me that migrating was a good idea. Although neither of us wanted to get married, it was necessary; otherwise, we would have had to separate and stay in two different migrant hostels: one of us in Sydney, and the other in Brisbane (not a good start in a country we knew nothing about).

I was twenty-seven when I arrived in Australia. By then, I had experienced many different and life-changing events, yet I had managed to emerge emotionally and mentally intact. Despite the many adversities in my life, I still felt I could do anything if I set my mind to it. If any obstacle blocked my progress going forward, I always found a way to get to where I wanted to be; I became a solution finder.

While traveling along the many different paths that life had taken me, my vision of working with horses never left me, and my passion for them never waned. Finally, after thirteen years in the horse industry, I was able to buy my own horse. She was a grey, warmblood mare called Monate, and she became the foundation of DVZ Stud. Today, almost forty years later, her great-great-granddaughters and sons are competing and continuing her legacy.

In 1987, I moved to Western Australia to work on, what was at the time, the largest warmblood sport horse stud in the Southern Hemisphere. There, I was introduced to my first network-marketing company by John Trevillian, a veterinarian. It awakened in me the possibility that I could do more than work for someone else.

I realized that earning a second income stream would dramatically improve my life.

Starting up a new company meant you're an entrepreneur, which required a different mindset and a new set of skills. I love learning new things, and my bookshelves bear witness to my quest for knowledge—my mind has always been like a sponge. I read books and listened to tapes by Tony Robbins, Zig Ziglar, Napoleon Hill, Dale Carnegie, and others of that era, and I soon became a self-development addict.

Everything I have taken on in my life, I have tackled with total commitment, because I believe in what I'm doing, and I want to know all about it.

For instance, there was the time I saw an advert for a part-time laboratory assistant in a high school. I was still in Queensland at the time and had no knowledge of science, but it looked exciting. I got the job. I loved it and did it for six years.

My "I can do anything" attitude and mindset gives me the confidence to go for it. I look at it this way: if you don't apply for the job you want, that's already a no. But if you take a chance and apply, you might get a yes. I've found that by just asking, I have often achieved the outcome I desired. I believe that if you want something badly enough, you should go ahead and do it.

Tony Robbins mentioned years ago that he had stopped using the words "I can't," so I no longer use them. It's as though there was a change in my brain chemistry. That way of thinking is now so much a part of my life that I rarely say those words; I stop myself when I do. Try replacing the phrase 'I can't do that,' with "I'll have a go," or "How can I make that work?" You see, when you remove such negative words and phrases from your vocabulary, your mind begins to react to your life situations differently, which in turn creates new outcomes.

Learning to be aware of how I talked to myself over the years has had a major influence on how I tackled life. Many people don't realize what they are saying and the negative effect it can have on their lives. For instance, imagine the impact of saying or hearing the following statements:

"You can't do that."

"You're not smart enough for that job."

"What are you thinking of, moving interstate?"

Remember the teacher I mentioned earlier, who told me that I wasn't smart enough to go to that other school? Well, I never let his words stop me from learning—in fact, I learn every day.

I believe any of us can be or do anything we desire. The biggest shift for me came in 2002 when I attended a two-day event hosted by Dr. John and more determined to continue towards my vision. I never gave up, nor will I ever do so.

These days, they call it grit. Looking back on my quite unconventional life, and what I have been through, I'm so grateful for all the challenges and the many experiences, as they have made me the strong-minded, determined person I am today—someone who can achieve whatever they set their mind to. And if I can do that, so can you. Everything in our lives is due to our actions and reactions to situations. It is about taking self-responsibility.

I've learned, through experience, that every situation has an opposite. There is always light at the end of the tunnel, no matter how far away it seems. You are braver than you believe, stronger than you seem, and smarter than you think.

Believe in yourself—because I believe in you.

BIOGRAPHY

Dolly van Zaane has been in the horse industry as a sports horse breeder for over fifty-three years. Her resilience has enabled her to take opportunities in pursuing her vision at all costs. Her story is of a woman with a deep love of horses and a zest for life. At seventy, Dolly might finally be retiring from working with horses but regards retirement as the beginning of a whole new chapter in her life. Her story will touch and inspire you not to let opportunities pass you by.

Dolly van Zaane's contact details are available at https://linktr.ee/dvanzaane

Demartini called "The Breakthrough Experience." At the time, I wasn't prepared for what would happen and how profoundly it would change me in terms of how I would come to view life and other people as a result of that weekend.

Demartini is a human behavioral specialist and educator, who teaches that we can lead inspiring lives. The Demartini methodology lets you focus on your core values and break through any limiting beliefs that kill your full potential. Thanks to his teachings and the Breakthrough Experience, I am a better person.

Horses have been my core value, and after fifty-three years in the industry and thirty-nine years of breeding under the DVZ brand, I am leaving a legacy with the horses I produced—I bred them not just for me, but for others to ride, compete with, and enjoy.

Now that I'm retiring from the horses as a seventy-year-old, I'm looking forward to leading my new team and becoming the best leader and influencer in my company. I may even do some public-speaking and write my biography. I'd like to inspire others with my story, to teach that it's okay to stumble in life, as long as you know where you're going, because then you can get up and move towards your goal. When you know your core values and develop your life around them, you will lead a fulfilling life. This is not some hocus-pocus talk, but something I have experienced and which I deeply believe.

Over five decades, I have been through the lowest of the lows and the highest of the highs. I overcame some major emotional, financial, and personal challenges that many people never experience in a lifetime. Many were due to both good and bad decisions, which has taught me resilience. I look back with a heart brimming with gratitude that I have lived such a full life already. Life is just one big lesson.

Not once in all those years have I sought professional help. Not a single tablet for anxiety or depression have I swallowed. I did not take to alcohol or any other substance. Through every hurdle, every unexpected event, no matter how traumatic, I came out the other end better, stronger,

CHAPTER 11

The Day I Took Control Of My Emotions

By Frederik van Rensburg

I remember the days leading up to me having to take control of my life: My wife was not happy with my attitude, and my children would become very quiet whenever I entered the room. Then one day, I was sitting at my desk in my excuse of an office, a former packing room, when it suddenly hit me like a ton of bricks. My emotions ran wild and I felt on the verge of losing my sanity. As I sat there, I suddenly recalled the look in my daughter's eyes when I made a stupid and uncalled for remark about something I couldn't even remember. At that moment, I started crying and felt like the biggest loser in the world. Everything that was happening resulted from the stupid decisions I'd made, or not made, during the last couple of years.

At first, I looked for any other reasons except my own behavior for having failed at almost everything. Finances were very tight just then, and all seemed lost and hopeless. I had just lost in a business deal, and the possibility of the COVID-19 lockdown was becoming a reality. It seemed inevitable that we would lose our household's biggest income because my wife's business would have to close down to meet the new social restrictions.

My work in the essential services area was the only hope, but the money I made was not nearly enough to keep us afloat. I felt so lost and had no idea how to handle the situation, and nothing prepared me for what was coming. The memory of the look in my wife's eyes the last time I spoke to her tormented me. I felt like giving up, but something inside me was guiding me to act faster than my mind was capable of thinking at that moment.

I kept hearing the hurt in my life partner's voice, which made me cry so uncontrollably that it hurt. After what felt like an eternity, I tried to pull myself together—I couldn't believe I could cry so much. My wife and I had been together for over twenty years, have three amazing daughters and a grandson.

Looking in from the outside, everything must have seemed fine, as if we were reasonably happy and content. By the way, if you asked me which word I hate the most, 'content' would win. So, it seemed we were doing all right in other people's eyes, but, in reality, financially speaking, our life was falling apart.

Many people didn't know that the bank had taken our house; I had to sell my car to free up some money. I was so broke and distracted that dealing with any of the mess seemed almost impossible. The financial strain was very intense, but one thing I knew beyond anything else was that my family would never see me in such a state again. I'd tried to be and do the best I could, but I couldn't seem to keep my emotions under control.

As I composed myself that day in the office, I wondered if anyone had heard me crying like a baby. Then, a horrible thought struck me—if one emotion could affect me so strongly and uncontrollably like this, what would happen if any of the other more dangerous ones were to act up?

After I managed to calm myself down, I felt clean inside for the first time in a long time. I remember it was terrifying but also a fantastic feeling. Looking around my desk, I saw the title of a book that is very close to my heart and one of my favorites. Part of the title is *'elevate your life.'* I'm thankful that, a couple of years ago, I decided to start reading books on success and motivation, which was how I thought of it at the time.

So, let's chat about emotions for a bit. According to the experts, there are six basic emotions: happiness, sadness, fear, disgust, anger, and surprise.

That's according to psychologist Paul Eckman's theory from the 1970s. But more confusingly, according to an article in *Forbes* business magazine, there are as many as twenty-seven different human emotions. No wonder some people need meds to help fix their lives! So, where do you start with trying to calm, suppress, or even control all of these warring feelings that can reap havoc and even destroy?

I could talk at length about all the many studies and conclusions that have been drawn on the subject, but I'm not going to do that here—I have to admit that I'm not that hot on details. But, for instance, take the whole well-known example of the glass that's half-full. Some would argue that it's half-full and others that it's half-empty. Here's my personal opinion on it—who cares about half-full or half-empty? Just drink it if you're thirsty.

But let's go back to my story. Emotions come and go and are neither good nor bad, but just the way we express our feelings. We never really get to learn all these things because life pulls us along—we learn in the 'school of hard knocks,' and everybody hopes and prays that things will turn out okay in the end.

For most of my life, I've been involved in the pharmaceutical retail industry, and working with other people is one area where you must learn that, sometimes, it's best to fake your emotions. For instance, in my job, I had to be alert, positive, and friendly towards others at all times so as not to upset a client or manager and get into trouble. However, there are many times when you're confronted with different emotions and aren't always sure how to react. Sometimes, you have to walk away to avoid dealing with something that isn't in your normal frame of reference.

One thing we must realize is that our emotions are normal and part of everyday life. We can't escape them, but here's a thought—what if we try to rise above them and start to control them? I always tell my kids that if you can focus your emotions and channel them productively, I believe you can change the world.

As I sat in my office that day, I realized I was in deep emotional distress, and those very words I had told my kids kept playing in my head over and over.

Sitting there with my head in my hands and praying for help and guidance, the answer suddenly came to me. I later realized it was that moment of feeling clean that was the turning point in my personal life. I thought if I could take control of my emotions, then I could take back control of my life.

Imagine what you can accomplish if you can dominate your emotions. Author Bohdi Sanders' best-selling book *Martial Arts Wisdom* is packed with wise words from great teachers to motivate warriors. For example, "When you react, you let others control you. When you respond, you are in control." I realized that day, learning to control my emotions meant I might, in time, become a much better version of myself and, with practice, the best possible version of me.

I once heard something about the different 'hats' we put on to deal with different areas in our lives. For example, at work, I put on my work hat, which comes with one set of emotions, and when I'm with my girls, I put on my dad's hat and another set of emotions; I wear a different hat that comes with different emotions as a husband. Thinking about this, I devised a plan to combine different hats with different emotions, and here's the kicker—it works!

It's important to understand at this point that this idea came to me in a flash but, as with anything in life and love, it requires the application of the 5 Ps: Prior Preparation Prevents Poor Performance. One saying that I use a lot with my team is that Focus creates Posture, and that creates Results. I decided back then to focus much more on the positive aspects of my situation and learn to dominate my emotions.

Some would say it's not that easy, or maybe it was easy for me. My professional response is: Suck it up, grow up, and take charge of your life. It means tackling it one day and one failure at a time until it becomes second nature. It means asking the people you love most for forgiveness and sharing your plan with them. But before taking that important step, you must forgive yourself. That's no easy task, but if you are dedicated, focused, and prepared to give it all you have, you will be amazed at the positive things that will happen in your life.

Here is the plan of action I drew up that changed my life for the better the day I took control of my emotions. First, I took the time to write down my personal goals and dreams. I also decided to always wait before I reacted to any given situation and choose to react positively with any emotions that came up. This simple formula has forced me to stay in a more positive frame of mind and see the world and people differently.

My biggest dream is to be a hero in the eyes of my wife and kids and try to make a positive mark on this planet we call home. So, I advise anyone in a similar situation to stop looking for external means to change things on the inside. I believe that what has happened to me as a result of making this change will help others make a positive difference in their lives.

Here's my formula to a happy life:

Focus + Positive Emotions + Posture + Hard Work = A Much Better You!

Taking control of your emotions can take you from where you are to where you want to be. It's not easy but possible. If those people who claim that we only have one life to live are right, then it's up to us individually to make it the best one possible. My experience is that maintaining a more positive frame of mind opens doors you didn't even notice were there, bringing fresh, exciting opportunities that were not previously available to you.

BIOGRAPHY

Frederik van Rensburg is South African born and raised. He is forty-seven years old, a family man with a passion for words and books. He has spent years working in the pharmaceutical industry, observing people and their behavior. He realized that people and their emotions are not always in tune. He is motivated by this fascinating truth and the desire to help and inspire other people to realize that the power of FOCUS is the ultimate weapon against a weaker version of you. Over the last two decades, Frik has been involved in different areas of business and now focuses on sharing life lessons that add value to the lives of people who are open to listening to him and adopting his simple equation for a fulfilled life: FOCUS creates POSTURE that creates RESULTS.

You can connect with Frederik van Rensburg at https://teamkaching.co.za/

CHAPTER 12

The Journey

By Gregory Stack

They say you know when you've hit bottom when you decide to quit digging. So many have hit bottom several times, including me. I've destroyed cars, valuable belongings, loving relationships with friends, girlfriends, and even my closest family members at times. I thought I'd hit bottom the first time I was arrested for drunk driving. But it wasn't long before I was off to the races again, drinking and using drugs.

For me, my drug use was mostly marijuana. I smoked marijuana every day but experimented with mushrooms, acid, and even cocaine. My drinking, however, caused the most damage. I didn't drink every day. Nor did I get drunk or get into trouble every time I drank. But whenever I did get into trouble, I had been drinking. Whether it was with the law, work, friends, family, or girlfriends, any trouble I caused or got myself into was always while I was drinking and drugging.

I was arrested for a second drunk driving offense less than two years after the first time, and in Michigan, where I'm from, that's an automatic license suspension for at least one year. Here's the catch, when you lose your license for drinking in Michigan, you must be sober (and prove it) for at least one year before you are eligible to apply to get reinstated. I ended up going nine years without driving—because I wasn't ready to quit digging.

I had hit bottom so many times before, but it seemed I hadn't experienced enough pain as a result. I share this because it's part of me, part of my journey to success. When I had finally had enough, when I finally experienced all the pain I could endure, when I was utterly fed up with feeling sick and tired, I finally asked for help. I was DONE! Done drinking, done using drugs, and done hurting the people I loved the most.

My mother used to tell me that she prayed for me every day; she prayed that I'd stop drinking and turn my life around. Well, her prayers were answered—and so were mine. I got involved with other people like me, and we helped each other in recovery. And I got on my knees every day and asked God for help and to keep me sober.

I'm now in my tenth year of recovery from alcoholism and drugs, and life has changed for the better in so many ways. Since getting sober, I have restored relationships with my family and friends. My parents got to see me turn my life around, which was such a gift.

Speaking of my parents, I lost both while I was in recovery—and I still stayed sober. Losing them was just about the most painful thing I've ever had to experience, but still, I never once thought about drinking. I was rock solid! I also gained massive respect from my employers and colleagues. I even started my own business just four years into recovery. Some of the other blessings have been new cars and new furniture!

Before recovery, all I ever had were used cars and hand-me-down furniture. Sure, these are just material things, but they meant a lot to me and seemed like true blessings. From that, I gained a real sense of accomplishment, which gave me the courage to keep going, knowing that I would have had none of it without recovery.

Most importantly, I now have a loving relationship with a beautiful woman who loves me for myself and the version of myself that I aim to become. She knows my story and loves me more because of it. So, nowadays, I continue to stay involved with the fellowship of others in recovery, and I continually strive for success.

I'm working at expanding my business and have also started a second business in network marketing. Some people ask me why I want to make so much money. For me, it's not just about the money, it's more about freedom and catching up for all the years wasted while I was drinking. I'm in my mid-forties and just getting started in establishing some sort of retirement plan. I know I still have a long way to go, but now I know I have what it takes to make a difference in the world.

My newest goal is to help people who are struggling with addiction. I recently had a conversation where I talked about how my family and closest friends know my story, but not even some of my best and longtime clients know it, not to mention all the people in the world I've never met. I said my story could help millions of people if I could share it with the world, and that's when I decided to make a difference by sharing my story with the world—hopefully, to help millions of people. It might help you if you're reading this right now, and even if you're the only person my story helps, then it was worth writing.

Writing this chapter is a part of my journey. There is no graduation in recovery; you're never done recovering. I want tomorrow to be better than yesterday. I want this week to be better than last week, and I want this year to be way better than last year. And I know I can accomplish that by helping others achieve success in overcoming addiction and watching the world unfold with blessings.

I am an expert in addiction because I've been there. And it doesn't matter what your addiction is; it could be alcohol or drugs, like mine was, or gambling, weight lifting, even working out. Believe it or not, something good for you like exercise can be addictive, too. Eating, sex, pornography, you name it, there are endless possibilities for addiction out there. And my addiction is part of me—it's part of my journey. But without my recovery, I would have nothing. I would still be living with roommates with addictions of their own, with no car, probably sitting and sleeping on that old, used furniture. Of course, that's all supposing I would still be alive, because the way I was living before recovery, there's a good chance I would be dead, in jail, or prison by now.

I was blessed that I rolled over two vehicles in my drinking days. Fortunately, I had no passengers with me, and I walked away both times, relatively unharmed with a few minor bruises. And here's the thing; I could tell you all day that I wouldn't drink and drive, as long as I'm sober. But get a few drinks in me—and I'd tell you I'm fine. Today, I want to help people, not hurt people. I value my recovery more than anything in the world because, without it, nothing else would matter. Today, I have a chance to make a difference in the world by sharing my story, hoping it would change people's lives.

It's not about what I have or what I want or where I'm going; it's about the journey. I live one day at a time, pushing myself to be better, setting goals for myself, and trying to get my story out there to make a difference. Another part of my story and my journey is what led me to my addictions in the first place—my childhood: I was the youngest of four siblings, and my parents started having problems when I was just a toddler. Moving around a lot, I struggled in school and had a hard time fitting in and making friends. By the fourth grade, I was getting into fights in the playground and, as a result, was placed in Special Education in a new school. On the last day of my fourth-grade year, my parents separated, and my mom, my sister, one of my brothers, and I moved out. We moved to a different side of town, in a new school district. So, I was now in my second year of "Special Ed" and yet another new school. Then, after a year, we moved again to another school district. It was tough having to adjust for three years in a row to being the newbie among a bunch of entirely new kids. I gravitated to the troubled kids. I guess because they were the easiest to make friends with and, like me, probably didn't have many friends anyway.

Luckily, I arrived in middle school, and with the help of some good teachers, I started to phase out of Special Ed and back into regular classes. But I was still mixed up with the wrong crowd, getting into fights, smoking cigarettes, smoking weed, skipping school, committing vandalism, and getting involved in other mischievous conduct that always landed me in trouble. By high school, I phased out of Special Ed altogether and was able to start making friends with jocks, preppy kids, and some of the smart kids, too. But I still gravitated to the troubled kids; it was where I felt most comfortable.

Looking back, I think this was because I had really low self-esteem, and I found comfort in hanging out with kids like me, who were doing stuff like drinking on the weekends, smoking pot, and being in places where they shouldn't have been. But, miraculously, I was able to graduate on time! I joined the US Navy after high school, something I'm very proud of, and as an American, I'm still very grateful for that opportunity to serve our country. However, that was when my drinking really took off because, after all, I was an adult, right? I was serving our country, so I figured I deserved to drink as much as I liked. That was my mentality, and, thankfully, despite the drinking, I was able to make it through and get honorably discharged, but not before rolling my first vehicle when I was home on leave drunk, and then getting my jaw busted in a bar-fight, while my ship was visiting another naval base in Florida. Within four years of getting out of the Navy, I had completely unraveled and gotten two drunk driving prosecutions, rolled a second vehicle, and lost my license for what turned into nine years before I finally got sober.

And, to this day, getting sober was the best thing I have ever done. I like to say that my worst day sober is far better than my best day drunk ever was. So, if you're struggling with addiction in any form, please know that if I can get sober and overcome my addiction, I'm confident you can, too. Since I was a kid and right up to my recovery began, there were many days when I thought about suicide. I would think about the different ways of doing it. How could it be done? Where? And what would be the best and least painful way to do it? But then, I would always think about how it would affect the people who loved me, especially my mom. Maybe that was because she was praying for me every day, even before she told me that she was. She was the best mom, and even though we didn't have much, she did everything she could to provide the best she could for me. It was only later I learned that those prayers were her biggest gift and that it's the prayers that give me the strength today to keep going, keep pushing, and keep striving for a better, more giving life.

I pray that this journey of mine never ends, and I continue to grow and help people by sharing my story and showing people that no matter how bad life is, no matter how bad it gets, *the pain can stop when you stop digging.*

You can choose your bottom wherever you are. You can ask for help and make a statement saying, "I'm done with this addiction"—and make your life a journey worth living.

BIOGRAPHY

Gregory Stack is a master of men's hair, salon owner, network marketing business owner, entrepreneur, and author. Gregory's background in men's grooming includes barbering in the US Navy, cosmetology school, advanced education around the country at prestigious academies, such as TONI&GUY, TIGI NYC, L'OREAL NYC, and Martial Vivot Salon Pour Hommes NYC, amongst many others. Gregory has been awarded a prize for Best Haircut by Allure magazine. His work has landed the cover of *HOT* by *Hair's How* magazine for his avant-garde masterpiece 'Patriotic Pulchritude,' which was dubbed a Sexy Salute to the USA.

Gregory Stack's contact details are available at https://linktr.ee/Gregory_stack

CHAPTER 13

The Gold In Consistency

By Hadassah Were

I had these fantastic genes: even if I thought about chocolate, I would immediately gain 20 kilograms. I recall my mother telling me when I was little girl, "Hadassah, you have the potential to gain so much weight." I didn't understand what she meant because I would hardly gain weight.

My mother is a self-made aerobics trainer. Growing up, I was her diligent assistant; I enjoyed helping her carry around aerobics equipment, and was always at the front row of her aerobics class exercising with energy. Sometimes I felt that I was showing off my flexibility to her clients, who were mostly mothers whose bodies had begun to lose their figures after their pregnancies. I recall them making comments such as: "Oh, your daughter is so flexible. Oh, how I would kill to have her body." I thought these mothers were lazy and weren't exerting enough effort; little did I know that I would be sharing this same pain at a later point in my life.

After the birth of my firstborn son, I began to slowly notice that it was becoming increasingly easier for me to gain weight. In our culture, a young nursing mother must have at least three good meals a day that comprises of protein and carbohydrates (to help with the stimulation of breast milk). With no exercise routine, and being preoccupied with a new baby, my weight was hitting unusual scales.

Then came my second, third, and fourth babies; and more weight. Just like that, I had passed the ordinary. Every year, my new year's resolution was to lose at least 10 kilograms; but I would lose the commitment after a month, and the year would go wasted. The thing about weight loss is that you know what to do, but in my experience, you haven't reached the breaking point or the motivation to sustain your regime.

Did I try? Oh, yes, I did. I would starve myself for weeks and lose weight only to gain it back once I started eating again. I googled various diets to try out, but none were sustainable. My mother came in to help with exercises and to make me healthy meals, but I would not follow through on the commitment. So, I would always lose a few kilos only to gain them right back. The interesting thing is that I exercised regularly: five times a week. But I wasn't aligning it with what I ate, so calories that were burned came right back. I was so frustrated, but my frustration wasn't moving me; Nothing was motivating me to lose weight. I had developed hypertension related to obesity; my back and knees were always aching; I was constantly tired and lazy; my skin was a mess; my metabolism was very poor, and I was frequently on tablets to loosen my stool. I am a confident person, but I felt that I had become shy and closed-in. Even the fact that my husband was seeing someone else wasn't reason enough for me to take serious action. I wasn't bothered about how I looked because I felt that my efforts weren't yielding any results. I had given up on myself.

One day, in 2013, everything changed. My youngest son was celebrating his birthday at school. During their break time, his whole class gathered to celebrate. I brought a cake and many goodies. As I sat on the front seat, the chair couldn't hold my weight; it broke, and I fell to the floor. As I fell, I looked at my son, and I saw a face of embarrassment and disappointment. Kids were laughing at his mother, and teachers were falling as they helped to get me up—it was a mess. Now, you must understand that it wasn't the first time I had broken a chair. This had happened in cafes and restaurants, but nothing was more painful than the look on my son's face that day. I felt I had let him down. I knew the kids in his school would have a field day with what happened. That was the day I decided to be serious gave me the push I needed to get out of the ditch and make strides every day. This led me to reach the top rank of the company in two years and seven months, already earning $100,000 annually.

These seven D's have since become my SUCCESS HABITS. Anyone struggling with anything (it doesn't have to be weight loss alone) can always apply these habits and find success.

So what are these success habits?

DECISION: Weight loss doesn't begin in the gym or a health plan, it begins with making that critical DECISION. I believe everything starts with a decision. Despite my many health scares and threats to my marriage, I still hadn't made the decision to embark on a weightloss journey. I hadn't decided, nor was I committed. Thus, I never gave it my very best. I was always on the fence. So what is it you want to achieve? Make that decision NOW!!! This habit is vital in helping you set yourself up for success. We are only wasting our time if our inner resolve hasn't been established because our actions move in relation to a commitment. Once a decision is made, the how-it-will-be-done begins to manifest. Looking back on that day when I fell off a chair, I had decided that night that enough is enough. That's when I remembered the doctor who had written about a weightloss program. I believe that this was activated by my decision.

DESPERATION: Les Brown talks about allowing your desperation to inspire you to take action. Burn every bridge so that you cant retreat; this situation will bring in amazing creativity. I remember telling myself that this is my only source of income, even though I had other businesses. That year, I decided to make a standing order that all my profits in my other businesses would go to a charity. So this network marketing business was my only source of income; if I didn't work, then I wouldn't earn. I wouldn't support my lifestyle, my children, and my mother. I was desperate, so all I would think about was making it!

DESIRE: This is almost similar to desperation, but as I explain further, you will agree with me that it needs its own place. Develop a WHY am I and make changes. I decided to try something new because everything else I had tried in the past did not work.

I had read about a doctor who ran a weight loss program at his clinic, so I decided to visit him. After taking several tests, he sat me down and asked me what I had done so far. It was the first time someone asked me questions such as, "What time do you have breakfast? What time do you have dinner? How many calories do you consume in a day?" I had read before that calories count for weight loss, but I was too lazy and unresolved to give it a shot. Everything he explained was making so much sense. I always wanted a quick solution to my weight problem, but there was no such thing. Now, this doctor was talking about a journey into a lifestyle-change.

My new regime covered all bases. It was comprised of portion-controlling every meal, eliminating all forms of processed sugar, a mostly protein and vegetable diet, juicing, and lots of water. He set up an exercise plan for me to ensure that I burned more calories than I took in. I started with walking and then jogging. I began to enjoy it. In a few weeks, I would run five kilometers daily. I hated the gym so much because I felt intimated by people who were doing so well. However, during this time, I took up kickboxing at the gym, and I fell in love with it.

During my first interaction with this doctor, he gave me seven words starting with the letter "D" which would be my blueprint for a successful weight loss journey. I was to write these words and place them on my mirror, and every day I would evaluate myself in relation to those seven words.

In one month, I had lost a fantastic nine kilograms. My physician even put me off my hypertension medicines. I found new energy, and my family provided terrific support. The program ran for three months, and I was a success story. I became an ambassador for their program. The three months gave me the jump start I needed to change my lifestyle. I moved from 145 kilograms to 75 kilograms in three and a half years.

In 2016, I joined a network marketing company, and along the way, I began to stall in my progress. I was getting frustrated, but then I remembered the seven D's. Just reading through the weight loss notes that I had taken doing this? Why do I want it? What is my desired outcome? Form images of what your future will look like if that goal was achieved, and let those images become your daily reason/focus to wake up every morning. This worked for me. I formed a visual image of the life I wanted for my kids and myself. Before joining network marketing, I had taken up a loan to build apartments; the interest was hefty on me. I visualized walking up to my bank manager and making my final payment. I visualized walking to the stage as a top income earner in Africa. I even wrote my speech down and placed it in my view every morning. The desire to achieve increased my focus daily; I wasn't leaving anything to chance. I was intentional and deliberate.

DETERMINATION: The decision I made, coupled with inspiration for desperation and growing desire in me to achieve, totaled to determination. Quitting was never an option, and this gave me more resolve to keep going. It kept me inspired even when times were very hard. I remember 21 days into my weight loss journey. I got a sugar-craving so bad that I developed a fever. My body was responding to the lack of sugar. The temptation to give up and promise to start all over again was so high, but I looked at how much progress I had made in 21 days. My husband called the doctor, and he advised me to take a walk; and if the feeling still persisted, I was to go see him immediately. It lasted for five minutes, but it felt like many hours. After the five minutes, I was good. I refused to give up. Tony Robbins says that determination is the wake-up call to the human will. REFUSE TO GIVE IN TO EXTERNAL PRESSURE. IF NEED BE, REST A LITTLE, BUT DON'T QUIT.

A famous quote from an unknown source says, "The greatest oak was once a little nut who held to its ground." AGAIN, DON'T GIVE UP ON YOUR DREAMS!

DISCIPLINE: Our business thrives on being disciplined. It's not something you buy; it takes practice and repetition to develop discipline. It thrives on consistency. It matters what you do daily. Every consistent action made daily is a step towards your harvest. Every time you don't act on your daily goals is a major set back; complacency begins to set in, and then BOOM . . . you are out of the game!

Mastering consistency in anything is a major skill for success. The discipline to keep planting during good and bad times is what compounds your harvest. I knew that my harvest doesn't care if my hoe had broken, or if the weather was bad. The day it rains, the seeds that were planted will sprout!

I developed zero excuses. I created my own consistent system. Every day, I planted; every day, I showed someone our deal; every day, I made a new list; every day, I read a quote. People who said "no" to my opportunity noticed my consistency. Any lack of it would increase their doubts. I knew I had to be disciplined in my daily activities. As time went on, I won their hearts because of my consistent action.

Guess what? Because of my consistent discipline, my team exploded. In less than three years, I had a team of over 5000 members.

Bruce Lee, the famous martial artist and movie star, said, "Long term consistency beats short term intensity."

People are energetic with their light bulb ideas but how to sustain that enthusiasm is the real challenge.

Starting is easy, but finishing is the battle.

Some tips to help with consistency:

1. Keep your eyes on the WHY, the reason WHY will align your focus with your set daily habits.

2. Pick your battles. Don't try to win many battles simultaneously; confidence comes from results. Try winning at one before you embark on another.

3. Stephen Covey says, "The key is not to prioritize your schedule but to schedule your priorities." How important is your WHY?? That is what you schedule

4. Develop emotional power to Ignore your feelings when that negative feeling comes; train your head to override it!

5. Catch that wagon. Every time you don't act on your daily goals is a major set back because it breaks your pattern. But don't beat yourself so hard and resign thinking all is lost because you have missed one day; it doesn't mean you can't catch up, you can run again and catch that wagon."

DEDICATION: My weakness was that I wasn't fully honoring my commitments to lose weight, which affected my efforts to remain devoted and dedicated. I failed miserably because I lacked this. Once commitment is present, there's always a way for the "How."

I needed to fall in love and be obsessed with achieving; nothing else mattered. I found a new love: ACTION. I became obsessed with daily activity. I never cheated on my love. I was truly dedicated; it did not disappoint. THE RESULTS WERE REMARKABLE!

Once you are dedicated and truly committed, you will find creative ways to achieve your goals. You become limitless and unstoppable.

DELIGHT: Find joy in the journey; celebrate daily progress; make it a fun process. Set targets, and once you accomplish them, reward yourself so that you keep looking forward to the rewards. I developed a fun culture in my team: we had dream days and nights where we didn't work but had fun activities. Birthdays were celebrated, great milestones were announced to the whole team, and rewards were given to top producers. This was a great tool in helping the teams remain motivated, and it created a lot of bonding.

CONCLUSION

I want my persistence, courage, determination, hard work, resilience, and consistent actions to inspire people to realize that it is only they who cause themselves to stumble along the path. So I train, coach, mentor, inspire, and I walk the talk.

ALWAYS BE IMPROVING . . .

BIOGRAPHY

Hadassah Were is a wife and mother of six children living in Kampala, Uganda. Having struggled for years with weight problems, she became an ambassador of the Slender Wonder Weightloss Program: a program that helps people make lifestyle changes for better health. She is also a founding member and trustee of Rahab Uganda: a non-governmental organization that helps restore the self-image of girls involved in sexual exploitation and human trafficking. Hadassah Were, a self-made lifestyle-entrepreneur, dedicates her life to helping people design their lives through her own life experiences. She desires that her persistence, courage, determination, hard work, consistency, and resilience will inspire people to know that they themselves are the sole obstacle to achieving what they have set their hearts to do. So, she trains, coaches, mentors, and leads the way.

Contact Information
Facebook: https://www.facebook.com/hadassah.were

CHAPTER 14

Tapestry

By James A. Railey

What is the measure of success? There I was, a twenty-three-year-old marine, my M-16A2 service rifle and several clips of death-dealing ammunition in hand, ready to pull the trigger and end it all. August 17, 1990 is a day I will never forget: My unit had just landed in the Kingdom of Saudi Arabia for Operation Desert Shield, prior to the operation turning into a storm. Don't expect to hear a story of a courageous marine, out to save the world and defend our way of life, although that story would make a colorful and compelling narrative. Just before our deployment, I had been demoted from a Corporal (E-4) to a Lance Corporal (E-3) and fined $400 at a nonjudicial proceeding. In my quest to make my mother my dependent—good initiative—I submitted fraudulent receipts to my unit—poor judgment. The words of my executive officer are as profound today as when spoken three decades ago: "Good luck, maybe you'll get your rank back out there."

I was released to my unit with those words, accompanied by my service rifle and cartridges of live ammunition. The uncertainty about my future provoked a range of emotions within me. There was so much potential for things to go wrong; most concerning, I was at risk for a mental health crisis.

Since that time, I've learned that feeling as though you don't belong, as if you're a burden to others, combined with having the means to carry it out are key ingredients for death by suicide. I had all three! Psychologically, I felt isolated and demoralized. The shame I experienced made me feel like I didn't belong. Within my unit, I had a position of leadership. After the demotion, I was suddenly subordinate to many of those marines I had overseen. Going to war, I felt like a burden to both unit and family. I'd lost my honor, focus, and commitment. Esprit de corps has longed captured the Marine Corps' ethos, it demands optimal accountability to self and unit, to execute its mission. With American forces forecasted to sustain heavy casualties, this presented additional stressors. At home, my mother was emotionally distraught; her only son was at war. It seemed so simple. I had the means to end it all, with one pull of the trigger. In hindsight, I raise the question, why am I still here?

March 11, 2020 was another day I'll never forget. My Momma, having survived two strokes and a ten-year residency in a nursing home, passed away. Overwhelmed with sorrow and grief, I also experienced a profound sense of gratitude. Gratitude!? I felt guilty and ashamed. Loss and gratitude are a great paradox. I understood loss; I lost the woman who gave me life. But why, gratitude? Like that twenty-three-year-old marine, three decades ago, I reflected on my dilemma. As a movie, I saw instances of tremendous pain, growth, and accomplishments. These pivotal events identified the measure of success and underscored my gratitude and why I'm still here.

So, what is the measure of success? What are its essential ingredients? Is it the human spirit's resilience to rise above obstacles and achieve levels of success that are both inspirational and aspirational? If that's the guidepost, then many people would consider me successful, an embodiment of human agency. I was born in Liberia. In 1980, a military coup overthrew the Liberian government. Momma, with access to a one-way ticket, chose to send her 12-year-old son, unaccompanied to the United States. Today, despite that fateful period in 1990, I remain a proud veteran of the U.S. Marine Corps. In May 2019, my mother lived to see a fulfilled dream when I finally received my PhD in social work after a fifteen-year odyssey.

I have no wish to negate the power of self-determination to achieve success. However, the highlight of my experiences interjects an often-forgotten component – mentors and guides. We often look beyond our communities for them when they are all around us, in our ecosystem, both in the human and natural worlds. God, with infinite kindness, graciously provides vertical help through horizontal means. People as social agents—they come to us and through us for others. It's a gift of spiritual generosity, a reciprocal engagement that allows us to build trust and be receptive to support. For me, success is both an individual and a collective endeavor. My idea of success is like an equation:

Success = <u>Quantifiable outcomes</u>
              Qualifiable means (i.e. self-determination, social relationships)

As the above equation suggests, the measure of success is like creating a tapestry, making tapestry a metaphor for moving forward, stepping back, pivoting, and embracing failure as an instrument of growth and development. Just as the construction of a tapestry includes many behind-the-scenes moving parts, social support, mentorship, and the pathways to transformative experiences and outcomes are strands woven together similarly. In retrospect, that fateful day in 1990 charted a blueprint for success and gratitude. It came at a time when I was most vulnerable, broken physically, psychologically, and spiritually. That seminal day helped me to internalize a method for success and created opportunities for growth and positive relationships with others. I once heard a sermon entitled, "I Know Why the Caged Bird Sings." Offered in the message were three points of intersection.

    First, the caged bird sings because she doesn't let external factors impact internal processes. Like the caged bird, I found trust and safety in a supportive holding environment, which permitted others to become fully attuned and empathetic. To build trust, I learned to overcome my fears and became vulnerable. Vulnerability provided shelter for me to live in grace, to be gentle with myself. I made a mistake and it was okay. To live in grace allowed me to be receptive to others pouring into me. My guides were attuned to my plight and provided access to resources and opportunities that have allowed me to live a life of distinction. They helped me develop the mindset to focus on clarity of goals and objectives, which helped me develop a growth mindset. It was a powerful experience to know that I was not alone. I rediscovered my voice. I became present for the moment. I assumed the power to choose to be what I wished to embody and the agency to pursue my goals.

Second, the caged bird sings because it's her nature to sing. She acknowledges but doesn't pander to the whims of emotional trappings. I am not dismissive of emotions, because being attuned to our feelings gives us the capacity to be human. The distinction comes from recognizing the difference between being joyful and happiness. I associate happiness as more of the result of external experiences, like your favorite team winning a championship or the euphoria being at a live concert.

In contrast, joy is an internal state of homeostasis, where you achieve a relative balance between many different elements. No matter what the external event, you possess an inner capacity for calm. With support, I became responsible for my wellness. I learned to objectively look at external events, without assignment of perceived meanings. For example, I could have used my demotion as an excuse to spiral further into depression and hopelessness. Instead, the synergy of an internal state of wellness, coupled with positive social support, was a formidable force that helped me overcome hardships and setbacks. Like the caged bird's song, being joyful was translated into an interactive, proactive endeavor. In the words of author Stephen King, "It's about getting up, getting well, and getting over." It became the empowerment and activation of voice, choice, and critical self-determination.

Finally, the caged bird sings because she knows that trouble won't last forever. Every situation has a beginning, a middle, and an end. Empowered by a social network of connectivity and reciprocity, I learned to sing. During Desert Storm, my executive officer's words waxed poetic; I received a meritorious promotion, approximately six months from demotion. One of my mentors, Corporal Hubb, asked if he could deliver the news to me. At my promotion ceremony, the commanding officer remarked that "Corporal Hubb's reaction to your promotion was as though it happened to him!" I was also successful in making my Momma my dependent while in-country! These accomplishments presented a philosophy for navigational capacity for empowerment, a conservative mindset—self as CEO, amid a liberal environment of support—a recipe for successful sustainable practices.

With the codification of the success equation, the tapestry of life's creation became like a journey of many destinations and ports of call. With applications to both individual and social contexts, my journey transcends my lifespan. Some ports have required me to refresh, learn, stock up, teach, and share with multiple destinations. Most significant, access to social capital has been instrumental; these relationships have provided cellular level reminders of achievements and support for transformational experiences. Also, the codification of success explains my feelings of gratitude when Momma passed away. Mentors helped empower the reality for me to be present, to care for Momma, and achieve a measure of success. This synergy of support and critical agency offers the insight of my essential ingredient for success. I attribute it as central to the single reason why I'm still here.

Internalizing my capabilities from the creation of tapestry has presented me with a blueprint to emulate and pay it forward. For many, success narrates a conservative mindset, driven by an internal locus of control to achieve individual milestones, often manifested by wealth or other material gains. But, just like me, what about people with internal and external conflicts stemming from traumatic events and self-sabotaging practices? Or others who are ready to rise above their circumstances, but lack the resources or opportunities for success? What if these people could be empowered to lead transformative lives of distinction? That means living unfettered from internal and external influences that negatively impact overall wellness.

Mentorship is the art of living in the existence we want to empower. It is an intentional, purposeful communication to meet people where they are. It is crucial to know that the past does not define but empowers us to experience transformative lives of distinction. Just as I discovered, people can be empowered to live optimally and lead self-directed lives, at scale., I seek better outcomes for those with similar challenges to live a life of abundance and wellness. With support, they can look beyond their present conditions and learn to internalize their unique capabilities to live optimally. To paraphrase the well-known words of the ancient Chinese philosopher Lao Tzu, "The journey of a thousand miles begins with the first step." I amended them to read, "The journey of a thousand miles begins with purpose." The reflection of my journey has given me purpose—an awareness from the universe: a divinely-inspired mission of service to others. My journey continues.

BIOGRAPHY

James A. Railey is a global-minded humanitarian citizen. A professional social worker with over fifteen years of practice, and a veteran of the United States Marine Corps. James' why is harmony-based, highlighting our shared human capacity for connectivity and reciprocity, through the lens of service. He has an extensive history of service during his time in the Marines and working with vulnerable populations in varied behavioral healthcare settings. James utilizes translational knowledge to crosswalk multiple domains to help people internalize entrepreneurial processes as pathways to wellness.

CHAPTER 15

What's Missing In Leadership?

By John N. Harris, Jr.

If you believe, as I do, that Jesus was a fisher of men, then you will understand what I mean when I say I also believe that God has called me to change and positively transform the "fishing industry"—and that's what I intend to do.

In chapter ten of one of the most famous books of the past century, *Think and Grow Rich*, published in 1937, author Napoleon Hill talks about the importance of creating a Master Mind Group to accumulate wealth and prosperity. During that period in the history of the United States, there were many outstanding captains of industry, the most famous being Henry Ford, William Wrigley, Jr., John Wanamaker, George Eastman, Theodore Roosevelt, Charles Schwab, John D. Rockefeller, F.W. Woolworth, Woodrow Wilson, William Howard Taft, and Alexander Graham Bell.

These great men went on to accumulate generational wealth for their families and for many of us who are living today. For example, the Rockefeller family left behind a financial and philanthropic foundation to benefit their family and many organizations doing non-profit work in the New York state area. The reputation of the Rockefeller family is seen as positive and is well-respected across the world. But all their good work would have been for naught had their good character been questioned.

This introduces a good point relating to the power, importance, and purpose of cultivating great character. We're all familiar with certain infamous leaders, who were once highly respected for their leadership ability and influence, but ended by their reputation being tarnished by one wrong decision, which caused them to fall from grace: Bill Clinton, Jim Bakker, Jimmy Swaggart, Bill Cosby, O.J. Simpson, Harvey Weinstein, Joe Paterno, Lance Armstrong, Richard Nixon, Marie Antoinette, to name but a few.

There have been a plethora of male and female leaders throughout history, going right back before the birth of Christ, a time when leaders of great character and spirituality fell from grace because of a major character flaw: Adam and Eve, Samson and Delilah, King Saul, and Judas Iscariot are good examples of this. I believe great leadership starts and ends with great character, one that is wise and intelligent, and a spirituality rooted in an understanding of God's word and His purpose for mankind.

Thousand of years ago, there was one man who was wise, upright, and obedient to God in all his ways. His name was Job. As the story goes, God and Satan had a conversation about Job and his integrity. This bible scripture comes from Job 2:3: "And the Lord said unto Satan, Hast thou considered my servant Job, that there is none like him in the earth, a perfect and upright man, one that feareth God, and escheweth evil? And still, he holdeth fast his integrity, although thou movedst me against him, to destroy him without cause." And although Job lost his health, wealth, family, friends, and everything he owned, he did not turn his back on God, nor did he curse God. And because he remained faithful to God, God restored to him everything he had lost twice over. How many of us today would have endured such a test of great character and spirituality? I use this story to make the point that, I believe, to be a truly authentic leader, you have to have a servant's heart.

Another great Bible story that exemplifies outstanding leadership is located in Mark 10: 43-45. The story's context is that two of the apostles, James and John, asked Jesus a question. They wanted to know if, when He came into His Kingdom, could they each sit to the right and left of His throne. And Jesus replied, "But so shall it not be among you, but whosoever will be great among you, shall be your minister. And whosoever of you will be chiefest, shall be servant of all. For even the son of man come not to be ministered unto, but to minister, and to give his life a ransom for many."

As a Servant Leader in this world, the people that you lead and serve must have confidence in your ethical judgment as a reliable guide. I believe one's "moral compass" amounts to a steadfast belief in God the Father, God the Son, and God the Holy Spirit. If you realize that your life's purpose is to love and serve others, then you must first love and serve God, the One who created you. You cannot give what you don't have, and, since God is love, you must first come to know and love Him. You cannot truly love yourself or others without loving Him first.

God revealed this wisdom to me twenty-eight years ago when I was twenty-eight years old. In 1992, I recommitted my life to Christ, and I have been serving Him and His people ever since, and my life's journey has been a blessing. In 1992, I showed my commitment to Christ by being baptized in water for the second time. As a seven-year-old boy, I was water baptized out of parental obligation. But, as an adult, I made a conscious decision to follow and live for Jesus Christ. In 1999, I became an ordained deacon in the Church. After twenty-eight years of biblical self-study, I now possess the biblical wisdom and knowledge of a pastor or evangelist. As an evangelist, you are called to spread the Gospel of Jesus Christ wherever you may be. So, today, that is what I do. I travel the globe, meeting new people from cultures all over the world, and I lead them to Jesus Christ; in pursuit of whatever purpose God has put into their hearts.

As John C. Maxwell so eloquently states in his book on leadership; there are Twenty-one Irrefutable Laws of Leadership: 1) The Law of the Lid; 2) The Law of Influence; 3) The Law of Process; 4) The Law of Navigation; 5) The Law of E.F. Hutton; 6) The Law of Solid Ground; 7) The Law of Respect; 8) The Law of Intuition; 9) The Law of Magnetism; 10) The Law of Connection; 11) The Law of the Inner Circle; 12) The Law Of Empowerment; 13) The Law of Reproduction; 14) The Law of Buy-In; 15) The Law of Victory; 16) The Law of the Big Mo; 17) The Law of Priorities;

18) The Law of Sacrifice; 19) The Law of Timing; 20) The Law of Explosive Growth; 21) The Law of Legacy. Mr. Maxwell goes on to say, "If you follow them, people will follow you." He also said, "… everything rises and falls on leadership." And although I believe his assertion is true, I also believe that if you do not possess great character and spirituality as a foundation of your personality, even if you follow the Twenty-One Laws, the building will come crashing down, and you will fall from grace.

A story in the bible that best exemplifies my point is in Matthew 22:37-40. The context of the story is that the Pharisees and Sadducees were trying to trick Jesus into saying blasphemous things against the Mosaic Law. So, they asked Jesus, in tempting him: "Master, which is the greatest commandment in the Law?" "And Jesus said unto him, Thou shalt love the Lord thy God with all thy heart, and with all thy soul, and with all thy mind. This is the first and greatest commandment. And the second is like unto it; thou shalt love thy neighbor as thyself. On these two commandments hang all the Law and the prophets."

Jesus very eloquently stated that to love God and to love others is the foundation of any Law that exists in this world. To be a truly authentic leader, one must follow the greatest commandments set forth by Jesus Christ. As a young man in my early teens and twenties, I can honestly say that, although I knew that story, my life back then did not line up with Jesus's teachings. I was living a "double-Life"; I was off to church on Sundays, but during the week, I was pursuing my own selfish, lustful passions, and focusing on my career, so that I could make more money and try to appear as though I was financially successful. Back then, I took all the credit for my success. I thought it was because of my own hard work, dedication, intelligence, and perseverance that I was a financial success. I was enjoying all the fruits of my labor, until it happened—"Pride cometh before the fall." The building came crashing down, and I lost everything: my house, my company car, my fiancé, my health, and my mind.

I had the "Job" experience and, although that experience happened to me, I never lost my faith in God. I stayed true to Him and others. I gave to others worse off than myself, even though I was living in poverty. I couldn't afford a place to live, so my car became "home" for six months. I would find something to eat every other day; usually, a generous hotel lobby worker would give me an apple or a cookie. I still went to church every week, and I still prayed for others and myself. And, because of my faithfulness, God restored unto me twice as much as before. However, I now give all the credit where the credit belongs—to my Lord and Savior, Jesus Christ. And I thank God the Father for creating me, others, and the universe.

My evolution as a Christian man has culminated in being wise, knowledgeable, and understanding of not only God's Word but also of people and what it means to be an authentic Servant Leader in my personal, professional, and public life. As a single man, I am so looking forward to being married and having a family of my own. Professionally, I have developed several income streams over the course of many years. Currently, I am a sales manager in the pharmaceutical industry, a licensed real estate salesperson in the real estate industry, and I am also an entrepreneur in the travel and leisure industry.

As Napoleon Hill suggested in his book, *Think and Grow Rich,* I have created a Master Mind Group of individuals, whom I utilize as my board of directors and advisors. Some of them are living, and some of them are deceased. However, the great character and spirituality that they possess, or once possessed, has been clearly documented and exemplified throughout their lives. I call them my "Conference Table of 12": 1)Jesus Christ; 2) Mahatma Gandhi; 3) Martin Luther King, Jr.; 4) Abraham Lincoln; 5) King Solomon; 6) Abraham; 7) King David; 8) Barak Obama; 9) Albert Einstein; 10) Dale Carnegie; 11) Bill Britt; 12) Dr. Myles Munroe.

To me, each of these men exemplify what it means to be a man of power and purpose. I believe that God revealed to them their purpose in life. I was personally mentored by Bill Britt and Dr. Myles Munroe for many years, and I was blessed by their wisdom and knowledge. Men and women of power and purpose can change and transform the world in a very positive way. For example, my core purpose in life is to develop and improve myself personally and professionally so that I can be the Servant Leader that God has created me to be. My ultimate goal is to positively transform the lives of ten percent of the world's population by helping others realize their God-given purpose in life and experience adventurous exploits by learning and sharing my faith, beliefs, and servitude with people all around the world from different cultures. I plan to create a legacy of multi-generational wealth, success, benevolence, and love for my family, the people, causes, charities, and foundations that are doing work building the Kingdom of God.

BIOGRAPHY

John N. Harris, Jr. has been a successful sales and marketing leader in the pharmaceutical, biotechnology, and medical device industries for over thirty years. He is an author of several books, mostly non-fiction. He possesses an M.B.A. in Management from Long Island University, C.W. Post, and a Post Graduate Certification from Hofstra University, Frank G. Zarb School of Business. He is also an entrepreneur in the travel and leisure industry. Mr. Harris is a world traveler and speaks several different languages. His favorite quote comes from the bible, from Galatians 6:9. "And let us not be weary in well doing: for in due season we shall reap if we faint not."

John N. Harris, Jr. can be contacted via https://linktr.ee/John_N_Harris

CHAPTER 16

The Refining Process

By Karen Westerman

Precious metal refining is an extreme process. Extreme heat, extreme pressure—the outcome of the product is usually identical chemically to the original, only it is purer. This process reveals the precious metal in its purest and most brilliant form. This is my refining process, the process of life.

Growing up has its challenges. More so, when growing up in South Africa during the apartheid regime. Add to this, being a pastor's daughter—now that was a different ballgame!

Being born into a "colored," aka mixed-race family in South Africa during apartheid meant that I was politically classified as a substandard human being. My racial classification was supposed to determine what level of education I should attain, what work I should do, and what socioeconomic status I should reach. Substandard human beings were expected to achieve less and be less. On the flip side, people in my faith community had unrealistically high expectations of me as the daughter of a pastor. Very few saw the real me, and I became frustrated with their preconceived ideas of who I was and should be.

My first real taste of tragedy came at the age of fifteen. My eldest brother died in a car accident. My world was shattered. Life after his death was tumultuous, and I was never the same. Suddenly, I was the eldest sibling and, as such, expected to be a role model to my younger siblings, a role I was never born for. I wasn't prepared for the responsibility and had to navigate uncharted waters.

I was angry with G-d! I went off the rails. The chaos lasted nineteen years, with each year becoming progressively worse than the one before. To the world, I seemed pretty normal. No one knew that I was fighting what felt like a legion of demons; the biggest one was my lack of self-approval. This led me to do things in the hope to fit in. Yet deep down, I knew I was not meant to fit in. I was born for something greater, but I wasn't ready to embrace that destiny just yet.

My parents and first mentors had instilled in me the belief that I was as good as anyone else, that I could achieve anything! However, their harsh experience of apartheid often led to them cautioning me about having too big a dream. Not because they didn't believe in my ability to accomplish my dreams, but because they didn't want to see me disappointed by the limitations the system imposed on certain people.

When I finally chose a career path that I was passionate about, I found myself being steered in a different direction. Even though apartheid had ended, the repercussions were tangibly etched into the minds of those who were supposed to be its victims. I was told that it would be harder for me as a woman of color to establish myself within the industry that I had chosen.

As a young adult, I couldn't understand why I could not pursue my dreams and goals. It went completely against what my parents had told me, and I was so angry. So, I developed a shield that prevented people from seeing the real me and the anger boiling inside. With a lot of determination and perseverance, I fought against the system, ended up studying hotel management, and enjoyed a great career while in the industry. To keep up with this career, I worked damn hard. Aged twenty-five, I bought my own home, owned a nice car, and could even afford a little bit of luxury. This was not the norm for a young South African—let alone a woman of color. But, back then, I was hardened by the system, and while my desire and intentions were always to ensure that others whom I mentored in that industry would achieve their dreams and goals, I often came across as being too hard. I believed I needed to be that way; my hard shield was my protection against the world and any pain it brought.

When I was twenty-nine, I got married, and, shortly afterward, my husband and I immigrated to the UK. I wanted so much more for my unborn children. I didn't want them to have to fight the same unnecessary battles in life as I had. My parents taught me that my job as a parent would be to provide, protect, and nurture my children spiritually, emotionally, and physically. They taught me that, as a parent, you need to leave a legacy for your children, and this is what I set out to do. My husband and I worked well together and were blessed with two beautiful daughters. I had become a stay-at-home mom during my daughters' early years, and, during the fifth year of our marriage, I ventured into the network marketing industry, moving around until I found a company with which I could resonate. It was there that I was introduced to personal development on a very different level. I was exposed to virtual mentors, some of whom have eventually become mentors in person. One such mentor helped me to channel my anger into passion. I learned how to embrace my passion, bold leadership, and unapologetic attitude in a way that was softer and more welcoming to those whom I had started mentoring.

But, ten years into my marriage, I found myself standing at hell's doors. Well, not standing in front of them—I had been shoved through them! I didn't see it coming, and I was engulfed in the inferno of flames. The flames consumed almost everything I held dear, and family life was something I placed at a high value. For a while, especially when I was on my own, the anger I felt for allowing myself to be blindsided took over. Those ever-familiar faces of my past showed themselves, more contorted than before. How could someone I love and who claimed to love me allow this to happen? We lost everything, our home, our business, our security, my girls' security—life as we knew it was over. I was angry that I hadn't been able to protect them, angry that they had to endure a tragedy of this magnitude at such a tender age. The flames grew out of control, and I realized that I had to do something before everything I loved was destroyed.

We went back to South Africa. I needed the support of my family. Almost as soon as we arrived, we found we could not remain in South Africa, as my daughters did not have dual citizenship. The thought of having to say goodbye to my lifeline and the comfort of our family home knocked the breath out of me. I asked myself, "Why me? What did I ever do to deserve this? Did I commit some kind of great sin? Why do I need to go through this horror show?" Before we headed back, a family friend visited and said, "Karen, you were chosen for such a time as this. G-d chose you because He knows you are the one for this battle." Her words encouraged me, and I understood what she meant, but, still, I was not ready to embrace it. The truth is, are we ever really ready?

Back in the UK, my daughters and I ended up in a homeless hostel. Arriving at the hostel, we had very little food, no bedding, just our luggage, and the clothes on our backs. I had to use the little money we had left for kitchenware. We were shown around and given a long list of rules about where we were able to have our meals, bathe, sleep, and play. We were not allowed to stay over at friends for more than one day per week—we needed permission for that. We needed permission to go on holiday, couldn't have people over after 10 pm, and had to sign in twice a day—the list goes on. I don't know what prison is like, but this sure felt as though we were in some kind of prison. It reminded me of the past system in South Africa that told "non-white" people what they could and couldn't do. Even today, I am still convinced that the beds in prison must be more comfortable than those we slept on in that hostel. I learned how to go to sleep hungry some nights, just so that my daughters could eat. But the hungrier one becomes (not just physically), the more clearly one's mind works. I quickly learned to be careful in whom I confided. I became guarded. I experienced the uncaring nature of some people and realized that very few people really do care. I started teaching my girls, "If people talk about you, you must be pretty important to be the topic of discussion." They loved that!

I realized that there was no time to feel sorry for myself—I had to pull it together for the sake of my beautiful girls. I started using the hours to develop and strengthen my spirit and my mind. I kept affirming myself and my children. I would teach them that we would not become a product of our circumstances and not fall into a victim mentality. I would teach them what my parents taught me: that we are overcomers, and that this was a temporary setback! After all, *circumstances do not make the man, they reveal him.* Children will do what we do, not what we say. I had to show them how to overcome—this would be my legacy that I would leave my daughters.

I started working on different jobs and kept building my network marketing business. I was working hard. At times, it felt as if I was going nowhere. I told myself that, while I could not change my destination overnight, I would change my direction—even when attrition was the order of the day. Every day was a mental and emotional battle to conquer. But I was taught to never give up, that not making it work was not an option! I determined that I was going to let my past guide me, not define me.

As a new year approached, I decided that it would be my year of plenty—the things I had put into motion the year before ensured that it would happen in this way. Energy flows where attention goes. I had focused on my goal to be out of the hostel within a year of arriving there. The tipping point of realizing my goals was when I took ownership of my part in why my girls and I found ourselves in the situation we were in. You see, even if you feel you have done nothing wrong, you also clearly haven't done something right. I called my then estranged husband to see if we could find a way to forgive one another. This was not necessarily about us restoring our relationship but being able to move forward in freedom. I wasn't prepared to tear him down so that I could feel better. I remember that I felt so much lighter after I spoke to him that night. It felt like a shift could take place in my life.

Although messy, it seemed that things started falling into place. We received news that a house had finally become available for my daughters and me. I experienced the Hand of G-d move in our lives through the doors opening, through the people brought across our paths—some of whom have since become like family.

When I look back on my journey and connect the dots, I am grateful for the struggles. I was never able to relate to people who struggled financially, but now I can empathize with them. Because of my own painful experience of being tempered in what I thought were the flames of hell, I can encourage others to become overcomers, too.

If—no, *when* you find yourself being tempted to wallow in the hell of self-pity, remember that you will only end up burning your tush a lot longer than you need to. Ask yourself if you're really in hell, or if you are in the flames of the metal refinery. Keep moving, the only way out is through it!

The season of abundant change is upon me. My calling is to help change lives one person at a time and teach people how to do the same for others. *Our hardships often prepare us, as ordinary people, for an extraordinary destiny.* Allow the heat and pressure of life's process to refine you like the precious metal you are.

BIOGRAPHY

Karen Westerman is a family-orientated entrepreneur who is a qualified Hotel Manager by profession. She graduated from The International Hotel School in South Africa. She is currently based in the UK, where she resides with her family. Over the last six years, she has started carving out a career within the network marketing industry and can usually be found helping others within the industry grow themselves and their organizations. Her mission in life is to serve people who want to transform their lives, but at the same time are willing to do the work required to achieve the transformation they desire.

Contact Information
Facebook: https://www.facebook.com/westermanliving
Instagram: https://www.instagram.com/westermanliving/

CHAPTER 17

Perspective Unlimited

By Kristie Jensen

Once upon a time, there was a very ordinary girl with a very ordinary name who had a very ordinary dream of a simple and ordinary life as a loving wife, home maker, and doting soccer mom. But this isn't a fantasy; this is reality, and reality turned out to be very different and more unexpected than I could have imagined.

On the worst day of my life, I suddenly and unexpectedly found myself in a figurative hole I couldn't get out of, not sure how I got there, staring at the ashes of the life I had planned, watching the sand shift under me and sinking down into it every time I tried to get out. All my goals, beliefs, and hopes were shattered. I now found myself a single parent, constantly on the defense, going to school full-time, caring for a child with cancer, all the while trying to care for my other children, who were feeling as lost and confused as I was. My world had collapsed, and I wondered not only how I had fallen into this hole but also how I could get out and put the pieces back together again. I saw the edge of the cliff—and wanted to go over, thinking it would be easier and better for everyone. I felt very alone and, although my faith had sustained me throughout my life up to that point, the pillars of that faith were threatening to crumble, and I was shocked to see it happening. My mental health became very unstable; I lived in fear and helplessness and displayed it through aggression. I never imagined I could get so low—not me.

So, are you wondering how I managed to get out of that hole and put my life back together? Well, for starters, I'm stubborn, and I don't know how to quit. Quitting makes me feel stagnant; it makes me feel gross, like a mosquito-infested bog. I needed to embrace the future, one day at a time, and learn from the past while setting boundaries to prevent it from crashing back into me.

I didn't give up on God, my children, or myself, even though that seemed easy at the time. Instead, I kept going. I was determined to be resilient. I was determined that I was going to receive my degree and change everything by becoming self-sufficient and independent.

That day finally came, and I received my master's degree in Clinical Social Work but, surprisingly, I didn't feel any different. I really didn't feel any more accomplished or successful than before. I was still just me. My problems didn't go away or become easier. In fact, I now had other problems to solve. So, I began to take a self-inventory and realized that I still wasn't happy, although I had achieved great success in some areas. I needed to change something, and I realized I had to change the way I looked at situations, at everything and, most notably, at that stage, I had to forgive. I had learned so much studying psychology to help others and began to find my own healing through that. Gradually, I came to recognize that I was already a great success, and I didn't need society to define what success was for me. I had been through hell—and I was still standing. I am proud to have successfully finished graduate school, but even more so because I received that degree amidst the fires of adversity. However, it doesn't define me or make me feel accomplished; neither is it the ending point of my success. I chose to define my success by my continual growth.

Perspective is a road map we create through life experiences that shape our perceptions of the world and the events that we experience, be they big or small. Everyone's perspective map is different and can be changed should we become vulnerable and, as a result, willing to choose a

different way. My life had changed dramatically, and I knew I had to change my perspective as well.

Henry Ford said, "There is no man living who isn't capable of doing more than he thinks he can do." I keep this quote on my desk. There is much power in thought, in perspective. Many philosophers and psychologists agree with that proposition. For instance, the bible (Proverbs 23:7) tells us that, as a man "thinketh in his heart, so is he." And Roman emperor Marcus Aurelius (121-180 AD) concluded, "We become what we think about." Thoughts become feelings, feelings become action, and all action has a consequence. Consequences are not negative or bad; they are simply the result of an active choice. They can be good, or they can be bad, positive or negative. Our perspective influences the way we think. "Life is perfectly fair" is a thought that helps me let go of being a victim and drives me to action; it's called radical acceptance. Sometimes, I receive what I merit, and sometimes I don't. Sometimes, that's positive, and sometimes it's not. Injustice does exist; it's very real, and how I chose to think about it moves me toward success or keeps me mired in emotional quicksand. Life events are often out of our control; other's choices are out of our control. Yet, we all have control over how we think about things.

Consider the notion of self-sabotage or self-fulfilling prophecy: If you think you're not sure about something, if you doubt or think negatively, your subconscious will make it come to pass because that is what you truly thought to do. You can say out loud all kinds of positive manifestations, ideas, dreams, and desires, but if you subconsciously decide it might not work or might go bad, it will make you doubt yourself further. Then, you have subconsciously made it come to pass. This way of thinking then becomes a vicious cycle of perceived failure. The solution is to change your perception.

Blame is another limiting perspective that is simply a deflection of our own fear and shame. In my case, I had to accept the responsibility for the circumstances in which I found myself. Ultimately, my life crisis was about my choices, my lack of boundaries, my wavering values and perspectives. I am able to forgive myself for that and all those who hurt me because our decisions, which we believed to be right at the time, were actually taken in response to shame and fear. I had to let go of shame and fear to become successful, to become whole. Faith isn't the absence of fear; courage isn't the absence of fear. Fear is a choice; faith is a choice. There is always a choice, not necessarily in what happens to you but how you chose to think and feel about it. Choose how you want to feel. It takes practice, daily practice to overcome the fear that comes from a sense of helplessness or shame. And, this we can overcome and transform into power; the power to take action to change ourselves.

I'm inviting you to challenge and change your perspective; I'm not asking you to view everything through rose-colored glasses or to become a positive Pollyanna, though there isn't anything inherently wrong with trying to be positive and making the best of things. What I'm asking you to do, what I came to realize myself, is that you need to see things as they really are and accept them as they are, which is not easy and takes courage, and then decide how you want to think and feel about them. I found success in creating the life I want rather than grieving for the life I thought I wanted and lost. I find peace and happiness in my changing perspective.

I realized I could stay a victim and let that stance slowly destroy me, or I could let go of my limited perspective, the negative mental map I had inside, and forgive. Forgive myself, my ex, my family, God, and all those who I believed had hurt me, whether they really had or that was simply how I had perceived it. Individually, we have so much potential, and too often, we excuse it away because of a limited perspective, either our own or of those whose opinions we value more than our own. Change is uncomfortable, sometimes even painful; however, it's possible to thrive in the refining fires of change to become who we want to be and reach our potential. I've learned to choose the perceptions that are most productive, those that build me a successful legacy, both in my eyes and those of God, and those are the only two opinions that really matter to me.

With any development training, there are basic skills that are learned upon which advanced techniques are built. When everything crashed down around me, I found that I needed to go back to the basic values and beliefs that I had once held dear; values and beliefs that had become distorted and obscured. I realized I had to redefine the boundaries I had allowed to crumble or blur. I had to go back to the basics and then create a new perspective. Some people believe success is defined by celebrity status, letters behind your name, degrees, and financial status. But I believe that success starts from within, or none of that matters. Find your values again; what do you believe in, and if it isn't working for you, how do you want to change it? How can you change your perspective?

I listened to a talk by an inspirational speaker who changed the word "FAIL" into an acronym: F-First; A-Attempt; I-In; L-Learning. This changed my perspective on my perceived "failures" and helped me forgive myself for my past mistakes and poor choices. Imagine; think about the future you want, broaden your perspective, and don't be afraid to FAIL. Successful people know they will FAIL at least once and often many times. Learning to walk wasn't accomplished at the first attempt. We don't emotionally beat up a child or call them a failure because they fall over and over, but that is exactly what we do to ourselves when we make a mistake, when we "fail" at what we want to accomplish. When you don't feel empowered, when you don't love yourself or forgive yourself and others, you will always question your worth. And that holds you back from reaching your full potential. I have found peace and success in changing how I perceive everything: You can change your life; you are more than you think you are.

If you are alive and kicking, you can become the success you dream of becoming. There is no instant formula. This world of instant gratification and entitlement is a curse that is preventing you from becoming your best self, from finding the lasting peace and happiness that is true success, which anyone can have, no matter what their economic circumstances.

Find the courage to be imperfect and make mistakes; let go of who you think you should be and embrace who you are; embrace who you want to become. If it doesn't line up with your values, change. Change your perspective, believe in possibility, risk failure, and seek out opportunities. When they come, take advantage of them fearlessly. They may not always work out or might turn out not to be the opportunities you hoped they were, but if you learn something from that experience, then you have achieved success, and you are that much closer to creating what you want. Stop playing inside the box. Get out; create your own perspective, your own idea of success, and get going. Ask yourself what you want your legacy to be—what needs to change for you to feel proud of the person you've been, who you are, and who you will become.

Believe you are enough, good enough, strong enough, worthy enough to be who you want to be.

I lost what I thought I wanted. The box of my life plan fell apart, but I found I was stronger than I thought; I'm empowered to create by a broader, ever-changing perspective as the boundaries of my old perceptions fade away. I have learned that I really can do more than I ever thought I was capable of. The only real control we have over anything is our control over how we think about everything.

BIOGRAPHY

Kristie Jensen, LCSW, has life experiences, which she highlights in this book. She has spent the last six years working professionally with men and women in addiction, challenging their perspectives and guiding them to achieve their goals. For her service with the Utah Department of Corrections, she received the UDC Institutional Programming Division Challenge Coin and UDC Certificate of Appreciation. *Life is perfectly fair* has become her motto, inviting others to change their perspective of everything, one thought at a time. Kristie has lived in four different countries and enjoys learning about other cultures and traditions. She is currently residing in the United States. She is a single mother of five amazing children, who are her joy. Kristie has devoted over thirty years of her life to serving and inspiring others. She continues to work to set an example through personal development and growth.

Kristie Jensen can be contacted via https://linktr.ee/jensenk

CHAPTER 18

Fight To The Finish

By Keith and Lakeisha McKnight

In times of uncertainty, change arises, led by revolutionary leaders. What makes a revolutionary leader? They maintain a strength that cannot be specifically identified. They possess the ability to press forward despite any obstacles that may arise. Great leaders possess the internal drive to push forward because they are not only thinking about themselves but also those closest to them, as well as people they have not even met.

Consider the life of Rocky Balboa from the famous movie series *Rocky*. If you reflect on the story of Rocky, you will understand that he came from a place where no one really knew him. However, because of his unique skillsets and his internal drive, he rose quickly to the top. In the film, Rocky considers the way his actions impact those around him; in his home and within his industry. He positions himself so that he can utilize his strengths to make the greatest positive impact on those he seeks to serve.

Thinking about the lessons taught through the *Rocky* movie series, how can you develop the Eye of the Tiger? How can you, as a leader, position yourself so that, when obstacles arise, you can bounce back and walk with amazing resilience?

Persevere, Even When You Can't Go Forward

Persevere in what you do. You can experience success through conviction, determination, hard work, and perseverance.

Perseverance has so much value that by merely showing it, you can make incredible progress. However, you must be backed by a strong conviction in what you are doing. If that is the case, you can boldly go forward.

Even when the going becomes tough, your perseverance will urge you on. All real successes have been the result of perseverance, as has been demonstrated in all significant achievements in science, military, political work, or public administration. It is to such a hard, persevering but rewarding life that we beckon you all!

Now, it is time to have a final recap of all the things we have covered. To make it easier for you, we have made it in the form of a list and have prepared an action plan that includes everything we have discussed so far.

We invite you to follow these simple steps to reach the pinnacle of glory, the glory that is the privilege of the leader in you.

Failing Your Way Forward

In today's society, no one wants to fail: failure is often viewed negatively. However, how would you know what success is without failing? Exactly! Let's take a look at the meaning of failure and the correct way to respond to it.

Failure simply means falling down or missing the mark and *not getting back up*. To live like a conqueror, you must change your perspective on how you see failure in business. Consider the case of the founders of the 409 Cleanser: these leaders tried their best to create a solution that would clean the most difficult stains and areas within a home. Have you wondered where the number 409 came from?

The name is significant to the lesson behind *failing your way forward*. The leaders of the 409 Cleanser project failed 408 times. They tried 408 combinations before they finally got it right on the 409th try. They tried and failed, tried and failed, relentlessly, all the way through an unbelievable 408 times. Therefore, you may try and then fail. The most important point is that you keep on trying. If you are a new entrepreneur seeking to start and grow a successful business, keep on trying. It will happen. If you are an experienced entrepreneur seeking to launch a new product or start a successful multilevel marketing business, do not give up. Your success is right around the corner. In fact, this is exactly what happened to us during our own entrepreneurial journey.

We never imagined that we would be the founders of an international leadership education and training company, or author books and travel the world speaking to new entrepreneurs and experienced business leaders to encourage them to live as winning leaders. And although we have now attained success, that status did not come without struggles and failures. We faced many personal struggles before our marital union, that could have led us down entirely different paths.

For example, I, Lakeisha McKnight, grew up in an inner-city, and my parents separated when I was a toddler. At that time, I also experienced incest that devastated my immediate family and caused psychological chaos within me. I struggled to know my worth, as well as my sexual identity. The struggles piled up as I transitioned into adulthood and fell in and out of various relationships. I was diagnosed with three diseases that were said to be incurable and impacted my ability to have children. During this difficult time, I questioned whether a man would accept someone with my past and who couldn't have children. We know the answer to this question, right?

And later, as a married couple, other hurdles arose. We faced struggles related to communication, as well as the right way to manage our finances. Yes! Debt became an issue. As a result, we had to overcome the trauma of the foreclosure of our first home and having our car repossessed. However, the problems that we'd thought would prevent the growth of our family miraculously disappeared! We believe God enabled us to experience a true miracle, since we now have two amazing children. But obstacles continued to arise both within our personal and business lives.

As business owners, certain marketing strategies and individuals involved in our endeavors created limitations for us. More specifically, the campaign tactics we implemented were not fruitful for many reasons, such as failing to adequately estimate the time needed for split-testing strategies and meeting the cash requirements for our campaigns. In addition to the search to find committed leaders and a solid strategy, our stretched finances also became a cause for concern in facilitating business growth.

Finally, we were able to join in business opportunities that enabled affiliates to build networks. The businesses enabled us to work from home, using a cell phone or laptop. Unfortunately, while the products and services offered were useful, the opportunities did not pay off for us, due to a lack of mentorship and poor leadership, and the companies did not remain afloat. That experience has helped us learn the importance of failing forward, while also discovering the following six keys to overcoming failure on the path to success:

1. Remember your humanity

No human being is perfect, including you. Some actions we engage in are not the best for us. We sometimes don't know what will work or what is best for us until it has been tried. Every outcome cannot be 100% predicted.

Action Step: Recall your last mistake or the moment where you experienced failure. Did this repel people from you, or were other people able to relate to you and the situation you encountered?

2. Communicate and be honest about what occurred

A major step to addressing failure is acknowledging it. Leaders are not perfect. Situations do not always work out the way that we have planned. In our minds, situations may play out one way, but reality doesn't always work that way.

Action Step: If another person has been impacted by your situation, verbally offer an apology. Failure to speak about what transpired could reveal a degree of pride.

3. Recognize the lesson learned

Within every situation (good or bad), there is a lesson to be learned.

Action Step: Identify what you have learned from the situations you encounter or the mistakes you make. Is the lesson similar to the one you have experienced in the past?

4. Begin to replace error with truth

Now that you've discovered the lesson, it is time to create an action plan and implement it. Move from learning to implementing, so that change can manifest. It is one thing to know something, but to implement a plan of action actually creates wisdom.

Action Step: Write down or review on paper what you have learned. Create a plan that helps you move from strategic thinking to implementation of that plan. Arrange support from someone to whom you will be held accountable, who will be completely honest with you.

5. Reflect on your growth

Between acknowledging the lesson learned and implementing a new action plan, it is important to reflect on how far you have come.

Action Step: Think back over the last thirty days and assess your growth in relation to the situation you encountered. You can also ask someone you trust whether they observed growth in you as it pertains to that truth.

6. Don't focus on failure.

Internal defeat is a mindset that has you believing that most new ideas will fail. You might think: "After all, what we tried last week failed, so there's no point in trying anything new."

Action Step: Whatever you focus on the longest becomes the strongest. Focus on the destination, because failures help you become stronger in terms of enduring the journey towards success.

Those six keys have propelled us forward together as husband and wife, parents, and now as full-time wealth mentors. Now that you know them, let's talk about where success truly begins—in the heart.

Big Heart Equals a BIG WIN!

How many times have you heard stories about a person who appeared to be weak and poorly qualified but has a big heart and finally wins out? Let's go back to my inspiration Rocky Balboa in the five *Rocky* movies. In the films, Rocky is a southpaw boxer from Philadelphia. Over the five-film series, Rocky's inspirational story builds to an astonishing climax. In the first, the boxer not only lacks confidence but also most of the basic essentials he requires to succeed at the beginning of his boxing career.

However, by obtaining solid team members for support within his power corner, the Eye of the Tiger, and the heart of a leader, Rocky rises to the top. He goes from nobody to somebody—the boxing heavyweight champion of the world! His life story teaches all there is to know about failing your way forward, taking risks, and pursuing your dreams. Whether it's professional training, a graduate degree, or business success that you seek, through perseverance, you will find a way to make your dream become a reality.

Rocky's story teaches us that we may one day hit rock-bottom after falling from the top, only to pull our way back up once more. His life truly reveals that there is a champion within every new entrepreneur, experienced business leader, and ordinary people.

Never give in. Keep the faith and press forward. You are unique and different as a leader. You have been called to influence nations. Do not give in to circumstantial obstacles. Do not give up in the face of challenges. Instead, see each new day as a fresh challenge. Embrace it. And realize that you are called to do something amazing.

Remember, there are going to be difficult moments in our homes, organizations, and our entrepreneurial journeys, but we must remember to continue to fight the good fight, whatever the circumstances. There will be many difficulties, but, as leaders, we will fight until the finish! Never give up on your relationships, your health, your goals, or YOURSELF! You must continue to break through the obstacles to get to the other side—success!

BIOGRAPHY

Keith and Lakeisha McKnight are the founders of The ILEAD Company LLC and Women of Elevation Career Services International. They have been educating and equipping leaders for over fifteen years. They have served as wealth mentors for adults across the globe for the past three years. More specifically, they provide mentorship for adults who desire to grow their influence, create residual income, accumulate appreciating assets, and build generational wealth from home. Their educational background and experience in wealth-building have given them the ability to help others attain lifestyles of freedom. Their commitment to wealth-building and leadership development is confirmed by members of Wealth Builders Worldwide, an organization dedicated to helping people achieve their dreams. Keith and Lakeisha especially enjoy empowering others to pay themselves first, with both physical and digital assets.

Contact Information
Facebook: https://www.facebook.com/BreakthroughWiththeMcKnights
Website: http://meetthemcknights.com

CHAPTER 19

The Vacation Principle

By Lee Murch

Back in the 1990s, I was a young man with a young family doing a job that I thought was the best I could do to support my family. But something was gnawing at me every day. Although I had no formal education or professional background, working as a truck driver and barely making ends meet was not exactly the dream career I had in mind when I first set out.

You see, I came from a blue-collar background, and so almost everybody I knew was either an auto mechanic, a truck driver, a factory worker, a cashier, or some such. But, even at elementary school, I sensed that I might be a little bit different, even though my grades in high school were just barely good enough for me to graduate. At the time, because of that feeling and my blue-collar background, I believed that going to college wasn't a possibility for me.

Time moved on, I married my soulmate, and we had two wonderful children together. But, while I was honest and hard-working, I still felt that I was completely out of my element. The thought nagged at me that I wasn't on the right path, despite there being no real evidence to back this idea. I had no other practical experience to suggest that I could do better than driving a truck. And, although I worked hard, we were forced to live hand-to-mouth, from paycheck to paycheck. So, as I said, the feeling of not being on the right path and that I could do better continued to gnaw away at me, and my feelings of despair grew when I looked at my young family and myself and racked my brains as to how we were ever going to prosper if things didn't change.

Fortunately for me, a chance visit to a friend changed mine and my family's lives very dramatically. My friend Phil called me one day and asked if I would do him a favor. Of course, I said yes. He asked me to come by his house, where he would explain it to me. When I arrived, Phil and his family had their garage door open, and their SUV was halfway loaded with every kind of camping gear you can think of. He announced that they were going on a camping trip to Yosemite, about five hundred miles away. Phil asked his children to load a few more boxes into the SUV, then motioned that I should join him to talk in the house.

We sat in the kitchen, and Phil asked me if I wouldn't mind coming by every day to pick up their mail, which he would collect when they returned from their trip. He apologized and explained that, although they had it on their list to notify the post office to hold their mail while they were away, they'd forgotten. "What list?" I asked him. He pulled out two pages of a legal pad with a "To Do" list on it that he and his wife had made for their trip. As I looked at it, I couldn't help but notice how detailed and specific the list was, as you can see from the examples below:

Map and driving directions to Yosemite—Get camping gear out of the garage and air it out for the trip.

Withdraw $500 in cash for the trip—Get the SUV's oil changed and fill up with gas—Pack kid's clothes.

Unplug kitchen appliances—Drop cat off at sister's house—Pay for camping spot in advance.

Borrow camping stove from brother—Clean the ice chest for the trip—Buy food for the trip.

And this was only a fraction of what was on the list. I praised Phil and his wife for their organizational skills, asking how long it had taken them to produce it. Twenty to thirty minutes, Phil said, adding, "Lee, we just stayed focused on getting the list right." Then Phil made a throw-away comment that hit me right between the eyes like a bullet and has stuck with me ever since:

"If you want to go somewhere, you have to know what you need and what you must do to get there."

I left Phil and his family to finish packing and drove home, but on the way, I couldn't get that sentence out of my head: "If you want to go somewhere, you have to know what you need and what you must do to get there." I repeated the words over and over again, unable to believe how revolutionary the statement was in terms of the place I was at that time in my life.

The next day, I did a lot of soul-searching and tried to analyze my life; I knew I was unhappy, that I wasn't where I wanted to be, and that I wasn't providing the income and the lifestyle that my family deserved. I also realized that if I stayed where I was, then nothing would ever change for the better. That scary revelation shook me to my core. It hit me at a time when, although I hadn't made any real changes in my life career-wise, I had started to educate myself by reading some personal growth books in an attempt to discover a better way to go forward in finding my place in the world. I wanted to get somewhere where I could contribute and, at the same time, change my life and provide more for my family.

There was one particular book by the late Jim Rohn that I read several times: *The Five Major Pieces to the Life Puzzle*. In the book, Jim Rohn writes about the process of change and how it begins; I quote:

> "Change comes from one of two sources. First, we may be driven to change out of desperation. Sometimes our circumstances can be so out of control that we almost abandon our search for answers because our lives seem to be filled only with irresolvable questions. But it is this overwhelming

sense of desperation that finally drives us to look for solutions. Desperation is the final and inevitable result of months or years of accumulated neglect that brings us to that point in time where we find ourselves driven by urgent necessity to find immediate answers to life's accumulated challenges."

He goes on to conclude the following:

"The second source that drives us to make changes in our lives is Inspiration. Hopefully, that is where you find yourself right now—about to become sufficiently inspired to make major and dramatic changes in your life."

Well, that was me to a tee; I was both motivated by the desperation of my situation and inspired by the effectiveness and simplicity of my friend Phil's list. That day, I sat down and made one of the biggest decisions of my entire life. This decision ended up changing the complete trajectory of my life and my family's future!

I decided to embark on a career in professional sales. It may not sound like a huge decision, but coming from a blue-collar family, going from driving a truck to making the jump to white-collar employment was a big deal. Fortunately, by this time, I had some success working part-time in door-to-door sales that paid by only commission.

Following Phil's example, I sat down and spent about thirty minutes writing my "To Do" list for my journey to a new profession. The list included the things that I needed, like writing a resume and buying new, professional-looking clothes. It also included the things that I must do to reach my goal, such as combing the classified ads for suitable situations, calling employment agencies, networking with sales professionals, researching companies that I was interested in working for.

Once the list was finished, I looked it over very carefully to make sure I hadn't missed anything. Confident that I hadn't, I went to work diligently, completing the tasks I'd listed one at a time. Remember, this was in the early 1990s when there was no Internet, so the library became my second home. I used the library's resources to research companies, educate myself about sales, and personal growth.

I'd like to tell you that everything happened magically within a few days from this newfound approach to life. Of course, that wasn't the case. I went through countless interviews —in person, and by phone—only to be told repeatedly that I didn't have any experience, no references, and lacked the right education! It was challenging, to say the least. Yet my determination to see it through was so strong that I mentally put my foot down and made the decision—I was going to go from driving a truck for a living to being a professional salesman—and nothing was going to stop me! I told myself that I just had to stick to the plan and keep working at it.

After numerous rejections, I'm sure many people would have given up at that point, but my belief in this approach was so strong that I had no choice but to continue until I reached my goal. Every time I considered tossing in the towel, I just repeated Phil's words that had become my mantra: "If you want to go somewhere, you have to know what you need and what you must do to get there."

Think about it— if you're headed for a destination in your car with your family, and you get halfway, would the fact that you're only halfway there be so discouraging that you'd want to turn back? Or would you be excited about the fact that you're already halfway there and continue to your destination? I think the answer is pretty clear, don't you think?

During this time, I had to continually remind myself that all my efforts would eventually be worth it—as long as I didn't quit, I would arrive at my destination. It so happens that I was reading *The Art of War* by Sun Tzu, in which he states: *"If you fight with all your might, there is a chance of life; where death is certain if you stay in your corner."* I would rather fight. Wouldn't you?

Within five weeks of starting my journey, I received a phone call from the general sales manager of an industrial parts distribution company. I'd contacted him weeks ago, and although we had a great conversation and I felt like we'd built up a rapport, he said they had no vacancies at that time. However, he'd keep my resume on file and, if anything turned up, he'd let me know. When he called, he told me that a sales representative had recently quit, so the firm had an opening for a sales associate. The phone call ended with an invitation to fly to Phoenix for an interview with the company executives. After three successful interviews at their location in Phoenix, I was finally offered the position. Although it meant moving from Southern California to Phoenix, Arizona, my wife Elizabeth and I decided that it was worth the move.

I did well at that company, but it didn't allow me to earn the six-figure salary I had in my sights. So, armed with a successful sales track record and some great referrals, I was soon ready for the next step in my journey. I'm sure you've already figured out what I did next: I made another list for my journey from a successful sales rep at an excellent company to my destination—finding an opportunity to earn a six-figure income.

Staying true to this approach, my family and I moved back to Southern California, where a machine manufacturing company had offered me a sales position that came with the chance to earn my target six-figure income. Within a year of accepting the invitation, I earned my first $100,000 annual salary. I can't describe how wonderful it felt to go from earning $500 a week driving a truck to earning over $2000 a week in sales—a staggering 400% increase in income!

At this point, I profoundly want to thank Phil for showing me his list. That simple action changed mine and my family's lives. My wife and I have used the "To Do" list approach with just about anything in life. It works just as well when you're planning a trip, as it does for planning a journey toward any life goal that you want to achieve.

Jim Rohn was famously quoted as saying: "The final result of your life will be determined by whether you made too many errors in judgment repeated every day, or whether you dedicated your life to a few simple disciplines practiced every day."

I hope that my story allows you to evaluate your position in life, whatever it might be. Based on my experience, I advise you not to hold yourself back for whatever reason and don't be afraid to make a move. Instead, I encourage you to make a "To Do" list! All you need to do is to take thirty minutes or so, sit down with your pen and paper, iPad, or whatever, and decide on your destination and how to get there. And while you're doing it, keep in mind Phil's words: "If you want to go somewhere, you have to know what you need and what you must do to get there."

Friends, I hope you find my story inspirational in traveling toward your own success. I wish you the very best of luck for your journey—or should I say list?

BIOGRAPHY

Lee Murch is a successful sales executive, sales leader, success coach, and entrepreneur. In his career, Lee has launched several businesses that produced six-figure incomes. He has coached, trained, managed, and mentored hundreds of sales professionals, sales managers, and entrepreneurs. From his humble beginnings in Southern California, Lee's enormous potential, focused determination, and eagerness to assist others in their desire to succeed in their chosen field has produced a life that he only dreamt about as a young man. Lee has remained dedicated to his true calling of educating and inspiring others to achieve their true potential. Lee resides in Northern California with his wife and soulmate, Elizabeth. They are blessed with a daughter Rachel, son-in-law Brent, and their teenage son Eric.

Contact Information
Facebook: https://www.facebook.com/Coach-Lee-272819266701854/
Website: http://www.leemurch.com

CHAPTER 20

Taking Full Responsibility For My Piece Of The American Dream

By Leslie K Williams

A few years after I dropped out of high school, I served 14 months in a federal prison camp for a felony charge of "misguided" ambition (aka credit-card fraud). After I was released from prison, I was to serve three years of federal probation in my hometown of St. Louis, Missouri.

Before my prison sentence, I had multiple run-ins with the law with both misdemeanor and felony charges on my record before the age of 21. My environment that was a low-income housing community in St Louis, Missouri fueled my ambition and illegal activity was going to be my way out. I admired the drug dealers, boosters, and hustlers in my community because they seemed to be living a lifestyle desirous to me. They indeed were the movers and shakers where I was from, so I guess I followed that path despite the options that my mom and dad laid out for me. More on that later ...

Back to my foolish ambition ... My friends and I would steal credit-card numbers to buy what we considered the finer things in life. One day we ordered multiple Chanel bags and had them delivered to a 5-star hotel where we were staying on a stolen credit card. Upon checking-in, we asked about a package that we had delivered; and upon our accepting the package, we were met by Secret-Service agents, arrested, and charged with three counts of credit card fraud. My dad bailed me out like he always did, and I would promise not to get in trouble again. But the truth was that my misguided ambition was too addictive for me to help myself. The day I was scheduled to turn myself in to serve the 14 months of my prison sentence, I bailed! I mean literally: a full-fledged fugitive on the run. My favorite movie at the time (1993) was *The Fugitive* with Harrison Ford and Tommy Lee Jones; I even changed my name to Natalie Gerard after the main character, US Marshall Samuel Gerard. Talk about hiding in plain sight. During my 10-month fugitive run, I had gotten deeper in, what some would consider, "white collar" criminal activities that led to my ultimate arrest.

I look back now at my time on the run when I was my most courageous self and wonder why I was so afraid to face the consequences of my actions. Somehow, I had bought into the social narrative led by today's culture that I was a victim and disadvantaged because I was black, so I felt entitled to the material things that I had stolen. This destructive mentality was my motivation to feed my lowest desires. I was an entitled victim of the oppressive, racist system. I would tell myself, "They set you up to fail, you are not responsible for your actions, and they owe us."

When I was only two years old, my parents got divorced. Although I lived with my mom and my two other siblings, my Dad, a Vietnam War veteran who served in the Air force, took excellent care of me. We were sort of like a poor, middle-class family (middle-class on my dad's side). My Dad was ordered to pay child support upon their divorce, which helped my mom, a single parent, to raise me.

My Dad's side of the family consisted of middle-class black professionals. My Dad and his siblings were raised in a two-parent household and lived the American Dream. My mom came from a broken household, raised by her mother in a single-parent household with multiple siblings. The subtle messages from both sides were so conflicting to me. My dad's side of the family modeled: hard work, pursuing education, marrying young & starting a family, pursuing a career and that honor and respect equal's prosperity. My mom's side modeled: struggle, you'll never have enough, manipulate to get what you want in life, steal, use your looks and body to elevate you in life, go to church, finish high school, and get a job.

I would live with my mom during the week and spend the weekend with my Dad. They both adored me by laying out what I would consider today a pretty solid foundation. I was my Dad's only child, so I was able to get everything I wanted. At 16 years of age, my Dad bought me a car, which was unheard of in the late '80s. My mom made sure that I got a solid Christian foundation through my different roles in the church, I sang in the choir, and served on the usher board. My mom made sure I was connected. Even when she had to work on Sundays, she would make sure I had a ride back and forth to church every Sunday.

Both my parents wanted me to have a good education, which is why they paid for me to attend a Catholic school in my elementary years. During my junior high and high school years, I attended a predominantly white school in St. Louis' school desegregation program (also known as the transfer program), where some black applicants were accepted and bussed out to better schools outside of the community.

Shortly after I was released from prison, I started to see the world differently. There was a shift in my perspective. This was during the OJ Simpson acquittal when racial tensions were high. The social narrative back then was similar to the one today: that of black reparations and victimhood. But I learned in prison that there was a code: a certain level of honor and respect in being accountable for your actions and that serving your time and accepting the consequences was an honorable character trait. There was no time to play the victim, it was widely understood that freedom comes from surrendering to the truth of your personal choices. I was motivated by what I learned in prison, and it became the catalyst for the foundational mental shift in my life. I decided I was going to take full responsibility for my actions and that I would always seek freedom through this lens.

Even with so much stacked against me (my felony record and being a high school dropout), I was passionate about turning my foolish missteps that were built on a faulty belief system into positive building blocks built on foundational principles of personal development and inward reflection.

While I was on federal probation, I coached myself into never buying into the narrative of being an oppressed minority again. Because of this mental shift I was able to flourish once I elevated my consciousness. I decided to put that same energy that I used for creating illegal activities into legal groundbreaking success, and I haven't looked back in over 25 years.

I have transformed from a serial criminal to a serial entrepreneur and change agent. Since I was able to change my mindset from victim to warrior, I've been able to accomplish my wildest dreams by reaching multi-million dollar success in government contracting, television production, the music industry, the beauty industry, and network marketing combined.

Building generational wealth through friendship, I decided to share my newfound mindset with my previous partners in crime: Dana and Kiki. They became my BFF's; and today, they are my partners in all of my multi-million-dollar ventures. Together we discovered and signed the first female African American country music singer to hit the Billboard charts in over 20 years! We traveled to India to get the best hair extensions and opened three retail stores to sell our own brand of extension hair. Essence magazine deemed our business to be one of the best venues to purchase great hair. I created and was the Executive Producer of the reality TV show, Amateur Millionaires Club, which aired on cable television. I started a prosthetic wig company exclusively for military veterans and active duty service members who were experiencing hair loss. This business venture with the Department of Veterans Affairs is the project that I am most proud of. Not only have I generated over $2 million with this venture, but I also got an opportunity to give back and serve those who have served us.

Today I coach newly minted entrepreneurs through my latest venture "Shebizness," a coaching platform for aspiring network marking millionaires. My previous experience with The Amateur Millionaires Club is what sparked my interest in Network Marketing. AMC was about 10 African American millionaires in the Networking Marketing Industry who had all earned over $1 million in one year while overcoming adversity. The star of the show, Stormy Wellington, a high school dropout became a great friend, mentor, and the driving force behind my passion to help my community grow beyond their circumstances. She is the highest African American female million-dollar earner in the network marketing industry.

I still struggle with my identity as a black woman in America with social economic conservative values, which don't always align with my community. I have a strong Christian foundation and I believe in moral responsibility. I do not buy into the current narrative of victimhood, which is the current mentality of our culture. I have to constantly remind myself of what true freedom really feels like, everything that I've been through, all of the hard work that I put in, the hardest task being breaking free from the mental prison of my faulty belief system, and the feeling I had when I finally surrendered and accepted personal responsibility.

I am now in my happiest state when I can look at a situation and not be influenced by the social victimhood narrative that predominates our media today. I've grown as a result of my past experiences and I have a responsibility to share with the world my story: How I overcame the odds of being black in America, and how changing your mindset has valuable rewards. I truly hope that the story of my success will be the catalyst for someone struggling with their identity.

The American dream is available to all of us, whether we are black, white, brown, etc. However, our paths may lead us astray for a while; nonetheless, it is YOUR path and decisions that will ultimately lead to a successful life.

BIOGRAPHY

Leslie K Williams is a reformed convicted felon, serial entrepreneur, "Star Power" personal development coach, and executive producer whose strategic leadership, empowerment, and passion have earned her the reputation as a visionary leader. She is widely known for discovering unique talent and helping women implement innovative business ideas that empower them to thrive both personally and professionally. For over a decade, she has garnered extensive industry experience as an executive producer in music

(Rissi Palmer Project) and reality TV (Amateur Millionaires Club). She is the brainpower and CEO behind SheBizness, a conglomerate that shines the spotlight on women entrepreneurs through a coaching platform for aspiring network marketing entrepreneurs. Leslie is working on the 2nd season of the Amateur Millionaires Club TV show, which highlights aspiring millionaires within the network marketing industry. Leslie and her husband reside in the Washington DC area and are Global Directors in Total Life Changes, a health and wellness network marketing company.

Connect with Leslie at www.yourcoachleslie.com

CHAPTER 21

The Power Of Choices

By Lynda Nabayiinda Were

"You truly amaze me," Sophie, my soft-spoken and graceful high school friend, said to me with a warm smile. She had stopped over at my workplace as she made her rounds in town, selling all kinds of women's paraphernalia from the boot of her car. "Why?" I asked in surprise, as I escorted her down the stairs from my office on the third-floor to the parking lot. We preferred to take the stairs to the elevator as it gave us some extra minutes to chat some more.

"Tell me. I'm always eager to hear about your new projects," she continued. "I am not into *projects!*" I rolled my eyes and laughed at her.

"Lynda!" She exclaimed as she whirled in a flash to face me. We were now literally blocking the staircase, with her on the rail side and me leaning against the wall. "You're such a busy bee. Each time I call you over the weekend or after work, you're going somewhere or meeting someone, at a party, or engaged in something."

I just kept staring at her and all I could say in response was; "Really?" after every few seconds.

"Really! What amazes me is how you do it all and are so happy and rarely exhausted." She said, as we continued down the stairway. Actually, Sophie was completely wrong: I was living in a state of perpetual happy exhaustion. This brief conversation kept creeping back into my mind during my solitary moments; as I drove home during the heavy traffic, as I took a slow bath, as I queued in the supermarket, or even as I wool-gathered in some lengthy meeting.

Indeed, after close introspection, I admitted that I was all over the place. I seem to be moving around as erratically as a ping pong ball! Silently I asked myself, am I effective? Am I achieving optimal results from all the activities I chose to undertake day by day?

I had an 8 to 5 job, which really meant that I was working from 5am to 7pm. I had a husband, who frequently worked out of town, and three daughters—a teenager with all the drama and anxiety that comes with that phase, a pre-teen, and a preschooler, each with unique demands; birthday parties, parent-teacher meetings, ballet practice sessions, the occasional illnesses, orthodontic appointments, coupled with household duties— this was enough to crack up a woman's sanity.

Throwing in the Toastmasters International public speaking club, where I serve on the executive; spice that up with my charity work at a local orphanage where I'm charged with the responsibility of resource mobilisation for the orphans' welfare – picture that activity!

Now, supplement all these with the responsibility of staying in touch with siblings, in-laws and friends attending extended family events and other duties surrounding these relations. Guess who the designated in-charge of organizing family events was? I loved it.

Organizing events and connecting with people comes naturally to me. I enjoyed getting everyone to participate in the unique get-together; picnics, themed parties, potlucks, cookouts, and holidays. Funfilled events and bonding moments motivated me to do more and more.

As if my life was not hectic enough being a wife, mother, employee, executive of a volunteer adult club, and supporting the orphanage, I rarely missed out on social outings, high school reunions, beach parties, weddings, bridal, and baby showers.

Sophie was right!

I was juggling everything and going about my life achieving small-time successes here and there. To the outsider, I was flying high. On the inside, the successes were minimal, and I was starting to crash.

Finally, it happened—I crashed.

One day, I forgot to pick up my daughter from school, only being alerted to the fact at 7:30 in the evening, when the school finally called.

I had forgotten my own daughter at school! My heart broke. I cried as I hurriedly hailed a motorcycle taxi, referred to as *boda boda,* to get me to the school across town in the shortest time possible. We weaved through the heavy commuter traffic, mindless of the speed limits, and fifteen minutes later arrived at the school. It was dark, cold, and devoid of students. I rushed to the amphitheater, which was the pick-up waiting area, and found my little girl with two other children still waiting for their parents.

It was a sobering moment. My eyes shimmered with tears again as I hugged her and asked, "Were you worried I wasn't coming?" "No. I know you're busy, but I knew you wouldn't forget me," she responded. I hugged her again. "Thank you for having faith in me."

"Nobody's perfect, so give yourself credit for everything you are doing right, and be kind to yourself when you struggle."—Lori Deschene

I learned a hard lesson that day—forgetting to pick up my daughter from school was crossing a line for me. Coupled with incidents of missed appointments due to tightly packed schedules, over-running, and colliding commitments, I realized enough was enough—it was time to take stock of my life. I desired to be the best mother and never have my children lose the faith they had in me. I wanted to be a fabulous wife, the woman described in Proverbs 31. I needed to be an outstanding employee, delivering over and above what was expected, to be the transformational leader Toastmasters needed in Uganda, to significantly improve the welfare of the orphanage where I served. I yearned for my businesses to flourish.

In a nutshell, I wanted to succeed immensely.

Inside, I was certain I could excel beyond my current outward success: If others could do it, so could I.

Henry David Thoreau says, "It is not enough to be busy. The question is: what are we busy about?"

Do not ever question the Law of Attraction: I craved - God and the universe responded. I was nominated amongst the company managers to attend a two-day workshop on Steve Covey's legendary book—*7 Habits of Highly Effective People*. With several other personal development books, seminars, and lessons from several mentors, Steve Covey's book brought about subtle positive changes that later escalated into results that caused a significant transformation in my life and translated into the lives of the people around me, changing for the better.

Choices:

Should I have a one-hour long lunch with snippets of office gossip here and there, or catch up with a close friend or business associate over lunch and keep my weekends and evenings free? Should I brave evening traffic for two hours, sign up for an evening language class, or build my business as I wait for the traffic to abate?

"Lack of direction, not lack of time, is the problem. We all have twenty-four-hour days."—Zig Ziglar

With a few changes in my life, within four years, I was able to:

1. Support my daughters in their extracurricular activities including ballet lessons, where we achieved a memorable milestone. Janelle, my eldest was awarded a summer holiday scholarship with the Florida Ballet School in USA.

2. Get an unexpected promotion at work against steep odds—going from leading a team of seven to a team of over one-hundred staff.

3. Get recognized on an international stage in front of over two-thousand people for performance achievement in one of my private organizations.

4. Be part of a vocational school board.
5. Join the Rotary International community and serve at the executive level.
6. Register two businesses and a partnership that are all thriving today.
7. Climbed Mountain Muhavura in South West Uganda.
8. Learned a new language, got certified for two French-language levels, and am currently pursuing the third level.
9. Formally registered the orphanage and currently serve as a board member.
10. Take three vacations each year for three years.

My Five Stop and Start Doing tips for achieving great results.

Five Stop Tips

- **Media Restriction.** I stopped reading newspapers and magazines and watching television. If the news was important, I heard about it over the car radio, through WhatsApp scrolls, or saw the headlines through my car window, as the newspaper vendors walked past during traffic.
- **Social Gatherings**. I stopped attending weddings and social events. It was either church service or reception parties. I usually chose church service. It was shorter and more intimate anyway. I stopped attending bridal and baby showers just because I was invited.
- **Fixer.** I backed out of being *Madam Fixer* or event organizer of anything, everything, and everyone. I learned to recommend other *fixers*, mastered the art of delegation, and learned to say no, or suggested a time that suited me.

- **Naysayers.** Anyone who saw the glass half-empty, I avoided like the plague, unless their company was unavoidable. And I considerably reduced the time I spent with people without direction in life.
- **Self-Limiting Beliefs.** I converted my self-limiting beliefs into positive affirmations. They were limiting my possibilities and holding me back from doing things that I wanted to do.

Five Start Tips

- **Prioritize and schedule goals for long periods**

    Review and prioritize your goals aligned to the critical aspects of your life:

    Family, Career, Finances, Spiritual, Fun, Health, and Relationship Building.

    From your goals, create monthly and weekly goal plans, feeding into a daily to-do list, starting with your big-ticket items from the goals list. Each goal must feature in the monthly plan. Residual time left after the big-ticket items are done can then be devoted to closing the important activities that can be accomplished in batches and in your off-peak productivity time; phone calls, personal emails, social media updates, or shopping, for example.

    At the end of each day, review the days' tasks because the most efficient way to live reasonably is to examine the results obtained every night.

- **Utilize idle time**

    This includes time spent in traffic, lunch hour, or early morning. I call these "ghost hours." Unless utilized well, one cannot account for them. I joined a morning rotary club that meets from seven to eight in the morning once a week. I transferred from an evening

Toastmasters club to a morning one that holds meetings from six-thirty to eight in the morning twice a month. I scheduled my business and relationship-building meetings over breakfast or lunch, thus killing two birds with one stone. Other relationships I opted to maintain by phone in off-peak productivity time. I undertook my French lessons during the peak commuter traffic rush hour, only setting off home later to avoid the traffic.

- **Personal Development**

    Clever people learn from their experiences. Brilliant people learn from other people's experiences.

    Make it your purpose to listen to audios and podcasts, read something educational and inspiring daily, learn about people more successful than you are, who have what you want—financial freedom, time freedom, thriving businesses, top company executive roles.

    Following successful individuals on social media channels is ingenious. It's tantamount to free mentorship and coaching. As such, your purpose is to emulate what they do, find out who they are following, what they're reading, where they're investing, and which circles they move in.

- **Build Networks**

    It's well known that networking is the key to a successful career and business. You can have the skills and education, but it won't be easy to get a job or even build a business without connections. Become intentional in building networks. Focus on the right people, those who hunger to become better than they currently are. Look for those working toward forging a better life for themselves, people with great marriages, careers, business growth, genuine community service, and healthier bodies. Create Win-Win situations, smile from the heart, make it your purpose to give before you receive, put yourself out in the service of others, choose associations that bring out the best in others, and join circles that attract positive, like-minded people.

- **Take a Breather. Have Fun**

    And remember, overall, you're making a good life—it's not all about making a living. Treat yourself occasionally, schedule fun activities with loved ones, enjoy your passions, within reason, of course. Whatever it is you want to do, go ahead and do it. None of us are getting out of this life alive.

    Once in a while, have quiet time, meditate and visualize where your life is headed. This refuels and gives you an energy boost for tackling the next goal in your life.

    As adults, most of us experience the same familiar demands in our lives: taxes, crazy families, relationships, challenging businesses, and jobs. So, how is it possible for some people to rise above all that to achieve more, while others don't? The power of the choices we make, what we deem important, how effectively and efficiently we utilize our time, the people we allow into our space and, most importantly, how desperately and how far we want to succeed in life. It is a choice.

BIOGRAPHY

Lynda Nabayiinda Were is a microbiologist turned Customer Experience Professional for the last nineteen years. She holds a master's degree in Financial Management from Uganda Management Institute. She attained the Competent Communicator and Leadership Award from Toastmasters International and is currently a senior executive in a leading telecom company in Uganda. She served on the executive committees of Toastmasters and Rotary International Uganda Chapters, and is a board member of an orphanage, a vocational school, and a book club patron. As the co-founder of Ascenify Uganda a management and consultancy firm, she mentors and trains individuals, social groups, and organizations on Customer Experience, Financial Literacy, Personal Effectiveness, and Leadership Skills. She lives in Kampala, Uganda, with her husband and three daughters, and enjoys watching family movies, reading novels, gardening, and traveling.

Lynda Nabayiinda Were's contact details are available at https://linktr.ee/lyndawere

CHAPTER 22

So What? Who Cares?

By Mary Etta Dockery

I'm looking at my patient and asking myself, "Why does he have such a peculiar look on his face?"

I am on the floor at a patient's bedside for the very first time ever as a brand-new student nurse. Elated and nervous, I had one whole patient to deal with by myself. Our "high tech" assignment for the day was to check and document vital signs, such as the blood pressure, pulse rate, and temperature of my one patient.

But there's one thing I must confess—it was 1963, a long time ago. In those days, we only had manual methods for measuring blood pressure, as well as glass thermometers, which we had to shake down with just the right flick of the wrist, holding on tight so as not to let it slip, fall, and break, spilling mercury all over the floor.

The patient still had that peculiar look on his face. Was it because I had to take his temperature rectally? Oh, no! I had forgotten to put lubricant on the thermometer.

My illustrious career as a nurse was off and running.

The years passed and, as a nurse, things happened, all sorts of things, I would tell myself that I should write a book because no one could make up some of this stuff.

Now, many years later, as I reflect on both the happy times and the sad, the funny experiences, and those that frustrated my inner soul, I pray that I helped my patients.

Medical attention through administering pills, IV's or wound care are good, as are the 'higher-tech' routine nursing skills involved in managing specific IV drips, tele strips; and especially being alert in patient care to avoid a stroke or calling a code. These are all fine aspects of nursing and are rewarding when there's a good outcome, by which I mean that my patient lived.

But my inner being was attracted to helping fill those needs that go beyond the physical, and I realized early on that medicine could sometimes only provide band-aid treatments on what were really psychological gaping wounds. But that is a story for another day.

Right now is about my reflections, and whatever light I may share comes "from me and my patients to you."

About that guy with the dry rectal thermometer—his temperature was good, he was cool, and we both laughed about it a little, after my sincerest apologies, of course.

I was such a klutz in those early years as a young nurse, dropping or tipping stuff over at the bedside, especially when trying to rush. For instance, while working in Obstetrics one afternoon, in my earnest desire to help my patient prepare to receive her baby for feeding, I accidentally knocked something over, which hit the floor and smashed to smithereens. It was another OMGoodness moment because the item was her religious statue. Yikes! I felt really bad and was super-apologetic. Thankfully, my patient was forgiving.

Right then, I decided to discipline myself to slow down and be more conscious of my movements at the bedside. I did that and found that I improved significantly over a period of time. That one decision plays a key role in my approach to nursing care to this day—don't be in such a rush but seek to continually improve patient satisfaction levels.

I have no need to be the fastest or the most knowledgeable. But don't get me wrong, timeliness is very important in any patient care setting, and

I certainly believe in being knowledgeable within my scope of practice, which includes acknowledging when I don't know something, saying so, and then researching it to find answers. But what good is speed and textbook know-how if I am leaving my patient lacking TLC? Today, people may wonder what that is—it stands for tender, loving care.

Let's go back to my decision to slow down and, more importantly, to up my game on giving my patients TLC. What excited me about it was the response I got from them, which made me want to give more and more. I wanted to put more energy into being positive for myself, for my patients, and their families regardless of what others said about the patient, the family, or me.

But change did not happen overnight. Often, there was a process of "detangling" from the negative conversations going on around me. I would find myself thinking, "Wow, why didn't I get up and leave when that group started talking?" However, to this day, the rewards of my growth have been immeasurable.

All my patients get a smile when I greet them on first rounds, no matter what I'm told during shift report. In my mind, I must find out for myself that they really don't want TLC. In addition, I must be authentic. A genuine smile works for me, although not all patients give me one in return. It's important to me for them to know that I'm there to take care of them, and they are not a bother when they ask for my help. That's why I'm always quick to remind them that they are the reason why I'm there. And yes, some patients do often ask me for little things that may seem unimportant, but I'm happy to do those things for them. My chief desire is for them to get better and return to their optimum health. I want them to have the edge, their fair share, and more of my positive input and encouragement. For instance, if I have to walk them to the bathroom five times in one night, then that's five times that they will return to a bed that has been straightened-out, with covers pulled back, and pillows fluffed. These little things make them feel better in their mind, and that's where healing begins. It's that knowledge that gives me satisfaction. My patients do have to work though, as returning to optimum health requires input from them as well, so I've learned to be a coach, a happy, pushy, cheering-squad of one.

There were two courageous patients whom I cared for the longest, one for one-and-a-half years and the other for three years. They both had accidental spinal cord injuries and could no longer move from shoulder to feet. However, they were fully awake, alert, and had clear thought processes. One could speak, but one had a high neck injury and could not speak. I cared for them at different times during their recovery back to life. Once transferred out from ICU, I assumed responsibility as their private nurse.

In these cases, physical care was crucial from the start to maintain healthy skin and optimal performance of all bodily systems. Simultaneously, major support was needed to help them positively direct the anguish in their mind when dealing with life's new reality.

However, no time limit can be set on the adjustment of a person's mind when dealing with and accepting the reality of being able to think clearly yet being unable to voluntarily use the rest of their body—like they were able to do just a short time ago. That is a sobering fact indeed.

As strength was gained physically, emotionally, mentally, and spiritually, and greater independence was achieved, I realized that I was giving them much of my positive energy and feelings. At the same time, I also expected them to work hard, to push through, and achieve as much as they possibly could to grasp the ability to direct their own care properly, no matter who the caregiver was. And I'm glad to say they succeeded. If you can give a little more and more each day, it lets them know you care. Quality care is the distinguishing feature of a good nurse.

Do I always have a happy outcome with patients? No, because stuff happens, usually on every shift. For example, Mrs. JD was already upset that it took so long for me to get into Isolation to take care of her needs. She had been a patient long enough to know that things like staff shortages, shift changes, and especially confinement to Isolation meant waiting longer than she desired. Before going in to see Mrs. JD, I had to plan ahead, be organized, ready to check her vital signs, do a physical assessment, have her meds, IV's ready to go, and remember to take freshwater. Plus, "gowning-up" is a time-consuming process that involves scrubbing hands, donning a gown, gloves, and mask.

I also vividly remember my early days in mental health nursing, particularly a patient called SD. She was twenty-six and a beautiful young lady, but so very sad. She was so severely depressed that she slipped into the realm of not wanting to live—she became suicidal. As her caregivers, we nurses sought to keep her alive, although, in her mind, she had decided to die. In addition to therapy, our nursing care was called 1:1, which meant that someone's eyes were on her every minute of every day, including while she was sleeping and attending to her bathroom needs. Our collective effort went on for several weeks, SD was still alive, still depressed, but we had hope.

That was when I was made to realize that "the best plans of mice and men" sometimes fail—SD was found hanging just long enough to be past life. She had been so determined, and she had found that specific moment and got away from us.

Heartbreak and devastation filled our whole unit, but, even as we grieved, we also had to pull ourselves together and continue giving our best care to the other patients. I don't recall all the details now, and they're not necessary, but that was one of those humbling moments when GOD reveals that He is the cause of everything that happens—period!

Now we come to today, when we have staggering global statistics that show millions of people are ill and suffering, thousands are dying or are already dead, supposedly due to COVID-19. Anxiety and fear grip the masses as daily activities around the world are disrupted, and folks desperately pray that they do not become a victim. But amid all this clamor and confusion, there is always someone at the bedside of the sick, sustaining them with life-energy, warm smiles, or a victory cheer.

Nurses around the world, you are in my prayers.

We are nurses and we can do anything! And, make no mistake, WE DO CARE! Okay, there are times when we may grumble and complain because of an overwhelming workload, but helping move our patients to their optimal health is *why* we care! That is the very reason why we are there. More than in any other profession, we care enough to match our determined and, hopefully, positive feelings with those patients whom we serve. And we know how to get the job done 24/7 x 365!

Writing these few words have helped me to realize that it takes time and practice to achieve reasonable mastery of a skill. And, though I often fought to keep smiling and maintain a positive approach to keep my patients' spirits up, I never thought of quitting my practice as a nurse. I often moved from one facility to another, looking for that "better place" to work. The outcome of finding that "better place" was clearly expressed to me by a seasoned nurse on my first job, who told me that it would be the same wherever I went. At the time, I didn't realize how profound that statement was.

The problem was not the facility, hospital, or clinic where I was working at any one time; it was me: I needed to change my mindset—and I succeeded.

I am still happy with my life as a nurse. Travel assignments take me to various areas of the country, and my comment to complaints about this or that place is simply to say that there will be problems everywhere you go. It is not always necessary to change the place where you work, but most often, your own mindset. And this serious change of mindset has to happen not just once but must be continuous throughout your life.

BIOGRAPHY

Mary Etta Dockery is a seasoned RN, having practiced for over fifty years and gained extensive experience in all medical specialties, except OR, ICU, and Pediatrics. Her favorite areas are Telemetry and Orthopedic surgery. Through the years, as her patients developed their physical strength, Mary Etta realized that she had to learn to help them fill the emotional and spiritual voids inside, which is so necessary for optimal recovery of health. Her degree in cultural anthropology has provided an ongoing, cross-cultural sensitivity that Mary Etta feels has been a perfect adjunct to her caregiving.

Contact Information
Facebook: https://www.facebook.com/mary.dockery.338

CHAPTER 23

Success As A Choice

By Moetini Tihoni

I recall all the years I've struggled with personal identity. I'm a native Polynesian pure-blood (huh!) with a bit of French, German, Chinese, and British blood thrown in. All these different cultures have forged my personality, with the most prominent being Polynesian. I'm an island-dude with multi-cultural aspirations, but I've always seen myself as a human living on Planet Earth more than someone with an immobile, categorized ethnicity.

Ever since I was a kid, I've always been a rebel, even though my surroundings forced me to toe the line and stick at doing things *their* way, be influenced by *their* thoughts and *their* lives, because that's how it should be. The educational system is quite simple in our islands. Even though we have a strong French academic school structure, the anchored Polynesian culture goes beyond that, dealing with emotions (actually not *dealing* with them), so it's pretty confusing and challenging to sort out. Well, at least, that's what I thought. The reality isn't as pretty as we make it out to be. Deep in our souls, we all have a bubble our minds have created to protect us and keep us from collapsing. I buried, deep in my mind, these horrible memories of the abuse I suffered; although I can't tell I was forced, I did lose my innocence way too early. I grew up hating myself, my body, for a very long time, and all of a sudden, one fine day, I finally stopped moping about myself and made the choice to be happy. I deserved it. Our mind is an inexhaustible source of strength and energy. I had found the power to forgive that disgusting act and live with complete serenity. I've never shared it until now.

I am the son of two middle-class administrative worker parents, pretty much like every typical family (dare I say), with simple goals to achieve: work during your shift, finish at 3:30 pm, then back home to get dinner ready, enjoy your meal while watching the news and sharing your day at work/school and get used to making them proud of having at least average grades in most subjects. Apparently, that would lead you to be able to live a sufficient lifestyle: owning a car and a house, with loans at the bank that you'd have to pay off for the rest of your life, isn't that inspiring? Yay! I was limiting my brain by accepting the average. "You can do way better than you know, but it's still a great result," my mum used to tell me, and she turned out to be right. I always dreamed of being someone special and aspired to have an "amazing" life, like those of movie celebrities and famous singers. I've had my dreams broken so often that I'd prevented myself from dreaming big, discouraged by criticism and harsh realities. Most folks are just happy with an average, peaceful life on our little island paradise without much ambition for anything save for what's needed to live happily ever after.

I had no complaints. I've cherished my life with my parents, who offered me everything I needed. I also have a half-sister who is older than me. She was a maternal figure to me. I remembered my dad taking us to resorts on some weekends, events organized from his work. That's when I started to enjoy leisure time, tanning in the sun lounger, sipping virgin cocktails, while the adults busied themselves with their own activities. I was in love with the idea of being lazy, and I swore to myself that I'd live this way forever. Daddy got me back in the real world and simply goes with "Scratch for daddy with your lucky fingers!" meaning if you wanna be rich. I thought he had the dream job—traveling around the world. Travel. WOW! He was actually traveling to other islands for his work. He was away for six to 10 months a year. My strong mum took care of me by herself most of my life; we'd been facing difficulties together. I always admired her forthright and unconditional love even though I was not an angel, I must admit.

Growing up with the thought of living a cozy future—"Daddy's job is pretty comfortable, think about it"—just wasn't for me, as rebellious as I was. When I came back from France, with a few marketing skills and an excellent knowledge of wine (not to mention night-clubs and parties), I decided to reroute to the hotel industry, perhaps unconsciously. Indeed, tourism is my country's main economic activity. I knew I'd be dealing with foreigners, Americans, and maybe I would be able to get close to the lifestyle I always wanted; who knew what opportunities would open up for me? I loved that idea, but if I had to put that feeling into words, I'd say that I didn't want to work for them. I actually wanted to be like them. Dreams, again! That was the unconfessed desire, deep inside my heart, that made me want to change my life into something I never really dared to think, or rather dream about.

I didn't have any other way off the islands except through success in my hotel industry career and setting my sights on a management position. So, I chose to move to New Caledonia for a resort opening, which would lead me out of my country for good, and perhaps a long-awaited better lifestyle. I actually found love there. I'm so proud of her because she has always stood by my side through thick and thin. Before leaving that beautiful "Kanaky Rock," I was shown what could have been—the opportunity of my life whose call I dared to refuse. Was I not ready? Did I mistrust network marketing? Who knows? I was sure that I couldn't bear seeing myself in hotels anymore; I had enough of that thankless job. Well, maybe I hadn't chosen the best year to quit my career.

It was a pretty challenging time for both of us (my mom included). My girlfriend and I were hit by a car while riding a scooter on our way to job interviews. That accident left Aurélia badly hurt and unable to walk without a walking-stick for months. We were broke, unemployed, and back living in my parents' house. My pride was hurt. I felt so ashamed of myself, but, of course, I tried my best never to let it show because my friend—Ego—thought of it as a weakness. Then, my dad had a stroke, a bad one, that had paralyzed him ever since. Watching that proud man being taken down so easily by those teeny tiny little blood clots—my dad, whom I'd been fighting almost my entire life to avoid resembling him, an uncontrollable violent man as soon as he drank, whom I learned to tame, often by force, to protect myself and my mum—was utterly knocked out by the stroke. It felt as if I was meant to come back home during that time. It seemed that maybe our guardian angel had driven us back home for that reason. As we say, life goes on, and what I recalled repeatedly in my mind was that my mum had retired for over 20 years and still struggled with money. My dad had only just retired. That made me feel bad for both of them. I couldn't help but wonder at the time if that was going to be my future as well: working until my 60s, only to end up sick and enjoying retirement in a medical facility with money issues.

But then, amid all that struggle, I had an excellent job interview and landed a sales job for one of the most luxurious Polynesian brands, selling our famous Tahitian cultured pearls. After a short time, I was promoted to head of the Bora Bora site, so we had to move back to paradise after having first settled everything for my parents. I couldn't help feeling doomed.

Back in Bora Bora, again! With our famous Tahitian style sarcasm! - *"Hoki faahau I Pora Pora!"*

While handling my job to the best of my abilities, I wanted to develop myself by learning new business skills. I thought I'd learn as much as I could about entrepreneurship. I got some good ideas for initial projects and even finalized business plans. I started the reprogramming process, thinking differently about my life and about the things that I might really be capable of. At that point, I had only taken a glimpse of my true potential just by making the right choice for myself and my family. When we knew we had our baby girl on the way, my mind went into overdrive with even crazier plans. What would we do to welcome her?

I'd respectfully chosen to ask my father-in-law his permission to propose to his daughter. Then I had planned a trip to Vegas to ask her to marry me with a personalized diamond ring. We found out about the pregnancy the day after I proposed at the top of Sky Tower. Thank goodness!

Otherwise, my story would have been different! I believe that these kinds of events that happen in our lives are not accidental. Law of attraction—that's the secret. I'm sure of it because Aurélia and I had openly expressed our wish to the universe to become a family, to be married (at least, I always wanted it secretly, but, again, didn't show my "weakness" or true self). Okay, so I wasn't going to be a celebrity after all, nor a famous artist in music or cinema.

As you may have picked up by now, my dream had always been to be wealthy-healthy, to travel all around the world visiting its the wonders, old and new, eat all the cuisines offered, and enjoy all the different cultures, while sharing it all with the people I loved the most. My closest friends and family will testify that I have always been a good person. Although it has to be said that I don't always keep my mouth shut, untold truths have slipped out. But, hand on heart, I have always welcomed people to my table, my house, and enjoyed company with whom I would share an excellent dinner and a few bottles of good wine.

Since the economic crisis caused by COVID-19 that hit us in 2020, I noticed that I started to become who I always criticized: the average man, always blaming life, bosses, the government, the school system, people in general, my parents, and my fiancé for anything I found faulty. I started to realize this even more when I began to listen to personal development podcasts, videos, and the training events I attended (thanks to the company that I'd finally chosen to enroll in). I was extremely grateful for having made that choice, the opportunity for a life change, and all I had to do was say YES. Well, my fiancé made me choose, to be honest. When they say 'listen to your women', just do it. So, who or what should we blame when life seems to make us average?

Previously, I'd always look at my life streaming by, without any purpose or any sense of having control over it. I thought I'd always be the dumb funny guy who loves to amuse his friends with jokes and stories, just an average man who is merely happy avoiding the stress of hard work, who will never overcome his untold fears, who drank until he forgot having a life purpose, and partied with no high expectations for himself at all. Did I truly have no other choice? I did! I've had enough of blaming others; I was done. I've proven it by becoming a better version of myself, the professional expert I am now, the super fiancé I am now, and, finally, the best soon-to-be dad I was going to be.

My beautiful little baby girl, Miss Lagresle-Tihoni Oranui Kyara UnaUnari'I, who was born on Saturday, July 4th, 2020, was the reason why I strived to be a better man—even the best version of myself thus far. Finally, I was unsure whether I had made a choice because I didn't really have the choice. That's how it should be. I have to be better because she deserves the best in everything—education, health care, lifestyle, vacations, etc. I want her to become an even better version of what we are now so she can play her part in enhancing the future of our world. I pledge and vow my life to be as inspirational, as committed to righteousness, as honest, as excellent a father and husband, and as helpful to other people as I can be in order to live positively and make our world a better place.

Changing our vision and perspective of life is simply a matter of being willing to convert a negative situation into a positive outcome. Have I mentioned that 2020 is a beautiful year? Let's continue to dream big—bigger than what we think our minds are capable of—by making the right choices for ourselves and our loved ones.

BIOGRAPHY

With a decade of expertise in the tourism and leisure industry, the "Maohi" Pacific Islander Moetini Tihoni made the choice of rerouting his career from regular employment to independent entrepreneurship in network marketing to help people achieve their life goals. He operates his organization in various countries around the world, especially in his home islands and current location, Bora Bora. While he has always been an authentic, high-standing, and professional person, he continuously tries to lift his colleagues and partners to the top in order to help them reach their true potential through trustworthy leadership. He shares with vulnerability and an open heart; that led him to a new path because he stands for truth and will always be true to himself. Today, he feels much gratitude for being a happily engaged man and a father.

Moetini Tihoni's contact details are available at https://linktr.ee/moetini

CHAPTER 24

Successful Thinking

By Paul Prinsloo

For every action executed, there is an equal and opposite reaction. That means when you choose to empower your disbelieving thoughts, there is an equal and opposite effect on your mind that positively impacts your way of thinking.

I choose to analyze my thoughts, craft better outcomes, and enforce my self-belief with an upgraded, more positive manner of thinking, as when you choose to say either "I can" or "I cannot." A person ultimately becomes who they choose to be based on repetitive thoughts that lead to action through an emotional response.

The subconscious mind is a powerful gift whose deep, dark secrets we can learn and apply to our lives.

We are only conscious for a few hours a day, but what we train the conscious mind to perceive as truth, we ultimately enforce and etch into our sub-self—the subconscious.

It is more powerful than the waking mind; it holds the key to either destroying or creating success. Therefore, we should look into the eyes of our subconscious and journey into the far reaches of its mystery, seeking to understand the origins of our limiting beliefs. Only then shall we become masters of our own precious and fragile design—the thoughts that program our beliefs.

As a child, I was taught that succeeding in life meant slaving away at every opportunity. For a few years, I believed that lie. The word "LIE" appears in the middle of the word "believe." Whether or not that is a coincidence, it is the truth: our self-belief is composed of the lies we tell ourselves.

That this system is a failure is proven by the fact that every life experience we go through, every inner self-talk we have, and every external opinion someone impresses upon us becomes the architect of our lives and programs our subconscious. The materialization process of success begins with the thoughts that program the subconscious, forcing an overpowering belief that is either negative or positive. The end result is an action that will strive to fulfill the programming—hence the materialization of one's thoughts.

It is in the finite capacity of the thinker's thoughts that success is either created or destroyed. I read a theory based on what thought is, and it made perfect sense to me. Matter is broken down into molecules, which are further broken down into atoms. After that come the components of atoms, i.e., protons, neutrons, and the outermost component, the electrons. When we further zoom into the subatomic parts, we discover a phenomenon called "quanta." Quanta, therefore, is the very essence of one's thoughts. If every material perceived by the naked eye is quanta at the minutest scale of existence, then it follows that thoughts can influence that matter. Absurd sounding, I know, but take a glimpse in your mind's eye on the possibilities of that and marvel at its complexity and mystery. It means that the materialization present in our lives is directly influenced by our very thoughts, be they negative or positive.

Goal setting is the most essential factor in reaching one's dreams. I cannot stress the importance of goal formulation that sets you up to perceive the goal as already being a reality. I advocate, first, deciding your goal: what it is that you want to accomplish, and then devising a step-by-step plan to achieve it. Of course, there will always be challenges, but overcoming those obstacles is what makes the rewards worthwhile. Then, aspire to become a superior version of who you currently are; always seek to improve upon yourself, even in the smallest ways. A good metaphor explains this: in order for a building to stand higher than the rest, it must have a deeper foundation than all the other buildings. In human terms, this means implementing a daily strategy of continual improvement. The power concealed in modeling oneself on another successful individual has been greatly overlooked, but much can be achieved by observing successful people and copying their traits, beliefs, and habits. With application, you too will become such a successful person. To attain this goal, it is vital to find a successful mentor—someone who inspires you to better yourself and implants a burning desire in you to go forth and conquer all your limiting beliefs.

Being positive is a state of mind and a product directly proportional to the amount of effort placed upon the decision to be positive. Negative self-talk is the number one destroyer of self-worth. Through negative thought, we can be our own worst enemies, so it's important to come to the realization that we, in ourselves, are enough. We hold within ourselves the power to either create or destroy the success we seek. If we continually pace up and down the road of repetitive action through ignorance, then how can we expect life to offer us the goblet filled with the elixir of fulfillment? Successful people know there is much more to life than merely the monotonous expenditure of useless effort. After all, life presents plentiful opportunities, and action-takers benefit from the fruits of their labors. Where do you currently stand? Do you perhaps have a follower mentality or that of a leader? When you choose to endure the challenges God sets out for each of us, be grateful for them and take them as blessings rather than curses. You will be rewarded more than you can imagine.

I would like to rewind a little and talk about a time in my life when I was clueless and stuck in a rut.

The story starts when I was in school. As I mentioned previously, I was taught that once an opportunity presents itself, then slave and slave away at it. During high school, I always worked hard and made sure I got good marks. I enjoyed the recognition and rewards that came with feeling accomplished. Towards the end of the school year, when I was 15, my father decided that, since the education provided in school wasn't on a par with what was expected in the working world, he would make me an offer. The offer allowed me to get ahead of my age group: I would go to college to study in preparation for a career in engineering. I was terrified and did not know what to expect. I felt the great unknown was waiting for me, slumbering, until it could reveal itself. I was a teenager embarking on an educational path that would, if rendered successfully, open up the pearly gates of a career path in engineering.

I remember working harder than anyone else because I was the youngest student on campus. All I knew was hard work and improving the skills I had to acquire to succeed in my future studies. That was when I learned that, even though something is new and we do not quite fully understand it, if we muster up the courage to set out to conquer, then conquer we shall. By venturing into the unknown, we step out of our comfort zone, the exact place where growth takes place. I began my studies and worked hard towards my goal with dedication. It was tough, but I stuck it out and achieved the goal I had set out to reach. I had successfully gained a career advantage over my school-fellows of the same age by achieving my goal with the odds stacked against me.

Being the youngest student on campus, with the title of top student, I then took on another challenge: obtaining a job. But there was one thing holding me back: I was too young to work for any major names in the industry. Eventually, my father struck a deal with my uncle and landed me a job; I had to work for my uncle at his company. It was a very difficult three months, working in the blazing sun at about 35°C, having only a water pipe to drink from when I got thirsty. General labor was my reality, slaving away to dig trenches with no protection for my hands. Every single day, I came home tired and mentally worn out, with blisters on my hands. I soon gave in and retreated back to my parents, but I quickly got another position working as a network technician. I remember the work as mentally stimulating, but the pay wasn't great. Plus, I was mistreated by my team leader. I begged God for an opportunity to earn a decent income and not have to deal with simple-minded individuals. Then, I got an offer to work in a coal mine for about three times my previous salary. Although I wasn't really sure I wanted to work in a mine, not because of getting dirty or working hard, but because of the working conditions. There are plenty of health risks associated with that type of work as one ventures into high-risk areas; you're continually placing your life on the line. Uneven floors make moving around a struggle. High temperatures can make you collapse, and don't even consider mine work if you're claustrophobic!

My friend then encouraged me to apply for an apprenticeship that would lead to my gaining a professional engineering qualification with letters after my name (the kind I could be proud of). Four years down the line, still applying my mindset of continual improvement and a strong work ethic, I finally achieved my goal and obtained the title I sought. After again being inspired by one of my mentors, I set out to further my studies, once more applying the belief that I am limited only by my own negative thoughts. Success is only a footstep away if you cultivate an attitude of positive thinking. Though challenges will present themselves, one can apply the combined key features of an unlimited mindset and follow through.

Life, at its fullest, can mean either harmony or agony, but it is within the power of each individual to become what they desire. There is a saying: "If you empty your wallet into your mind, your mind will soon fill up your wallet." I believe that to be true for any individual who pursues the mindset of a conqueror. There is a famous quote, the origin of which is unknown and is often wrongly attributed to Albert Einstein, that, nevertheless, perfectly illustrates my point: "Everybody is a genius. But if you judge a fish by its ability to climb a tree, it will live its whole life believing that it is stupid." Everybody has the ability to achieve greatness, but there are, sadly, only a select few who pursue their dreams and aspirations. We are entitled to lead a life worth living; we have to realize that we are worthy of such a life. Desire drives the passion that emanates from the belief we can pursue and achieve greatness.

My message to the determined, driven, aspiring leaders out there is always to seek to better themselves by pursuing the aspirations that others say you cannot achieve. Make believers out of skeptics, inspire others to take on the tasks they want to achieve but think impossible because of their limiting beliefs. Encourage them to be open-minded. After all, the only time a parachute works is when it is open. Present yourself as a beacon of hope to others, change your negative beliefs, and construct new and inspiring ones. Ultimately, you must ask yourself the very important question: "Is the juice worth the squeeze?" When you decide the answer is yes, then stick to your decision with dogged persistence. Don't just dip your toes in when working toward your goals but immerse your whole being. Let's make a dent in the universe!

BIOGRAPHY

Paul Prinsloo is a keen observer of what drives people and how they can continually improve themselves. His purpose is to empower people, to awaken their true selves, and conquer their limiting beliefs. He always keeps the following maxim in mind: *Keep moving forward and push through your pain to prosper.*

Paul Prinsloo can be contacted via https://paulandkellylumenjade.com/

CHAPTER 25

The Power Of Authenticity

By Priscilla Olson

If we want to be great, it's time we get over ourselves. Has anyone ever told you to *just be yourself?* We must admit that our culture really likes that phrase. Today, you hear it just about everywhere, you see it everywhere, and everyone believes it to be great advice to live by. I'll admit I've been there before, and who would argue with that advice? Like many people, I fell victim to bullying as a child and throughout my early adult life. Never feeling accepted or "fitting in" felt normal to me. But ironically, I was always that person people would go to for advice on relationships. This helped me understand that you must be able to deal with rejection to get connection. Having a fear of rejection will only hurt our ability to connect with people. The fact is, not everyone is going to like you, and that's okay. To be fair, I do believe it is important for one to develop a healthy self-esteem and a good sense of well-being. But what I want you to notice is that, as a society, we are seeing an over-inflation of self-regard—an obsession with self-entitlement that has fueled narcissistic behavior. Sure, there is a significance to 'just being yourself' and 'following your heart.' Those phrases tell us to express our individuality and not conform to someone else's personality, to be confident in who God created us to be, to be optimistic about our life, and to develop an authentic sense of self. All those things are good. But what happens when we fall off the tracks and 'just be yourself' becomes unscrutinized and goes unquestioned? What happens when a culture like ours takes it too far and starts to believe that, above all else, 'you' are what matters most? Leading us to ask, does the digital age help us to connect or compare ourselves with each other?

If we want to achieve big things we need to collaborate, one mind is not enough. Fear kills empathy. Harboring fear towards 'difference' triggers an 'us vs. them' way of thinking, and when we draw a line between us and others, the mechanisms of empathy shut off. Lack of emotions leads to a lack of empathy. Our emotions carry highly significant information, and if we don't receive this information from others, it's very difficult to understand each other and genuinely connect. If you want to know how to connect with others, you first must be strongly connected with yourself. It isn't until we're able to accept and embrace ourselves for who we truly are, that others can do so as well.

A respectful approach towards others is important, despite any differences throughout this process. As much as we like to focus and acknowledge our strengths, it is just as important to recognize and accept our weaknesses. By embracing our weaknesses, we become stronger and more grounded as an individual. If you don't know or if you're having trouble identifying what your strengths and weaknesses are, I assure you it's well worth devoting some time to finding out: they could be professional or personal and are what make you an individual. Write them out and try to create a plan for improving them. We always have room to grow and become better as individuals, and working on your personal development should become a daily discipline. Don't just be yourself. I encourage you to go outside of yourself so that you can serve this world with your talents and traits that make you unique. Decrease your fear of the unknown, and you decrease your fear of difference.

Walk in their shoes. It's in getting out of your comfort zone that really challenges you to grow. One of the best ways to develop a strong connection is to find a common ground. Avoid small talk by asking questions that are universal (meaning anyone can answer them). Ask deep, thought-provoking questions to empower them to come to their own powerful conclusions to make better decisions for themselves. In turn, they will feel inspired and motivated. Remember, having a genuine interest creates a safe space to open up. So, a good conversation with another person should be around 80% about them and only 20% about you. Be an active listener, support them by listening without interrupting or being judgemental. This is huge. When we listen and are attentive instead of thinking of how we will respond, we can focus one hundred percent on going deeper in understanding one another. Sure, people come from all sorts of different backgrounds, but we're all in need and want the same outcome—love and acceptance. All relationships enrich our lives and give us new perspectives and new lessons.

What strengthens the relationship? Trust. And how do you get trust? Through a combination of effort, honesty, integrity, and vulnerability over time. You can't fake it, and you can't force it. This becomes especially important in the virtual world we live in today that thrives on inauthenticity, and where personal disconnection is at an all-time high. Research suggests that a relationship begins naturally when we determine whether a person is trustworthy or not. That's why it's so critical to start off with the right intentions because it has never been easier to spot the fake interactions and which relationships are transactional or relational. Much of the problem lies in the fact that being genuine is devalued in our culture, while success, personal achievement, and avoiding criticism are highly praised.

We're all somewhat starved for authenticity. For relationships to be authentic, we have to genuinely share our inner self in the present moment, regardless of the consequences. Vulnerability in relationships is what deepens and strengthens them because it's about taking steps together. When we open ourselves up and are willing to be vulnerable, we tell them that we trust them, and naturally, this will make them feel like this is a safe space to become more open and trustworthy with you. Every relationship requires equal effort on both ends to sustain its health. No one can relate to those who try to come off as perfect because they won't seem real. So, don't try to diminish your authenticity because it will constrain your growth and self-esteem. People will want to get to know you if they know you are a caring person. Until you get close enough to connect to people and relate to them on a personal level, you're not going to have influence as a leader. A servant leader knows that they must relate more to those that they lead. People will want to let you help them when you're sincere about really wanting them to achieve success and when they see you as an example of what can be.

There's a reason why people get coaches, personal trainers, and instructors. It's because we want to be shown how to do it the right way, and we want to be challenged to be our very best by someone who walks the talk. As a coach, I've had the opportunity to work with people from all walks of life under a variety of circumstances, and the greatest way I found to connect with them was through empathy and humility. This was because every client I worked with had to be vulnerable with me from the beginning for me to help them. I would ask discovery questions like, what are your short- and long-term goals? Why are you doing this now? What have you previously tried that didn't work? What challenges have you faced or overcome in life? What are your limitations? What do you expect from me as your coach? And the list would go on, until I could completely understand where they have been previously, where they are currently, and their expectations on where they wanted to go. But for them to see results, they needed to be honest with me about their daily struggles with the process. We established trust and a "we're a team" partnership from the very beginning because I never made it about me; it was always about them. They put their trust in me because I showed them how much I cared about them. Learning their weaknesses helped me understand just how hard I could push them. And in return, they learned a lot about themselves in the process, realizing they were much stronger than they thought they were. Anyone can obtain a degree or certification to achieve a level of status, but when you start to apply what you've learned and get results, you gain the experience that positions you as the expert.

I believe taking your time to get to know someone is an important thing to remember. Real relationships that last aren't built in a hurry; it's not about quantity but quality. Building connections takes time, effort, commitment, and courage. Give people some breathing room to get to know you first and ask if they want your help before you offer them any kind of solution. Always give before you take. I believe that over-delivering and going above and beyond will gain trust and likability with people, especially with those you meet for the first time. We need to recognize that every relationship is different. Whether you're networking or building relationships, there's no magic script to follow. It takes two to build a connection, and it's not always what you say, it's how you say it. Research states that 7% of communication is verbal, 38% is in your tone of voice, and 55% of communication is in your body language. Your message and your tone should always stay the same. Keep it simple, but be honest and genuine and allow yourself to be real and not scripted.

Being consistent with those you've built relationships with is vital. You need to be someone who holds themselves accountable. Have integrity, keep your word, take full responsibility for your actions, and hold fast to your morals and values. Even if this means ending up in uncomfortable situations or having to make tough decisions, ask them for feedback on how you can better support them and be open to receiving it. Not acknowledging our mistakes can make us lose trust and credibility. Create a culture of sharing your failures as well as successes. Reward the act of risk-taking, then come back and celebrate the results regardless of whether it was a success or not. Define the limits and figure out what risks and failures are acceptable. Learning how to communicate challenging matters delicately and compassionately opens the pathway to an evolving relationship. We might not always agree with or approve of the decisions of others, but when we have empathy, we treat them with compassion, openness, and kindness. Nurture your relationships by practicing acts of giving. This can be in the form of giving your time, attention, resources, information, etc. Giving something of value will help you establish trust in your relationships.

Now more than ever, leaders must utilize the power of humility and empathy towards others, and steer away from all the selfishness and entitlement to get us back on track as a society. Many of us have experienced the effects of poor leadership in our communities, our homes, schools, jobs, even in sports and politics. Leading with your ego is the effect you have on yourself, but leading with humility is the effect that you have on others. We must surrender our ego and stay away from this "me, me, me" mentality and replace it with "how can I be of service to you?" We need the kind of humility that inspires people to lead lives that are gracious, humble, and character-driven. Such leaders understand they're not the center of attention and believe in listening and understanding, as opposed to a pretentious performance for others. It's about making a difference to give more than you receive. Be focused on being significant, not on over-achieving personal success.

Great leaders inspire you to create the next best version of yourself, encourage you to grow, and allow you to be who you're meant to be. Their lives are grounded in love and service towards others. I truly believe that authentic relationships are good for our well-being and the key to living a significant and meaningful life. If we can change the way we connect with others, together we can change the world.

BIOGRAPHY

Priscilla Olson became obsessed with her vision of freedom at an early age. She is a former independent women's health coach, who traded the billable hour for more time and financial freedom through a career in network marketing. Her visionary leadership has mentored many around her to experience massive success in business and life. Her mission is to unlock the untapped potential in others, so they too can choose how they live, influence, work, and play. Priscilla's passion is supporting others to reclaim their most energized relationships with their peers, their bodies, and life itself.

Contact Information
Facebook: https://www.facebook.com/Priscilla-Olson-102210191489839
Instagram: http://www.instagram.com/priscillaolson_

CHAPTER 26

Change Your Thoughts And Change Your Life

By Rick Dorr

When I was approached about joining a new business venture, I jumped in with both feet. It's one of those businesses that get you excited and cause you to lose sleep at night. Instead of counting sheep, I was counting endless possibilities. I had these explosive, "what if?" thoughts: What if I could create a second income stream? What if I could become a top leader? What if I could help and mentor hundreds of people? What if?! Over time, I began to lay the groundwork for a substantial business and gained recognition as a rising leader. I was able to influence people one-on-one and also mentor crowds of hundreds.

But overnight, it all came crashing down. One of my mentors called me to tell me that the Federal Trade Commission (FTC) had closed the company down and chained and locked the doors. I made the three-hour trip to the corporate offices, only to find the information was correct. A few hundred people had gathered outside the corporate offices and stared at the doors sealed with chains and locks.

It turned out that the company was involved in less than ethical business practices, and the CEO had been shipping corporate funds to an overseas account. It was true; the company that so many of us loved and had been working hard to help succeed was gone. In a flash, thousands of people with previously lucrative livelihoods, fueled by their residual incomes, were left with crushed dreams.

Who of us hasn't had our hopes and dreams crushed? Maybe it wasn't a business venture, but a marriage that started with so much promise, then, in one conversation, you found out your spouse was in love with someone else. Or, you found out your teenage son or daughter, the one with so much potential, was addicted to drugs or alcohol. Or, even though you felt fine, your doctor found a lump in your breast, or you were diagnosed with cancer or some other debilitating disease, or someone close to you died.

Life has a way of testing us to see what we are made of. What do we do in these times of setback, loss, and disappointment? How do we handle the bad news, the bad breaks, the shattered hopes? Do we crawl on the couch like a spoiled child holding tightly to their "blankie" and suck our thumb because things did not go our way? Do we retreat into some small corner of our mind and nurse the bad news, fuel the raging fire within us, and feed the negative monster that wants to take over our lives? Do we check out of life and vow to never start another business, love again, hope again, or dream again?

Of course, the choice is ours to make. It is always ours to make. We cannot control many of the things that happen to us, but we can control how we react to them. The bible's Proverbs 23:7 states, *"As a man thinks in his heart, so is he."* We choose our thoughts. We choose what we dwell on. We choose what we allow to penetrate our minds. There is an adage that says, "We move in the direction of our most current dominant thoughts."

Now, forgive me if this sounds too simplistic because I know it's not easy. I speak from personal experience because I have had my fair share of setbacks, lost thousands of dollars in business ventures, survived a broken heart through a divorce, lost a home through foreclosure, had my kids go off track, and have my own collection of shattered dreams. But I still have to be the one who chooses in which direction I want my life to go. One of the bible's authors wrote: *"I call heaven and earth to witness against you that today*

I have set before you life or death, blessing or curse. Oh, that you would choose life; that you and your children might live!"—Deuteronomy 30:19.

I cannot dwell on two dominant thoughts at the same time. I only have the ability to focus my attention on one thing properly. So, when the hurts of life come, when the setbacks occur, when the doctor's report is not what I'd hoped for, when my relationship did not turn out the way I dreamed, when my kids get off course, when I lose my job, I can choose to dwell on the negative report (death) and move in that direction, or I can choose to think positive thoughts (life) and move in that direction. I have the power to control the course of my life.

I am not saying we should stick our heads in the sand and deny the reality of the situation. I am not saying we should act as if nothing has occurred. What I am saying is, we can acknowledge that something terrible happened but choose to look at it in a different light. Yes, I lost my job, but I know that another one and a better one is right around the corner. Yes, my marriage did not make it, but I know that love still awaits me, and I look forward to meeting that new person. Yes, my kids got off track, but I fully believe they will get back on track again. Yes, that business venture closed, but there are plenty of new opportunities awaiting me. Yes, I do have that illness, but discoveries in medicine are happening every day.

Choose to focus on your preferred future, not your past. Yes, feel the pain of what happened but choose to move past it as quickly as possible by focusing on what you want. You are not powerless! You have the power within you to make those choices. You have the ability within you to move forward.

Shortly after the company I was working for was closed down by the FTC, a group of leaders, choosing not to be deterred in their quest for financial freedom, began to look for another home, so they could rebuild. I was invited to be a part of that team. Having found a place to call home, we all went to work again to build a preferred future. Over the next few years, I rose to the top of that company, becoming one of the top leaders. Once again, I found myself in rooms of hundreds of people, mentoring and influencing others to rise to their full potential. Eventually, I became the company president. If you find yourself in a tough situation, choose to set yourself apart from others, and be an example of what is possible. No longer choose to be a victim but choose to be victorious; no longer choose to be conquered but choose to be a conqueror. When the negative thoughts begin to crowd your mind, stop, refocus, and think about the possibilities, not the impossibilities. I love this statement by Joel Osteen: "Your setback is just a set-up for something greater." Isn't that statement powerful?

My marriage of fourteen years had fallen on hard times. After numerous attempts to make it work, we both knew divorce was the only option. I'll spare you the sordid details; suffice to say that my wife and I both realized that trying to move forward together was a task not worth pursuing. Losing in business was hard, really hard, but failing in marriage was the toughest thing I ever had to go through. Of course, it was a long and painful process, with many emotional lows. The truth is, I was emotionally numb for almost a year.

I'll never forget the day when I was driving home from work; it was one of those wintery, foggy days we sometimes have here in the Central Valley of California. My life felt much like that day. I was living in a gray fog, trying to navigate the road directly in front of me because I could not see much further than that. On that day, I cried out to God, "Please help me!" Shortly after saying that simple prayer, a small opening appeared in the sky, and it was as if God had poked his finger through the fog to let a little ray of sunshine hit my face. At that moment, I realized God had not forgotten about me and knew what I was going through. It was a sign for me to finally break out of my depression and begin to move forward.

From that day forward, I chose not to stay in that heartbroken condition forever. I took the advice I am giving you and began to turn my thoughts to a better and preferred future. I considered all the new possibilities before me and was ready for anything that might come my way to lead me to a full and total recovery. Days later, while driving, I heard a commercial on the radio talking about a divorce clinic that helped people through divorce recovery. I knew that the commercial was meant for me. However, I was driving and unable to write down the information. So, I said a short prayer: "If that is meant for me, Lord, let that commercial come on again," and almost miraculously, it came on again. So, I quickly pulled into the closest parking lot, got out my pen, and wrote down the information. I called the number, enrolled in the class, and later discovered it was one of the best decisions I ever made. But that is not the end of the story.

What I learned at the clinic gave me the ammunition I needed to change my thinking and walk out of my pain and heartbreak; it did give me a new way of looking at things and helped me realize my divorce was not the end of my story. I realized it was okay to admit there were some areas of my life where I needed someone else to help me see things differently. It's okay to have a life coach, a mentor, or a friend, someone who will walk through life's challenges with you. We don't have to do it alone. It's okay to ask for help.

In that divorce recovery clinic, I met Sandy, my current wife of almost thirty years. She truly is my soulmate and life partner. Had I not chosen to put the past behind me and move forward, I never would have gone to that clinic, and I would never have met my life partner. That setback was a set-up for something greater.

I could give several examples of how changing my focus and redirecting my thoughts have changed the trajectory of my life. After my foreclosure, I did get a new home, better than the one before. My children, who went off track, are now doing great and living successful lives. My financial setbacks have turned around, and I am living a successful and prosperous life.

You have the power to choose. If you choose to live in the past, then so be it! If you decide to move into your preferred future, then so be it!

CHANGE YOUR THOUGHTS AND YOU CAN CHANGE YOUR LIFE.

BIOGRAPHY

Rick Dorr, hailing from the Central Valley in California, is a national and international speaker who can make audiences laugh and cry with his dynamic speaking style as he teaches them about life, business, spirituality, and creating the right mindset for facing life's challenges. He has spoken to audiences across the United States, Mexico, the Philippines, and South America for over four decades. In 1980, he was named as one of the Outstanding Young Men of America. He developed his leadership skills as a veteran staff sergeant in the United States Air Force, the president of Travel 2000 Network, the vice president of America's Travel Companies, the owner of his own business, and a top trainer and leader in several network marketing companies. Rick has helped thousands of people regain their dreams and recapture their vision for a preferred future.

Contact Rick Dorr via https://linktr.ee/rickdorr

CHAPTER 27

From One Acorn A Thousand Forests Are Born

By Ry Fry

It was a chilly night and well after sundown, as I pulled some Dungeness crab out of the Puget Sound off the Edmonds Pier, just a short drive north of Seattle, Washington. It was January 2015. I was 39 and had two of my beautiful children alongside me. My son Jagger, just four years old, and my daughter Lake, two, enjoyed helping their dad do a little crabbing. But what may sound like a perfect family experience was, in fact, far from it.

You see, the crab limit in the Puget Sound was only five male Dungeness crabs per day. I was pulling at least ten to fifteen female and male crabs that evening, as I'd been doing every few nights for the last month. While my children were excited and enjoying our weekly ritual, I was terrified the game warden was right around the corner, preparing to deliver a hefty fine for pulling way over the legal daily limit. I'm not usually a lawbreaker by nature, but I wasn't crabbing for sport—it was the only way I could think of to feed the three of us. I was down to my last options, with less than a hundred dollars to my name. Once we were home safely, driving a borrowed car from a friend, we would crack open each crab and cook them, adding rice, and that would sustain us until we needed to make another late-night run to the pier.

I'd love to say that I was broke at the time through no fault of my own because that would be so much better than the actual truth. The truth was, not only was I down to my last hundred dollars, but I also had over five hundred thousand dollars-worth of debt. Between my two failed relationships that had left me with five beautiful children, I was behind the eight ball, staring at mounting back taxes and child support. While my young son and daughter were pulling up crab from the Edmonds Pier late that night, they were all smiles and loved spending time with their father. But, despite the smile on my face, inside, I was sobbing. I had absolutely no clue as to how I was going to get out of the desperate financial hole I found myself in, support my five children, and become whole again.

As I was sitting on the pier, feeling more and more depressed as desperation grew in my mind and heart, I suddenly heard my grandfather's words: "From one acorn a thousand forests are born." This quote had changed my life in the past and set me on a successful journey in network marketing. I'd had tremendous success in network marketing, starting at age twenty-seven, so what went wrong? How the hell did I end up on the pier, completely broke, in massive debt, dodging game wardens in the middle of the night with two kids under the age of five, and barely seeing my older kids? Then it hit me—and I instantly realized what I'd been doing wrong all those years and the lesson my grandfather had desperately tried to teach me. I had completely missed the point.

Let me back up. Earlier in my life, growing up, I always knew that my grandfather, Donald E. Pickett, was a very wealthy man. In 1958, my grandfather started a network marketing company named NEO-LIFE. To this day, NEO-LIFE is one of the top network marketing companies in the world. I had a wonderful relationship with my grandfather growing up, as he taught me many invaluable lessons. He helped our family and many other families in infinite ways that are truly immeasurable. He grew up in the Great Depression, stood in bread lines, and was the youngest brother to eight sisters. What I found so fascinating when I was about ten, were the stories he would tell me about his distributors who started with his company and began sharing the products from NEO-LIFE. He would talk about how they would completely transform their financial futures. He would speak of the schoolteacher, the nurse, the post office worker, and even those struggling to get a job. He was so proud of his distributors, as they would work their way into a better life. Although my Grandfather gained tremendous wealth from what he had created, for him, it was always about other people and how he could help them have success, too. He was truly the best man I ever was blessed to know. When he was 98, I knew his time was about to end on earth, but he nevertheless gave me his final lesson.

'From one acorn, a thousand forests are born.'

As a young man at the start of my working life, I had no desire to do network marketing, despite what the industry had done for our family. It never really occurred to me to try. I was already living a fairytale life working for my brother, who had started a beef jerky company, which my grandfather had helped him launch. With the high protein diet trend going crazy, sales were constantly increasing, and, working in the family business backed by my grandfather, I knew I had complete job security. Life was great. I had two beautiful daughters, with another daughter on the way. We were living in a half-a-million-dollar home in Utah. I thought I had the world all figured out. Then, the beef jerky company was suddenly lost to venture capitalists, while I personally made some bad investments. I lost everything and realized for the first time that the financial spigot had been turned off. The control I had over my financial destiny turned into being an employee, trading time for dollars.

At that time, I received an invitation and found myself at my first network marketing meeting, along with twelve other people, listening to a guy in Dockers and a button-up shirt in someone's basement. He said that the company he was with was going to grow from 1 billion to 5 billion in sales and was looking for a few good leaders. I thought to myself, "I have a high school education and a lot of desire, so let's do this!" I only really joined that first network marketing company so I could go home with a plan.

I was 27, went right to work, and my first month's check in network marketing was $263. I thought to myself, "This works!" I put in some time and effort, and I got paid. I haven't looked back since, and I've been working full-time in network marketing for many years. Within fourteen months, I was one of the fastest to achieve the highest rank in the company, which took me all over the world. I traveled and grew my business in Israel, Hungary, Romania, the U.S., Mexico, and Canada. I was growing as a person, increasing my skills, and becoming a true professional in the network marketing space. Unfortunately, my obsession and pursuit of continuing my grandfather's legacy in network marketing created a lack of balance with work and family, to the point of losing both.

With the loss of my family and network marketing business, most of my closest friends, and even some of my family, strongly advised me to get out of the network marketing industry and pursue a 'real' job. But, instead of pushing me away from the industry, I was driven to succeed in network marketing at the highest level. I promised myself that I would never give up on my goal, whatever the journey ahead looked like.

During the next decade, I continued to self-improve and sharpen my skills to become a seasoned professional networker. This consisted of consulting, assisting existing distributors in growing their networks, and working on the corporate side of network marketing. This experience gave me knowledge and understanding of both the distributor's and owner's side of the business. I truly started to grasp every aspect of network marketing and understand what my grandfather had created so many decades ago.

But despite my increased skill and understanding of the industry, my work wasn't paying off financially. I'd been successfully consulting other distributors and companies to grow their businesses and increase their revenue through my experience. I was trading time for dollars once again. Don't get me wrong, there is absolutely nothing wrong with the security of earning a wage as an employee or consultant. None of us would have the opportunity to earn a network marketing check without the cooperation and support of the employee. I've been so grateful for that regular check from my employer in supporting my family, but that was not my goal in network marketing. My goal was to have time freedom and financial freedom to continue to build my legacy. But instead of enjoying those freedoms due to all of my experience and success, I found myself on a pier in Seattle, crabbing illegally.

My grandfather's words hit me right in the face again on that pier in Seattle: 'From one acorn, a thousand forests are born,' and I finally understood what he had been trying to teach me. I am the acorn! You are the acorn! We are all acorns! The moment I realized that every acorn has the ability to turn into a four-hundred-year-old oak tree, I knew exactly how to achieve my financial and time freedom goals and help others do the same.

What I discovered from studying the acorn now seems so obvious. Every acorn has the same DNA. EVERY single acorn has the DNA to be a four-hundred-year-old oak tree. The acorn's perfection and elegance are equally impressive as the strength and power of a fully mature oak tree.

The Acorn symbolizes potential and strength.

Thinking of my own journey, I have stood my ground against divorce, custody, debt, bankruptcy, the ORS, the IRS, blackmail, eviction, scammers, defamation of character, false accusations, failures, rejections, deceptions, fear, attrition, and loss of friends and family. Even though every acorn has the same DNA to become a mighty oak tree, some decide to stand their ground, while others surrender to the challenges of life. I decided to continue to stand. Every single one of us has life challenges similar to the ones I've been through, so it's easy to see why so few become the oak tree they have inside of them and continue to live out their lives as an acorn.

Napoleon Hill said, "The strongest oak of the forest is not the one that is protected from the storm and hidden from the sun. It is the one that stands in the open, where it is compelled to struggle for existence against the winds and rains and the scorching sun."

'Oak trees are built strong, allowing them to live for hundreds of years—tannic acids in the leaves and bark guard oaks from fungi and insects. Oaks send up new sprouts from their roots if they are burned down or eaten by animals. Many oaks have thick bark that protects them from fire. For these reasons, oaks are among the most important species in the many forests, woodlands, and other ecosystems. Harvested oaks, which have stored energy, or strength, down in their roots, sprout again and form many new, thin branches'.

Although the acorn and the mature oak tree are equally impressive, an acorn only affects a few, while each oak tree becomes an entire ecosystem, shedding ten-thousand acorns per year, which creates thousands of forests. So, why do some acorns become four-hundred-year-old oak trees, while other acorns never take root?

The only reason the acorn becomes a magnificent four-hundred-year-old oak tree is because it gave a hundred percent to not giving up, regardless of the storms and scorching sun that life delivers—and it's a hundred percent accountable to the outcome.

I made my decision on a pier in Seattle to be a hundred percent accountable to my life and decided to become a four-hundred-year-old oak tree in the network marketing industry and, hopefully, leave a lasting legacy, just like my grandfather. Over the past few years, I have never been prouder of the legacy I'm creating in the network marketing space. As a result of deciding and being accountable, my personal life has never been more rewarding. I have become debt-free, am completely current on child support and back taxes while sharing the most fruitful relationship I have ever experienced with my fiancé and our little acorns.

Will you decide today to become the four-hundred-year-old oak tree you were destined to become?

BIOGRAPHY

Ry Fry is the owner of LV Coaching. He is an entrepreneur, venture capitalist, top network marketer, and influential coach. Fry is known for breaking down the sophisticated basics of network marketing and establishing systems that allow the average person to win in network marketing. In nearly seventeen years as a top networker, Fry has built massive international organizations within four companies. His teams have generated more than two-hundred-and-fifty thousand customers, producing over five-hundred million dollars in lifetime sales. Fry develops inspired training and tools that support network marketers. Ry Fry is defining the future of MLM with new technology that gives individuals personalized evaluations of self-awareness to improve business and personal performance. Fry's passion is developing leaders who share the same vision of creating balance and time freedom between business, adventure, family, and friends.

Ry Fry can be contacted at www.ryfry.com

CHAPTER 28

Letting The Cat Out Of The Bag

By Sandy Lowe

I arrived in the world in November 1959 at Lady Chancellor Maternity Home. If the administration staff back then had known of my ancestry, my parents would have been turned away because I was a mixed-race kid and, therefore, shouldn't have been born there.

My Mom was three days in labor with me, and after I was born, she had a bad case of baby blues and didn't want to feed me. The nurses and my dad had to coerce her. She had only wanted boys, so when I came along, a girl, she was disappointed. I guess that's why I had a special relationship with my dad, who often spoiled me and gave me a little bit of extra fatherly love to make up for my mum's lack.

My mother, Shirley, was born out of wedlock to a mixed-race mother and an Irish Father. Back then, it was considered a shame for a child to be conceived out of wedlock, so my mother lived out at her grandmother's farm in Gokwe called Sikombella. She was very fair, with light-colored hair, green eyes, and a chip on her shoulder that made her question why she should have to hide in the bush away from civilization, learn the vernacular language, and be so different in color to everyone around her.

My granny later married and my mother grew up in the small gold mining town of Que Que, attending the local school for mixed-race kids, together with her stepsiblings. At that time, there were separate schools and communities for whites, mixed-race people (called coloreds) and Indians. Then, of course, there were the townships reserved for the black-only community. Everyone had their place, and no one could cross the racial barriers or break the rules of the country.

After leaving school, my Mom met my dad at a local dance one night. He was very fair, handsome, could dance well, and had just moved to RISCOM in Redcliff, near Que Que. He had grown up in Beaufort West, a small town in South Africa, with his brother and three sisters and had come to what was then called Rhodesia because, being mixed- race, his career choices were limited. He was looking for a better life in a new country. He had been engaged to a schoolteacher, but because he was a mere bricklayer, the union wasn't approved.

My Mom and Dad decided to get married and pretend to be white. This meant that they had to give up their jobs, take on a new name, destroy all their identity papers, and start a new life in the capital city of Salisbury.

They raised five of us children. My dad built the house we called home in Waterfalls, a European-only suburb while working for the railways. Mummy worked hard, not having servants as all the other neighbors did. We children went to the local school and, to the ordinary person, everything seemed fine. But my siblings and I knew we were harboring a secret that we had to keep through hell and high water, or else we'd be thrown out of the community.

All my Mom and Dad wanted was for us to have a better life than they had. Was that a crime? I can remember Mom telling us a story once about the time when she lied about her race and took a job at a local fashion store as a shop assistant. It was her first job. One of her jealous relatives spilled the beans to her employer that she was a colored girl and, therefore, wasn't allowed to have that job.

Consequently, she had to resign with immediate effect. I can remember when I was seven years old going to South Africa to meet Dad's relatives and seeing that the public toilets had a sign saying "Nie Blankes," meaning only whites were to use the facility. The segregation was real, as real as our huge family secret. We children always had to wear a hat to avoid sunburn, as our complexions in the sun turned tan instead of pink like those of our friends and neighbors. Mom refused to let us participate in sports because of the sun factor. We were very competitive, so this was hard for us and was one of the things that we rebelled against. We were always arguing against the rules, regulations, and strict laws Mum laid down. Yes, she wore the pants in the household, and you dare not cross swords with her; she ruled with an iron rod.

One cold winter night, at around one in the morning, our doorbell rang. It was a policewoman and a police officer bringing the news that my older brother, Nev, had been involved in a head-on car accident and died on the spot. He was only nineteen years old. Apart from the grief of losing Nev, I was shaken up by the fact that I was supposed to go with him that night in the car and had only decided not to at the last minute.

From that moment on, Mom was never the same. She was devastated. Nev had always been her favorite child, the fairest of us all, and such a cool kid. He never let my Mum's rules get to him. He'd always find a pot of gold at the end of every rainbow. He was so popular at school that everyone wanted to be his friend.

My Mom started on tranquilizers and sleeping tablets after that and never quit. Life continued in our household, but there was a whole different atmosphere.

The house got sold and Mom and Dad moved to town. By now, we older kids had left home, mainly because home was never a pleasant place to be. Only the youngest sibling, Heather, remained. She is the gentlest, kindest, and most tender-souled human being I know.

When Dad reached retirement age, he became bored with life, which comprised tinkering about in the garden, playing putt-putt over the road, working at the racecourse on a Saturday, and trying out new recipes.

One rainy day there was a terrific storm. Dad took the opportunity to go to the garage in the garden, connect the hose pipe to the car exhaust pipe, feed it through the car window, and breathe in the fumes. My sweet little sister found him dead. She was only thirteen at the time. As you can imagine, her life has never been the same since then. Understandably, she was mentally traumatized and, as a result, has had to rely on medication to function over the years. Thankfully, she's married to a great guy, who cares for her, and she loves life.

Unfortunately, when Heather left home to get married, Mum got empty nest syndrome and couldn't take life anymore; she drank rat poison and ended her life.

These tragedies affected me, too, and it seemed to me that, from an early age, my life had been dominated by feelings of embarrassment and shame, and I had a very poor self-image. I always seemed to be having to deal with catastrophes, for instance, like the day I received a call to say that my older brother, when running in his flat in Bulawayo, had slipped on a rug, hit his head, and instantly broken his neck. He lay unconscious for two days, only waking up to find he was paralyzed from the neck down. He had called out for hours and was only rescued when a neighbor's little girl eventually heard him. The door had to be forced before he could be reached. He was turned away at the hospital because his medical aid was insufficient for him to be treated. We had to have him airlifted as quickly as possible to a hospital in the city of Harare, where doctors removed the bone from his spinal column. Sadly, this was to no avail, as he died four months later in St. Giles, a rehabilitation hospital.

Another incident where life threw me a curveball was when I had to deal with my husband having a nervous breakdown on our honeymoon. He has a hereditary condition and has been diagnosed as being bi-polar.

Thank goodness that, earlier on in my life, I found Jesus and gave my life to Him. I've had to rely on Him to get me through the tough times. Am I perfect? Heck no. I've blundered so many times that I've often had to go to the cross and repent for things I shouldn't have done, thoughts I shouldn't have thought, and words I shouldn't have uttered. My life has been a daily walk, but I'm confident that, because I know whose I am, I can face tomorrow.

How many of you know that there's no word in the English language for a parent who buries a child? A child who buries his parents is an orphan.

A man who buries his wife is called a widow. A woman who buries her husband is called a widower. I had to bury my adult son. For sure, it's the hardest thing I've ever had to do. He, too, took his own life at the age of twenty-six.

I had done everything the Word of God instructed to break generational curses, bloodlines, anything, and everything to stop bad things from recurring. I couldn't believe I had to face yet another enormous blow in my life.

Why do bad things happen? We will never know the answer to that question, but what I do know is that life is twenty percent of what happens and eighty percent about how I deal with it. I realized a long time ago that it's my attitude towards events that's important. I still have three beautiful children, all of whom I love dearly. I don't have favorites as my Mum did, and try to make sure none of them feel as though they don't matter. I pick myself up each morning and get working at the business I started almost three decades ago. I decided to make the most of my life and integrate as much fun into it as I can. The mantra I live by is, "I master the art of living," and I make little distinction between my work and play, my labor and my leisure, my mind and my body, my education and my recreation, my love and my religion. I hardly know which is which. I simply pursue my vision of excellence at whatever I do, leaving others to decide whether I am working or playing. To me, I am always doing both.

As Theodore Roosevelt said, "Far better is to dare mighty things, to win glorious triumphs, even though checkered by failure . . . than to rank with those poor spirits who neither enjoy nor suffer much because they live in a gray twilight that knows not victory nor defeat."

I've found it's been so important to find my tribe that spurs me on and accepts me with my flaws. My tribe lets me be who I am, my authentic self, and always encourages me not to stay the same but urges me on toward better and greater achievements. I've found that keeping my nose to the grindstone, setting goals, and dreaming bigger dreams make me want to be the first member of my family to create a legacy that will enable me to change my family tree forever. I believe that God has always had my back and continues to help me make my dreams happen step by step.

BIOGRAPHY

Sandy Lowe writes books you won't be able to put down. Living in Zimbabwe, she has experienced first-hand challenges spanning over three decades of providing service in the real estate industry and successfully running her own business during times of turmoil, uncertainty, and unpredictability. Sandy is a world traveler who lives life to the fullest and seeks to enrich others.

Contact Information
Facebook: https://www.facebook.com/sandy.lowe.336

CHAPTER 29

When Adversity Came Knocking, It Was Game On This Time!

By Steven Stemberger

This time it was different: I had taken a lot of lumps along the way, but now, there he was, Mr. Adversity, staring right at me. Oh, I've seen him so many times before that I've lost count. It always seemed that just when I'd got things rolling good, then, Pow! —he smacks me right in the kisser. That's what my father used to tell me when I was a little boy growing up in the little old town in Michigan called White Pine, where everybody knew everyone. The population was around a thousand souls in that little copper mining town.

Back then, school days started with Dad turning on the lights, announcing it was "daylight in the swamp," a military phrase meaning get up and at 'em, time for school! Those are the kinds of things we tend to take for granted—having great loving parents.

I was the middle child. I have two sisters who said I was spoiled because I was the baby of the family, something which Mom confirmed just the other day, lol!

We certainly weren't born with the proverbial silver spoon in our mouths, but we always had food on the table, clean clothes, and a cozy home.

Early on, I developed a love for ice hockey, and I played from age five. Boy, I recall Dad taking me to almost every practice and all the games. Back then, we had to flood the rink and scrape the snow off before every game. I remember playing with a teammate, Mike. We always knew where each of us was on the rink at any one time. His dad was the coach and very meticulous, which is why we used to win games, even though we sometimes had fewer players than the competition. That's just the way it was; no complaining, double shifts, and the ice. We succeeded by always finishing what we started and competing with the best the other teams had to offer—and often came out victorious.

Then, it seemed just a blink of an eye, and I was in my forties, with plenty of road bumps and bloody noses along the way. I've had lots of jobs, but I guess you could say I didn't do so well with most of them. First, at the age of fourteen, I got a job pruning Christmas trees for good ole Buster. I was average in high school, went on to study at Northwood Institute college, and progressed to taking culinary courses. My dream was to work on cruise ships, but the trouble was, I never heard back from all the requests I sent in those big manilla envelopes. I knew it was time to work hard, just like my father did. So, I became a night buffet chef, then a chef at various restaurants.

My life changed completely when I went into construction, doubling my income, and eventually traveling all over upper Michigan. But soon, I found I had little money, I was just married, my step-daughter was only three-years-old, gas prices were soaring, and I was out day and night in search of a Carpenters' Union. Many doors slammed on me, but the thing I had going for me was that I didn't have a "quit bone" in my body.

Eventually, all my hard work paid off; I met a Supervisor guy who told me that I couldn't just "climb aboard" but had to go through the proper channels to get where I wanted to go. He said he was sorry that people had lied to me about the best route to take into the industry. Pow! Mr. Adversity again. But the Supervisor guy saw such determination and persistence in me that he gave me the number of a guy he knew to call about getting an apprenticeship in Wisconsin. "Tell him I sent you," he said. So, that's what

I did. I studied and got extra tutelage from my father-in-law every night after work. He was a great man who worked at General Motors but built homes on the side, which enabled him to retire early. As a result of my determination, later on down the road, my hourly pay rate rocketed from nine dollars an hour to almost twenty-two.

Those were great times, but then; Pow! Mr. Adversity landed me another hard blow when I was laid off. Having just got married, my wife and I decided it would be a good idea for me to transfer elsewhere, and we moved down to Indiana, where there was less snow, for my career and to help my sister. The first chance I got, I grabbed the local phone book and started calling all the carpenter halls but had no luck. Then, in the third week, I decided to make my own luck and walked on to a jobsite to ask if they were hiring. The foreman asked if I had my own tools with me. "Yes, Sir," I said. And he said, "Then go get them—you're hired." He immediately called the business agent, and I signed the reciprocity papers for my transfer from Wisconsin to Indiana right then and there, on the hood of a Ford Explorer at the jobsite. It's funny when people relate someone winning at something to just being lucky. It's also interesting to note that, when you work your butt off, the luckier you seem to get. Every time Mr. Adversity has come knocking, I've learned to deal with him, no matter what the outcome.

For years, I loved building things. I worked in the commercial and industrial construction sectors. For nine further years, I worked in the field. I did so in extremes of heat and cold. What was also challenging is that the industry is more about *who* you know rather than *what* you know. After a while, it started to become just a job, trading time for money; in essence, a paycheck. It began to have less meaning in my life. I began to go into robot mode, with little emotion about what I was doing. So, the fun element of my job became less important to me. The powers that be took away my passion for doing quality work and made it more about getting as much work out of you as possible—without any pay increase.

For years I struggled with the regularity of industry layoffs. It was very evident to me that, even though you might have great skills and experience, you weren't immune to being laid off, often because the other guy who wasn't ,had a friend in charge who protected him. I remember once, I was building a scaffold, doing a modification 350 feet up, when a call came through on the radio telling me to hop back down to the office. Two supervisors rode down in the elevator with me. At the office, the guy I had just finished the modification for told my supervisors, "You better hold on to this guy. He does a fantastic job". That's when the supervisor said, "Tell that to the man in charge; we're bringing him (me) in to get laid off." You see, the guy in charge liked to randomly pick out people to be laid off by their social security number, so, no matter how many times I had volunteered to work overtime or drive through storms to see if they were able to keep me for a few hours, it didn't matter. I think the guy just got a kick out of playing games with people's lives. Disappointment struck hard again; it was really wearing on me, as I really needed the job to support my family, especially since it had been tough to find a job at all the previous year. We had been unable to keep our home during the national recession in 2008-2009.

Anyway, being laid off this time was the defining moment for me. I was laid off for six months and started to feel the adverse effects in many ways. For one, I felt diminished as a man, not being able to provide for my family as I knew I should. That was rock bottom; it really hurt and weighed heavily on me. My marriage suffered and wasn't as strong as it had been. I was crushed. I started to think that I didn't want to be around anymore. But I looked up to the heavens and said: "God, please! Give me a sign that everything is going to be alright? Please!"

Two hours later, my left hand started itching; Dad always said money was coming in or out, depending on which hand it was. Several hours later, I was in my bedroom watching hockey on TV when my phone started sounding text alerts repeatedly. I checked and saw that nine messages had come in from a friend I used to hang around with in my high school years. He was telling me about an opportunity that would mean I could travel the world and make extra money—if I was interested. "Janice," I said to my wife, "this is my sign from God that I asked for. I'm doing this!" She replied,

"It's your baby!" She knew what it was all about and what I was getting into. Of course, it was, yes, you guessed it, network marketing!

The thing about it was that I fell immediately in love with it. It meant I got to go out and meet people I never knew existed; kind, happy, positive, and caring people. It suited me down to the ground—and still does!

Immediately, my life had meaning again. And, to this day, I keep working on improving myself every day, trying to be a better version of myself every day. I thrive on meeting like-minded people and have goals and dreams to help as many people as I can before I leave this world. I've grown so much as a husband, parent, grandparent, son, family member, and friend because of network marketing. I feel blessed beyond measure.

That was around five years ago. I knew I had finally found my vocation, my purpose in life, which is to help others looking for help, to give of myself to the maximum, with no strings attached. God certainly answered my plea that day, and every day since, I feel as though I've been born again.

For six years now, I've been writing a Facebook post almost every day, under the title, "Our Good Morning People." In it, I love sharing with people my daily thoughts, and many folks have thanked me for the daily inspiration my posts provide. So, my message to you is that there are messages all around you that you will see right before your eyes if you just take the time to listen and look.

Since that one purposeful evening, when I welcomed the opportunity to get into network marketing all those years ago, I have read over seventy books on inspirational personal development. That reminds me to thank my friend Donni Kay, who reached out to me with that opportunity—it was a life decision gamechanger.

Every day, I try to add a little value to people's lives, even if it's just through a passing smile. I recall a quote in my school yearbook that said my smile was like a villain's from Shakespeare's play *Hamlet*.

That is something that has stuck with me to this day. It adds fuel to my passion for helping others. Thank you, Mr. Valesano. If you're reading this, those words you wrote so many years ago have positively impacted me!

But then, Big Adversity hit me right in the kisser again, this time with a big, life-changing event—a car accident.

It happened while I was going home from the gas station, just cruising along at no more than fifty miles an hour, when Bam! Another car decided to take a shortcut through mine. I was struck and spun into the opposite lanes of traffic. The pain was immediate; my back and neck were in agony. I went straight to the hospital emergency room to have x-rays, sure that the injuries would prevent my regular working out sessions. I had just finished my personal best Twenty-One Day Challenge, working back to back, with no days off, and I was closing in on ninety days straight. But, in the blink of an eye, I was completely knocked off course. In all, the accident took me out of sync for a year and a half. I went from being a super-healthy person to needing help walking. One time, I tripped on a storefront threshold and, luckily, another guy caught me before I planted my face into the floor! He happened to be mute, and when I thanked him, he just smiled. I believe he was my guardian angel in disguise.

After having had seven steroid shots, countless neck and back physical therapy sessions, and constant doctor follow-ups, I was getting more and more frustrated. Where would it all end? Where was the light at the end of the tunnel? All the time this was going on, I stuck with my personal development and was grateful, as I knew things could have been so much worse.

It was January of 2020 when my doctor said that the medical team had done all they could for me. She told me that the pain would come back, but she cleared me to exercise again. I said, "That's great, thank you, Doctor Amanda. From today to the end of the year, I'm going to be doing pushups to strengthen my body. I'm going to do one pushup increase per day until the end of 2020." She said, "You know how big you're going to get?" But, of course, it wasn't all about that; it's about driving through this adversity through daily commitment for a year and proving to others that, when you want something bad enough, you don't quit, no matter how long it takes. You've got to be persistent and consistent and finish the task at hand.

Now, I started doing five pushups—that's all I was able to do when I began, and I'm happy to say that I'm at 260 pushups per day as of the ninth of September. Tomorrow will be 261, the next day 262; you get the picture.

So, my message is: Whatever you do, keep moving forward, don't QUIT!

BIOGRAPHY

Steven Stemberger is known for his extreme dedication and tenacity. Once he commits to something, he finishes the task with integrity. His purpose in life? He describes it like this: "The way you grow is to jump right in and help others by sharing knowledge and wisdom while adding value to others by lifting them up and adding support." He has a passion for entrepreneurship and the network marketing industry. Mentoring people has been his lifelong goal. He has mastered the art, knowing that the gift of giving is the prize of life. Be better today than you were yesterday: "Move on and grow." Steve served for six years in the Army National Guard, where he became a Squad Leader. He has been married to his wife Janice since 1992. They are blessed with a daughter, Jessica, and two beautiful grandchildren, Isabella and James Michael Scott. Steve was born in White Pine, Michigan (Upper Peninsula) and currently resides in Indianapolis, Indiana.

Steven Stemberger can be contacted via https://linktr.ee/steve_stemberger.com

CHAPTER 30

Awakening

By Winston Broderick

Stepping off the plane at JFK airport that windy October day, I can vividly recall the chill that ran up my legs. As my younger sister and I walked through the airport, we were in awe. This was our first-time leaving Jamaica and everything here seemed brand new. As we entered the baggage claim area, we could see our parents. It had been months since we last saw them, and I remember thinking, at seven years of age, "I'm not prepared for this." While my sister and I were still in Jamaica, our parents traveled back and forth to the United States for about two years, establishing a home in preparation for our immigration there. In their absence, unbeknownst to them, we were being verbally and physically abused by our caregivers. This included being slapped and having forkfuls of food forced down our throats when we refused to eat, to being told to stay quietly in our room alone for hours while their boyfriends visited the house.

A few years later, around the age of 10, I was sexually assaulted by a close family member. I don't remember our first sexual encounter, or why it stopped three years later, but when it did, I created a story that she no longer desired me, which ultimately led to feelings of rejection and abandonment. It would be almost ten years later, sitting on a therapist's couch while in college, that I would begin to unpack the anger, self-loathing, shame, guilt, and hate that lived inside me as a result of things that were done to me. In therapy, I started to address the insecurities I felt in my relationships and tried to figure out why I struggled with inconsistencies in my character and fidelity. I had been trying to protect the little boy inside me who was afraid of people leaving him.

My school only offered six free sessions with a therapist, which meant once it ended, I had to do the work on my own. Unfortunately, I was too undisciplined and ignorant on how to, and subconsciously, I believe I liked the story I had created about being the victim. I was the damaged boy who had his innocence stolen. I shared this story countless times with the women I dated, and it made them want to fix what was broken. Unbeknownst to me, I was reinforcing a poor self-image and became trapped in my own story of weakness and self-pity.

"How you do anything is how you do everything."

Soon after graduating from college, I started a career as a real estate agent at a firm in Manhattan. Within two years, I became an associate broker, and soon after, due to my personal productivity was promoted to vice president. My poor self-image didn't just affect my sexual relationships; It also affected my professional ones. Eventually, I started getting into verbal altercations with some of the agents over my style of management and my inability to have crucial conversations. I even had one agent tell me to "go fuck myself" and storm out. Emotionally, I wasn't prepared for the rejection that soon followed by those I once called co-workers and how it would trigger my feelings of unworthiness. Despite all this, the office generated huge profits, and my managing partner was pleased. However, there were many nights when I was so ashamed at who I had become, that I would sit in the office alone, unable to bring myself to go home. I didn't realize it then, but the anxiety and guilt I was feeling inside made it impossible to sleep most nights.

About a year after closing on a two-family house with my little sister and her husband, my firm lost its exclusive listing of a fifty-building portfolio. Within months, our doors were closed. Two years into the recession of 2008, I was unemployed and had to find work. I bounced around from firm to firm, eventually landing another managerial position, but when I couldn't duplicate the level of success I'd previously enjoyed financially, I just quit.

Not too long after my brother in law also lost his income, we found ourselves in pre-foreclosure, and my car was repossessed. Over the next four months, I fell into a depressive state. I did not want to accept what was happening and began spiraling down a path of numbing my emotions through the distractions of working out, playing video games, porn, and drugs. The bills continued piling up as I was eating through my savings, and the creditors called relentlessly. With money running out, I reached out to my mom for a loan, and she suggested I invest a portion of it in learning a new trade. Acknowledging my many hours spent in the gym, she encouraged me to become a certified personal trainer. Her logic was, if I was going to spend so much of my time there, I should be compensated for it. Severely unmotivated, I reluctantly agreed and enrolled in an online course.

After months of putting it off, I passed the necessary exam and began looking for work. After interviewing with four different gyms, I received an offer and started working with one of the top gyms in the city. Within a few weeks of starting, New York was hit by Hurricane Sandy. The club closed for about three weeks as the city dealt with the aftermath. I used this situation to my advantage and started working on my skills and getting additional certifications to enhance my marketability to members. Three months into the new year, I was able to acquire 27 new clients. That year, I was named *Trainer of the Year* at our club and made the company's *Top 100 list*. At last, I had gotten my swagger back and started to feel confident again.

Shortly after my resurgence, the creditors I avoided paying while unemployed, resurfaced aggressively and began garnishing my paychecks. We'd also made multiple court appearances with the bank and were denied several modifications of our mortgage. They concluded that our household debt to income ratio was simply too high. At the behest of our lawyers, I, having the majority of the debt, needed to file for bankruptcy. This was my rock bottom; the act of filing for bankruptcy was like a public admission of financial failure.

Crying out to God

About a month after the bankruptcy was finalized, we reapplied for a modification and were approved on a three-month trial basis. Unfortunately, even after making the required mortgage payments, due to circumstances outside our control, we were again denied. I laid on my bed for hours with the letter, staring at the ceiling and just praying, "God, please don't let them take our house, please just give me something I can do to change this. I'll do anything, please just give me a chance." I felt so broken and defeated. The next day I was approached by my manager about a newfound business opportunity that she had just started. We had often discussed opening our own gym together, as well as various other businesses, and, on account of my circumstances, I was eager to hear what she had to say.

She sat me down in her office and had me watch a video. What I saw involved two of my favorite endeavors, travel and money, and was in the field of network marketing. It would require me to reach out to individuals in my network to share the product, enroll those interested, and for those also interested in making money, teach them how to do the same thing. "No," I answered. I needed money now, and what she didn't know then was I had tried these types of business models while in college and never made any significant money.

Days later, she summoned me to her office again and insisted that I REALLY watch the video, noting that I was disengaged the first time. She was right; I'd watched it with an underlying limiting belief and false narrative that "people like me" just didn't succeed in "things like this." The video ended, and I was prepared to say no again, when she put her cellphone on speaker. The voice on the other end said, "*Hey Winston, it's a pleasure to meet you. I've heard amazing things about you. Winston, I'm not sure if you're a man of faith or not, but God doesn't put things in our lives for no reason.*" I gazed up from the phone, handed her my credit card, and signed up for both the membership and business. Could this be God's answer to my prayer?

We immediately got to work, making a list of 20 people who knew me, trusted me, and whom I had either discussed starting or actually done business with before. She instructed me to share the video with at least 10 of them that night. I went home and started calling. My first seven exposures were all NO's. After that, I mentally quit, and planned to resign. The following day, after exchanging pleasantries, I told her I needed my money back. She asked if I had called the ten people, to which, I reluctantly admitted I hadn't. Frustrated, she asked for my list, called the next person on it, and handed me the phone. With minimal enthusiasm, I explained to my former colleague, Mark, that I had just found what he and I were looking for and had discussed countless times while we were real estate agents together. Before I could utter another word, she snatched my phone from me and shared with him what she and I were about to build with the business.

Boom, five minutes later, I had my first enrollment. Over the next two years, the team, led by my manager, had massive success, enrolling over 450 customers in a relatively short period of time and enabling her to walk away from her position at the gym. Due to our combined effort, I was able to hit multiple paid ranks within the organization and gained national recognition, which afforded me the opportunity to walk the stage at one of our national trainings to celebrate with our company's CVO and founder.

Soon after, there was a major falling out with my former manager and another leader on the team, resulting in us parting ways. I took the team made up of my enrollments and decided to lead them on my own. However, without her leadership and interpersonal skills, coupled with my poor relationship habits, we saw a decline in the retention of new enrollments. Internally, I started to resent some of the key producers on my team who were out-performing me each month; and when it came to building relationships with the new team members, my ability to support them emotionally was nonexistent. I was fixated on everyone and everything else, blaming the company and my upline leadership, while failing to realize that the regression of my business was because of ME.

I started looking for answers. I went to personal development seminars, listened to various podcasts, and started reading books on leadership and personal growth, like "Letting Go," "Crucial Conversations," and "As a Man

Thinketh." These books helped me ascertain that instead of trusting God, I was blaming him for my poor past experiences, and the decline of my business. I awakened to the truth that if I was going to fix the relationships with those around me, I needed to revisit the broken relationships that caused the damage in the first place, the one inside myself and with God. I was finally able to see that the negative emotions and feelings I had towards others were the effects of my own misguided ideology, and that my source of validation was from people and things.

I now know that only a sincere and authentic relationship with the creator can truly validate us —a relationship that builds us up and helps bring out our true self, revealing that we aren't the sum total of our mistakes but rather something far greater. Many of us lack the understanding of how to effectively speak to ourselves, because we aren't aware of who we are, and more importantly, whose we are. Start asking more empowering questions. How do I reconcile the shame? Without; my job, money, family, or physique, WHO AM I?

BIOGRAPHY

Winston Broderick is a Network Marketing Entrepreneur and coach in the fitness industry. He has spent thousands of hours working on himself and gaining a deeper understanding of human nature and learning how we think. His passions include spending quality time with his fiancé and children, improving self-efficacy in others, both physically and spiritually, and challenging the status quo of who we believe we've been told we are. He has a vision of building up others to live lives of purpose and not just quiet desperation. His leadership has helped thousands of people experience success in life and the networking marketing industry.

Contact Information
Facebook: https://www.facebook.com/winston.broderick.jr
Instagram: https://www.instagram.com/wbroderickjr/

CHAPTER 31

There Is Light At The End Of Every Tunnel

By Yeliz Nuray

Achieving success is not the end of the journey. Life tends to throw way too many curveballs for us to be able to rest on our laurels. Success isn't the end of the story, just the end of a chapter, which can end in ways you weren't prepared for.

Before I had my children, I was a proud business owner. I started my own business from the ground up. With support from my parents, I turned my dream into a reality. I loved my salon. I spent my whole life building it. I had a huge client base. I could work my own hours, and, most importantly, I was in control. I opened my salon at the age of twenty-one and enjoyed seven happy years in the industry.

But, as I said, things can change, often in the most unexpected and tragic ways.

As we approached the end of 2006, I was nearly nine months pregnant. I was due in two weeks; as far as I could tell, it was going perfectly. And then I lost her.

I lost my baby girl. I still don't know how, and I don't think I'll ever know why. They told me it was a freak occurrence, a condition that only affected one in a million. But I didn't hear any of that. All I knew was that

I had gone from the happiest point in my life to the lowest point, over the course of one conversation. During my last scan, she had been perfectly healthy, so to say this came out of the blue would be an understatement. I expected to leave the hospital that day with my baby girl in my arms and all the future joys that came with her. Instead, I left that day on my own.

I returned home. Instinctively I walked straight into her bedroom, the one we'd spent weeks painstakingly preparing for our little girl's arrival. And that was when I lost myself. I felt that, suddenly, all the darkness in the world had gathered to consume me. When my hope for a child fell apart, all the other parts of my life quickly followed suit. I had to give up my salon; the thing I had spent my entire life working towards—was gone in an instant. There was no way I would've been able to carry on. I was severely depressed for months afterward. I wasn't in the right mental state to continue.

So, I did the most important thing I could've at that point. I gave myself time to recuperate, reassess, and take stock of where I was. And, eventually, time to start rebuilding. I wasn't just rebuilding a business at this point. I was rebuilding myself, my life, and my confidence, too. But still, there was a big hole in my life. We had all this love for a little girl, and we had nowhere to put it.

Then my son came along. Erel had a perfectly healthy birth, and we enjoyed some of the most memorable years, full of joy and laughter. And I cannot exaggerate how much it meant to be able to be there for all his "firsts." It meant the world to me. So, I made a big decision. I wanted to go into the profession of foster care. Everything had gone so well with Erel and, as I wasn't working, I felt I still had time to make use of and love to give. Someone deserved to feel the love we had in reserve for our daughter, and with so many kids out there desperate for love, it wasn't a hard decision. The funny thing about foster care is that you go into it to help heal children who've been neglected and tossed aside by life. What you don't account for is just how much those kids will heal you in return. But most importantly, it renewed my faith in the fact that I was supposed to be a mother.

As luck would have it, my first placement was a baby girl. We loved her as if she were our own and were on the verge of adopting her, before her father reappeared, and the local authority gave him back custody of his daughter. But I'd taken knocks by this point and lived through far worse, so I kept going, with the only goal in mind being to provide as many kids as possible with a safe, warm, loving home. And then came Eyshan: My beautiful daughter, with enough character for two kids. And with that, my perfect little family was complete. My kids had helped pick up the pieces of my life and put me back together. Now, I love being a mother, and I'd do anything for my kids. But, as the years went by and my days as a businesswoman slipped further and further into the distant past, I could sense there was still something missing. I missed working. I missed interacting with customers and feeling useful beyond looking after my kids. But, at this point, it had been years since I'd been part of the working world and, to be honest, I just had no idea how to re-enter it, let alone negotiate it.

Then, one day, I came across an online ad inviting people to start training to be members of cabin crew for commercial flights. Better yet, you could do most of the training from home. As a kid, I remembered how I had always fancied myself as an air hostess. I think I saw the job as something glamorous and an opportunity to see the corners of the world. The prospect was exciting and alluring. So, I bit the bullet and jumped back into the world of work, completing my training, and beginning my new career. My time as an air hostess was incredible. I saw so much of a world that I'd never known. I learned so many things about different cultures, different people, and different places.

But it wasn't the same as the salon. I had a boss to answer to, which was a new and rather unwelcome adjustment. Owning my own business had not only made me feel secure and proud of what I'd done, but it also made me feel I was in control. Having a sense of control over crucial parts of your life, from my experience, is central to a healthy state of mind. I'd been in control of my own business for seven years. Letting go of that business was one of the hardest things I ever had to come to terms with, but I knew that if I didn't get myself back into a position where I could dictate how I spent my time each day, I wouldn't ever feel true fulfillment again.

So, I started looking into new opportunities online, and I found something. Well, that's a bit of a lie. I was looking for puppies at the time when I stumbled across this new opportunity—the chance to work from home and be your own boss, to eventually run your own team. This seemed to tick every box, and, soon enough, I was beginning my journey working for a travel agency. My family gave me all the support I could have asked for, which was priceless at a point where I was still severely lacking in confidence. My time as an air hostess had given me a good enough peek inside the industry for me to feel confident about approaching this sector, and I took to it like a duck to water.

As an independent travel agent, I work from home during hours that I choose, meaning that I can keep up my commitments to caring for my kids. There is no feeling quite like taking a sick day off and not having to explain yourself to anyone! Besides, it was in an industry I was passionate about. And, most importantly, I was my own boss again. And, to make things even sweeter, this business provided me with even more opportunities to get away, to see the places I wanted to see, and fulfill the wanderlust that I'd discovered I had during my time as an air hostess.

And then came COVID-19, with all its restrictions, shutdowns, and bankruptcies. But, by this point in my life, I'd learned a valuable lesson: I'd added a priceless skill to my armory—the ability to see the opportunities in setbacks. The pandemic left me with a wealth of time, so I decided to further my career and strengthen my position within the company. Four months of hard work led to four successive promotions, an achievement I couldn't be any prouder of if I tried. One of the most important things about this job is that it gives me the chance to run a team again. A team that, I'm happy to say, is growing by the day. But running a team again wasn't just for my benefit.

I remember how it felt to be stuck at home, feeling useless and forgotten. A lot of people can't work in typical work environments because of disabilities or mental health issues. This business provides the chance to feel valuable, important, and make some cash! I wanted to make sure as many people as possible would benefit from my discovery. As my team grows and I see the positive changes that people experience, I'm reminded that I made the right decision. Finally, the future looks bright again.

My story is many things: At some points, a tragedy, at others, a comedy. My story is one of redemption. Most of all, my story presents some important and invaluable lessons about traversing the world of work and others that are widely applicable in nearly every part of our lives.

I learned to take time for myself when I needed it. The world is as busy as it's ever been, and we often feel there's a compulsion to keep up with the traffic of day-to-day life. The reality is that it's vital that, every now and again, we take a step back. It not only gives us time to reassess but some much needed time to relax and re-energize.

I learned that the only way from rock bottom is up. I was able to negotiate the most trying time in my life—and a situation that I never thought to encounter, but I did not let it take over my life. At least, not for too long.

But by far, the most important lesson was about how to see those fleeting moments of opportunity in situations that seem utterly hopeless on the face of it. I am living proof that a setback need not signal the end. It can often present us with new opportunities for growth that we otherwise would not have stumbled upon. No one's life is one long upward trend. There are ups and downs, peaks and troughs, setbacks, and triumphs. They make you a better, more accomplished, and grounded person. Without them, life would get boring pretty fast.

BIOGRAPHY

Yeliz Nuray is a British-Turkish Cypriot and mother of two who talks about her search to discover her calling by pushing past pain thresholds and becoming a business owner while always keeping her family at the heart of everything she does. Her journey has been an emotional roller coaster of highs and lows, from battling depression following her daughter's death, having to relinquish a much-loved profession as a result, and her unyielding quest for self-actualization to find her purpose in life. She is living testimony that by keeping things real, being true to yourself, and having compassion, things can be rewarding, gratifying, and life-changing. Today, Yeliz has surpassed her own expectations and is exactly where she wants to be. She cannot wait to share her experiences to help a multitude of others realize theirs.

Contact Yeliz Nuray via https://linktr.ee/Liz0808

CHAPTER 32

The Person You Fight To Become

By Inez Kuz

My family is just a typical, average family. There's me, Mom, Dad, and my sister. And, of course, we always had a dog. As far back as my great grandparents, we have mostly been a healthy lot, not sickly and no diseases . . . until I came along. My body has betrayed me many times over the years, starting with chronic belly pain in my early twenties, which didn't disappear until my hysterectomy last year, three-foot surgeries to remove a bunion, emergency gall bladder surgery and, finally, being diagnosed with both Crohn's disease and Fibromyalgia in the same year, aged thirty-eight.

That first year following the diagnosis, I saw every specialist, physiotherapist, and nutritionist available to me, and joined support groups to understand and deal with these diseases. It turns out that Fibromyalgia is intricately linked to gut issues and, not surprisingly, they plagued me six months apart. One thing that every person I encountered had in common was that none had the same combination of diseases like me. I wondered how any of them could help me or know my struggles. How could they understand my pain, my thoughts, feelings, and my fears?

Things came to a head one day during an information session on Fibromyalgia at the University of Alberta Hospital in Edmonton, Alberta. As I looked about the room at fifteen other sufferers and their caregivers (mine was my oldest daughter Alyssa, God bless her soul. I couldn't have gotten through those early years without her), I saw just how differently this disease affects different people. There were three speakers that day: a doctor who explained where Fibromyalgia comes from; it's kind of a spin-off to arthritis, except its nerve pain triggered in the brain and, therefore, without a physical cause; a physiotherapist, who told us if we exercised more we would feel better; and another doctor who was adamant that painkillers don't work. Question: If you cannot have a pain killer and the pain is so awful as to leave you bedridden, how are you supposed to exercise? I didn't understand. None of the speakers had Fibromyalgia or, for that matter, anything wrong with them. I was puzzled about how they felt they could instruct sufferers like me how to live their lives when they couldn't possibly understand how we feel. As Alyssa and I left the meeting, I vowed that someday, somehow, I was going to help people like me fight to become successful in life.

Following the diagnosis, except for hospital appointments, I stayed in my house for a full year. I didn't make plans, as I didn't know how my body would be feeling on any particular day and might have to cancel them at the last minute. I tried different medications and recipes. I was exhausted all the time, as I was still following my old routines, even though I had all these new challenges to deal with. At physio, I tried "needling" (the Western version of Chinese acupuncture) to alleviate the pain in my elbows, but it left me with terrible bruises. The nutritionist tried her best to help me, but the diet plans she gave me didn't work. Of course, I was grateful that all these people were willing to help me, but people are so different, and there are no hard and fast rules that suit everyone. I knew one big change had to occur before I could start to become the person I was meant to be: that was to look deep into myself and accept the person I now was. Acceptance seems to me to be the hardest part of living with any disease, but I found that the sooner you accept it, the sooner you can start addressing the goals and dreams you had in life before the disease. I have discovered some wonderful methods of coping, achieving happiness, and even realizing my goals that I would like to share with you.

Back then, my father was so upset that his baby girl was sick that he focused his attention on finding a way to make me better. His solution? Find the diet that matches your blood type. The internet came in handy for this. I found the right blood type diet for me, printed it off, and followed it to the letter. Success! I didn't feel so bad, and I still follow this diet very closely—my favorite part is that I'm allowed red wine. I would suggest everyone looks into their blood type diet because something as simple as ingesting the wrong acid, like the citric acid contained in oranges or lemons, can make a profound impact on how you feel.

I also signed up for the Fibromyalgia Newsletter, as I knew I would be more powerful with knowledge and could help others understand what I was going through. I found a fantastic article on the internet that recounted what a person going through Fibro feels like. Then, I made every person close to me read it, and understand it. That look of pity quickly disappeared from my parent's faces, and I was ecstatic. It helped me realize that I'm still me, even though I hurt every SINGLE day 24/7.

On top of that, I started having family meetings, with Facetime proving a great help when we couldn't get together physically. During the meetings, we discussed the challenges I was facing, appointments, or just everyday stuff. This kept everyone in the know and on the same page. It took a ton of stress off me not having to explain everything about the disease multiple times, and stress is the absolute worst thing for chronic pain sufferers. Those who wanted to help were part of the meetings, which enabled us to stay on course and grow as a family.

I also started a journal, recording what worked, what didn't, food, exercise, activities, treatments, etc. After six years of that, I know my body so well. Over time, I've learned that I am the best advocate for my own health. Many practitioners I encountered during this time believed every pain I have could be attributed to Fibromyalgia, but I argued that is just not the case. When I came across such people, I learned to move on quickly and find someone more understanding. This disease is still relatively new, and many health professionals don't understand it. The day I was referred to a pain clinic was the best. The professionals there are trained to understand your pain and use different methods to help you cope with it. I've tried everything from Prolotherapy (sugar/water injections into joints) to PRPs (platelet-rich plasma injections) to calm the pain. These people really know their stuff! Unfortunately for me, the injections didn't work, but I was put on a slow-release narcotic that doesn't affect my mood (no highs and lows) but certainly makes dealing with the pain easier. I can now take walks, go fishing, and even play golf on a good day.

I believe it's also important to surround yourself with positive, loving, and understanding people. This is hard to do because, at first, all you want to do is hide under the covers and talk to other people who feel just as bad as you do. Support groups are great, but you should feel better when you leave the group, not worse or confused. If the people around you aren't willing to try to understand or don't want to and can't accept the new you, then I say, simply move on. For instance, I have immediate family members with whom I don't associate anymore because my chronic pain was too much for them. But that's okay because I believe we're all better off now.

I was very fortunate to meet a great man who wanted to understand my pain and take care of me. I married that guy, Dave, this past summer. I wasn't letting him get away. A couple of summers ago, he bought me a dog—which, for a chronic pain sufferer, was a game changer. My puppy's name is Jax, and he's a MinPin crossed with a dachshund crossed with a chihuahua. He's so adorable. But the greatest thing for me is knowing he's always there for me and accepts me just the way I am. To my mind, there's no better affirmation of love or reassurance that you're going to be okay than having a fur baby by your side. Jax and I are inseparable; we go on walks, truck rides, and even on trips to visit my family or business trips staying in a hotel. He's so good, and everyone adores him, but I know deep in his heart he's all mine, which means the world to me. I thank Dave every day for the wonderful gift he gave me. I know I wouldn't be as productive without Jax.

Finally, the most important thing I can tell you about living a full and prosperous life while living with chronic pain is to Be Good to Yourself. When we're growing up, we're told there are all these things that we must do. For instance, women were expected to stay home and take care of the house, the children, their husbands, and go out and get a job. But such tasks seem very daunting when you're stuck with chronic pain, never knowing how you'll feel from day to day, or even minute to minute. You cancel engagements at the last minute, take too many days off from your job, and often seem tetchy to others. I never liked telling people about my health issues, as I thought it made me seem weak. I'm quite a private person, but once I feel I can trust someone, then I might tell them. However, over the years, I've come to realize that if you don't open up, then you never truly know how understanding and accommodating some people can be. That means you risk missing out on learning or even helping someone else who is going through the same things as you.

Of course, there are still days when the pain means I can't get out of bed or do something as simple as open a jar, button my shirt, or figure out how to fold a towel (Fibro fog—it's a real thing)! My motto now is: "Spend one day in bed and be good to yourself." I find that by doing that, I won't have to spend a week in bed because I pushed myself too hard. By being kind to yourself, I mean stuff like taking a bubble bath, reading a favorite book, watching a funny movie, burning your favorite scented candle, wearing the most comfortable things you own, or treating yourself to food that is guaranteed to refuel your body. I also snuggle up with baby Jax and turn the phone off. Those who know me understand my need for peace, and I always return unanswered calls when I'm ready to be me again. Many people might say they don't have the time for that or see it as selfish behavior. But I listen to my body and not what others have to say. I believe it's very important to understand yourself and your body and what makes you feel good. My chronic pain means that I must fight every single day, and refueling my mind and body makes that fight seem not quite so daunting. To me, it's no big deal if I don't get all the laundry done or clean the whole house in one day. Neither the house nor the laundry is going anywhere. These are not life-threatening things, but worrying about them can be. That's why I don't plan months in advance anymore; it's just too stressful. Instead, I go week to week and make sure my loved ones are on board with the plans. They're all so fantastic now at adjusting on the fly. My advice is to take time to smell the roses, visit with a friend, try something new, and genuinely love those around you. Try not to let your disease be the only you that people know.

BIOGRAPHY

Inez Kuz is a person living with Crohn's disease and Fibromyalgia. Inez has spent the last six years testing different treatments and plans to combat chronic pain. Although there is no cure, Inez has found ways to be a successful entrepreneur, wife, mother, and contributor to the wellness of others through coaching, mentoring, and writing. She believes everyone, no matter their physical or mental challenges, can make their dreams a reality.

Inez Kuz's contact details are available at https://linktr.ee/inezkuz

www.ingramcontent.com/pod-product-compliance
Lightning Source LLC
Chambersburg PA
CBHW031918240526
45464CB00021B/238

Acknowledgment

My most sincere and profound appreciation goes to the Most High God for giving me the inspiration for this work.

I like to appreciate my wife, Favour, for her love, encouragement and strong support to me in ministry.

I, also, wish to appreciate my great friends in the RCCG FCT Province 7 Prayer Champion Department, Emmanuel Idu, Gabriel Nimmak and Bode Adebola, who are very supportive in the course of my work on this book.

I cannot fail to mention members of staff of KHMS Jahi Abuja, who created enthralling relationship environment. Thank you!

I like to say a big thank you to my mentor, Pastor Ededet Otu-Bassey, whose love and support has become one of God's sustaining pillars in my work and ministry.

I like to specially appreciate Jennifer Ajukwu and Joy Chia who invested time to straighten some of the ideas in this book.

I, also, appreciate all my numerous friends in church, home and other places, pardon me if I do not mention your name here, but you are very wonderful and looking at my relationship with you, I have come to understand that in relationship one must be guided.

Forward

Laws are principles and regulations which have been established to guide or guard people or the doing of a thing. We find that laws are targeted to influence the life of a people and that seem to be the cardinal achievement of any good law. All laws derive from God drawn mostly from the sensibility of mankind.

The author of "The Laws of Relationship" has adopted in his book this basic cardinal for influencing the reader; by helping the realization of the need to live within God's ordained life principles. Laws regulate and act as a guard and guide and these principles have been broken down here in the most appreciable way, in this book.

This book is written in a very unique way and in the most simplistic format that makes reading easy also makes comprehension very easy too. Life principles are broken down for the ease of practice and should make the readership accept it as a practical guide to a good and rewarding life to the individual reader in particular and the public in general.

It is a must read for everyone mindful to live a God pleasing life as we do not live life alone at any point in time. In the book the Questions for Reflection systematically arranged following every topic will be useful guide and help to drive the understanding deeper: practice it!

I encourage you beyond reading the book to retain it as a guide and a regular check; and as a monitor in all our work while on the surface of this earth. It is a book quite revealing, interesting and suitable as everyday guide. It is as good for the old as it is for the young men and young women whose life we owe God to help to form. Read it and keep it close always.

Ameh Franklyn Adejo.
Legal Practitioner & Pastor in Charge of Area

Introduction

Life is all about relationship.

We are surrounded by people. Our happiness and effectiveness depend on how well we get along with them. We work with our head but relate with our heart. We may lose effectiveness when our heart is troubled as a result of friction or strife with people.

The fear of pain associated with relating with people and how it affects our work, has caused many to shut the door to their heart, hoping they can get on with their lives without being affected. They starve themselves of true happiness that comes with heartfelt relationships and the joy only love brings; denying themselves the opportunity to build quality relationships and store up beautiful memories.

When you open your heart to people, this challenges them to reciprocate. When you understand how to relate with people, they will be ready to go to the ends of the earth for you, not minding the cost.

We all have reasons why we relate with people. The following, to a large extent, are true about relationship:

- Our happiness depends on how well we can relate with our friends and families.
- Our joy depends on how sincere we are when we share our time and resources with others.
- Our effectiveness depends on how well we get along with sub-ordinates, colleagues and boss.
- Our character is influenced or tailored by how well we understand the people around us and handle conflicts.

Therefore, our daily lives, effectiveness, health, happiness and joy, to a large extent, centre around relationship.

Arguably, the primary objective of education is to make you better in relating with people. If you lack basic relationship skills, you are not schooled.

I have written this book to challenge and build you into personality capable of sustaining quality relationships, and also, to give you tangible ingredients that will ultimately make you a better person. This book brings to your hands laws that guide relationships, thoroughly explained for easy assimilation, and laws that will become our lifestyle.

I charge you, read diligently every line, paragraph and page. Testimonies await you in Jesus Name (Amen).

1
The Law of Proximity

Closeness and availability increase fondness.

Falacy	Absence makes the heart grow fonder.
Fact	We tend to love those who are close and available to help us when we need them the most, not necessarily the best people in the world.
Basic Truth	It is true that not every body is a hopeless romantic, but if you love or value a person, the only way you can show it is if the person is close by. Distance is one of the constraint to building love and respect. If you are not able to push past the barrier of distance and invest time in those you love, your love has little or nothing to offer.

When it comes to increasing fondness, do not say it; just make effort to be as close as possible. Actions enhancing proximity can light the fire of affection in anyone.

You cannot light the fire of affection in a person, if you maintain great distance from him or her.

Most people erroneously believe that this law only applies to people who are trying to initiate a relationship. The law has stronger effect on a well-established relationship than the one that is yet to begin. If a married man, for instance, leaves home early and maintains late nights, he will get home one day and discover that his wife and children are all gone. Similarly, if a woman keeps too much distance from her spouse, it is very likely that another woman will take her place. Proximity does not only ignite the fire of affection, but also determines it sustenance.

Required

Push past the barrier of distance; close gaps between you and the people you love, this will reveal your heartfelt intentions towards them.

Questions for Reflection

1. What three (3) things have created relationship gap between you and those you value/love. (The people you value may include your colleague in the office, church members, your associates, friends and family relations) You may list more than three.

    a. ....
    b. ....
    c. ....

2. List three (3) practical steps you can take to remove these barriers. (Your action step may include: regular visit, paying of a

colleague's child school fees; spending more time with those I value; taking a walk once a week/month with those I value, etc.)

a. ....
b. ....
c. ....

2

The Law of Dedication

Concentration improves quality.

Falacy	Familiarity breeds contempt.
Fact	It is not the quantity of time we spend with those we love that matters but the quality. Let your commitment to expressing your love to your loved ones, be profound.
Basic Truth	When we choose to spend time with people, we must think of all the ways to make the moments memorable and time together remarkable. Prepare the gift to give, the words to say and the ways to lift the persons' spirit. These things have lasting effect on people and make them willing to see us again.
Required	When you are with those you love, give them your undivided attention.

Question for Reflection

1. Mention five (5) things you can do to make the time you spend with people memorable.

   a. ....
   b. ....
   c. ....
   d. ....
   e. ....

3

The Law of Common Language

Consistent mutual understanding brings growth.

Falacy	Good relationship involves people naturally speaking the same language.
Fact	The world is made up of people from different walks of life and tribes, with different personal experiences and innate abilities—no two people are the same. To interact effectively with other people, we must make conscious efforts to understand them.
Basic Truth	In close relationship, we do not just communicate, we relate. People must understand each other in any kind of profitable relationship, if the relationship is to stand the test of time. In the real sense, they must speak the same language. They must be ready to lend helping hand, caring, loving and appreciative. These elements make people to be willing to read and understand you, and when you make positive moves, they make moves to meet you there. The law of the common language comes into play when these elements are present. When

Required

they are absent, people only play along, they don't relate.

People may be excellent communicators, yet lack the ability to speak the same language with those they truly value or love. If you cannot speak the same language as another, you cannot keep that person close to you, for a long time. You cannot enjoy the company of people with whom you cannot relate with a common language.

Relationship has its own language. To enjoy relationship with people you must strive to speak a common language with them.

Questions for Reflection

1. Mention three (3) ways you can improve your relationship with people by communicating at their frequency. (Your answer may include: identify with their loses; know their weaknesses; render helping hands; give advice on ways to solve their problems)

   a. ....
   b. ....
   c. ....

2. What three (3) things can you do to help people who value you communicate at your frequency. (Your answer may include: tell them my personal history; tell them about my likes and dislikes; tell them my best and worst experiences; be patient with them)

   a. ....
   b. ....
   c. ....

4

The Law of Clarity

Communication is the fuel of relationship.

Falacy	I can get along fine without much communication.
Fact	Poor communication starves relationship.
Basic Truth	A relationship is as good as the communication between the parties involved. People often take this fact for granted in their interactions with others. Most times, leaders communicate without clarity leaving followers to their assumptions and expect result at the end of the day, only to be disappointed.

Good communicators ensure clarity. When they communicate, they are precise and leave no room to ambiguity. They say what they mean and they mean what they say. When you fail to be clear, you are preparing yourself for conflict, whether you like it or not.

Communication is a two way traffic; you must seek to understand first, to be understood. You have to show patience when interacting with people; so that it will be easy for

> **Required**
>
> them to express their feelings and opinions, also correct them with love and respect where necessary—criticize constructively.
>
> Whenever you communicate, seek to be clear, precise and listen for feedback.

Questions for Reflection

1. What five (5) things must you have at the back of your mind to communicate most effectively? (Your answer may include: say exactly what I mean; mean what I say; I will not interrupt people when they are still talking; I will not be judgmental; I will make effort to understand what a person is trying to tell me before I respond, etc.)

    a. ....
    b. ....
    c. ....
    d. ....
    e. ....

5

The Law of Common Goals

Common goals give value to relationship.

Falacy	Relationship is necessary simply to have somebody to talk to.
Fact	"Two are better than one; because they have a good reward for their labour. For if they fall, the one will lift his fellow: but woe to him that is alone when he falleth; for he hath not another to help him up" (Eccleciastes 4:9 – 10, King James Version).
Basic Truth	Relationship draw strength from common goals which people must consciously seek to achieve. Two of the most common goals in relationship are joy (or happiness) and getting help in times of need. People do not always go into relationship knowing exactly what they want from it, but when relationship cannot make them happy, they simply want to cut off.

However, if you make up your mind to make other people happy, you will find happiness in most of relationship you engage in, and be positioned to break off any relationship you think is toxic.

We cannot do everything by ourselves and even the things we can do for ourselves, we sometimes are unable to. Many times we have shortage of time, money, materials and physical strength. If we do not get help when we need it, it may appear the world is coming to an end; especially, when the people we consider to be our friends and families are not willing to help. It is, therefore, important that we make it our goals, to make people around us happy, be ready to render help when the need arises and to avoid emotional attachment with people who are not willing to reciprocate.

Required

To give value to your relationship, give it goals to achieve.

Questions for Reflection

1. List five (5) goals you want your relationship with your spouse to achieve.

    a. ....
    b. ....
    c. ....
    d. ....
    e. ....

2. List five (5) goals you want your relationship with other people to achieve.

   a. ....
   b. ....
   c. ....
   d. ....
   e. ....

6

The Law of the "Life Goal"

A man's biggest desire defines his relationship.

Falacy	People can relate without any concern for their personal desires.
Fact	People's life goals influence the kind of people they seek out for relationship and the relationship they maintain.
Basic Truth	People's life goals are their biggest singular desires. They cannot sacrifice them on the alter of relationship; life goals serve as the basis for their relationship. When people discover that a relationship has not met their life goals, they immediately seek out another relationship that can. If a person's life goal is to acquire a lot of money for the sake of having money and the pride it brings, he can do almost anything to acquire that money. For instance, Judas betrayed Jesus for money and Gehazi betrayed his master's trust for some pieces of silver. The end of both Judas and Gehazi were, however, disastrous. When your life goal has no objective of adding value to people you are heading for destruction.

Some people's life goals are shallow. Picture a man whose life goal is to always have clothes for Christmas. If he is broke in December, he may go and borrow money, or even steal, just to have Christmas clothes. Without any concern for the injury he inflicts on the people who care about him. This is the problem with shallow life goals; the costly price we have to pay for something so small. If your life goal is small, you may give up the relationship you cherish for a plate of porridge or a piece of silver.

No life goal is bigger than quality relationship with good people. The truth is a solid relationship is worth more than gold. Bishop David Abioye tailored his life goal around Bishop David Oyedepo, the founder of Living Faith Church Comission. He stood by him all through the tough times until the ministry became a huge success. Pastor Enoch A. Adeboye of the Redeemed Christian Church of God, expanded the vision of the founder, Reverend Akindayomi, even after the founder was long gone. Bishop David Oyedepo and Reverend Akindayomi understood the secret – a quality relationship with good people is worth more than gold. Building a solid relationship for a lasting legacy became their life goals.

Required

Whatever you want to achieve in life, make it one of your life goals to seek out good people and build quality relationship with them. Whatever you achieve in life is secondary to the relationship you keep. Good relationship is good business.

6

The Law of the "Life Goal"

A man's biggest desire defines his relationship.

Falacy	People can relate without any concern for their personal desires.
Fact	People's life goals influence the kind of people they seek out for relationship and the relationship they maintain.
Basic Truth	People's life goals are their biggest singular desires. They cannot sacrifice them on the alter of relationship; life goals serve as the basis for their relationship. When people discover that a relationship has not met their life goals, they immediately seek out another relationship that can. If a person's life goal is to acquire a lot of money for the sake of having money and the pride it brings, he can do almost anything to acquire that money. For instance, Judas betrayed Jesus for money and Gehazi betrayed his master's trust for some pieces of silver. The end of both Judas and Gehazi were, however, disastrous. When your life goal has no objective of adding value to people you are heading for destruction.

Question for Reflection

1. Mention three (3) ways you can always relate with people so that they will be willing and able to help you achieve your biggest goals in life. (Your answers may include: Spending more time with people who are of great value to me in order to understand them better; Solving the problems of those who work for me; Making my vision beneficial to people who are ready to be part of my success)

   a. ....
   b. ....
   c. ....

7

The Law of Sacrifice

Sacrifice is the required price for improving relationship.

Falacy	A good relationship is cheap.
Fact	The degree of sacrifice defines the quality of love. Unwillingness to make sacrifice result to lack of interest or love.
Basic Truth	There is no relationship without sacrifice. Infact, it takes a great deal of sacrifice to maintain close ties.

    The prodigal son was tired of making sacrifices, so he demanded for his inheritance and it was given to him. After which he went to a far away country, where he squandered everything he had. Seeing that he had nothing left, and with no where to go, he chose to return home. In the light of his actions, he believed he had lost his place and begged his father to accept him as one of his servants.

    In a relationship, when we do not make the appropriate sacrifice as at when due, we relinguish our rights.

| Required | To build and sustain relationship you must ascertain the required sacrifice per time and respond appropriately. |

Questions for Reflection

1. What are the prices you are willing to pay to improve your relationship with those you value? (Mention the first five (5) that comes to mind)

   a. ....
   b. ....
   c. ....
   d. ....
   e. ....

8

The Law of Responsibility

Responsibility gives staminer to relationship.

Falacy — People who love you, will continue to love you whether you behave responsibly or not.

Fact — No man will do everything for you.

Basic Truth — You must take responsibility for relationship. If your relationship is to stand the test of time, you must be consistent in playing your part and showing appreciation. It is bad and irresponsible to neglect your responsibilities, while you watch your partner shoulder all responsibilities. It is a gross irresponsibility, to allow your partner in a relationship to do everything.

People will not continue to shoulder all responsibilities to sustain a relationship without their partner's support. All parties must be able to pull their weight in being supportive of one another for the relationship to work. Anything short of this, will lead to the dearth of the relationship.

Relationship is like fire, being irresponsible

Required

is taking out one of the elements that keeps it burning.

It is your responsibility to seek out your role and make tangible input to keep relationship going and mutually beneficial.

Questions for Reflection

Please check.

1. Do you take responsibilities for your lack of performance or blame others?

    - ❏ I take responsibility for my shortfalls and lack of performance
    - ❏ I blame my inadequacies on people close to me

2. How prompt are you in returning calls?

    - ❏ Very prompt   ❏ Not Prompt

3. How often do you deliver on your promises?

    - ❏ Always   ❏ Seldom

4. Who pay the bills in your relationships?

    - ❏ Paying the bills is always a joint responsibility
    - ❏ I take responsibility for paying the bills
    - ❏ Others pay the bills for me

If any of your answers is anything other than "i", you need to step up and start taking responsibility to give your relationship stamina.

9

The Law of the Pillar

One person always loves more.

Falacy	People have equal ability to love.
Fact	Everyone is capable of love, but some more than others.
Basic Truth	Our ability to love differs, but we all can love most sincerely (from our heart). We can love and be loved in return.

Those who love more are the pillars of the relationship, while those on the receiving end are the dependants. The pillars are love givers, while the dependants are love seekers. The pillars often find love wherever they go, simply because they love freely; but the dependants feel unloved until they find pillars.

The pillars are the burden bearers in relationship. They do everything in their power to keep the relationship going. Once a pillar is tired of a relationship, the relationship is through.

While two pillars can be very intimate, two dependants cannot maintain intimate relationship. However, the dependant can feel fulfilled when with a pillar. If you are the pillar in any relationship do not feel terrible as long as the other party is not making effort to make a mess of your feelings. But if you are the dependant, make the pillar know, by your appreciative action, that you care and you will always be there.

Required

If you cannot equal your partner in showing love, you must match him in reciprocating love.

Questions for Reflection

1. Mention three (3) things you can do to prove to others that you love them. (Your answer may include: be the first to make a call when you care about a person, teach a person to give by giving quality gift, always be ready to forgive when the one you love offends you)

    a. ....
    b. ....
    c. ....

2. Mention three (3) ways to reciprocate love. (Your answer may include: be quick to return calls; saying thank you in a special way – may be, by giving gifts; avoid careless words which make people feel cheap for loving you)

    a. ....
    b. ....
    c. ....

10

Law of Mutual Consent

There is no relationship without a mutual consent.

Falacy

You can bully people to stay loyal to you as long as you have a special advantage over them.

Fact

You can buy a hand but not a heart. Loyalty is optional.

Basic Truth

You cannot make people your friends if they are not willing to be. No matter how much you love a person, it is the person's prerogative to choose to walk by you. You do not have such power to make someone your friend against his will.

No amount of money can buy a man's heart. However, when people see your sincerity and patience, they may get to like you and open their hearts to you. You must give the people you love, the time to consider if they want to love you in return or not.

For instance, when it comes to choosing a spouse, you must be sincere with yourself. You should not marry someone who does not truly care about you. Give the person you love the chance to prove if they want the same with you, otherwise your marriage will end on paper. The same is true about a loyal follower or a friend. If a person does not want you, give him space and lighten your emotional burden.

Required

To be sure about where you stand with people in your life, give them the chance to be sure they want you around them.

Question for Reflection

1. Mention three (3) things you can always do to gain or sustain the loyalty of those you value. (Your answer may include; empathies with them when they have a bad experience; share their joy when they have a major breakthrough; always find a way to help people solve their problems)

   a. ....
   b. ....
   c. ....

11

The Law of Ignition

Great courage and tact are required to make people like what we have to offer.

Falacy — Every good relationship starts by accident.

Fact — You must have the courage to present what you have, stand and listen, read the other party and strive to appeal to the party's emotion or reasoning. You must say what the person likes to hear and not what you feel like saying. You must do what the person wants you to do in the manner he wants it, not what you want or the way you want it.

Basic Truth — If the ignition process is very successful the relationship gets a smooth take off and possibly ride, as though the people have known each other for a long time. If the ignition process is not very successful, the people may struggle and continue to make amends until they settle in the course of the relationship. If it fails completely, people may detest each other and may even become enemies.

More so, the ignition process may be

successful but the person(s) that initiated the relationship might have paid a price too high that they may not deliver on their promises or meet expectations in the course of the relationship. It is, therefore, left to the second party to cover up or give up.

When the ignition process fails, you have two options: the first is to invest time, money or other resources to motivate the other party, and the second is simply seek out other people available and willing.

Required

To initiate a relationship, read the other party and count the cost before you take a leap. Patience and tact are, therefore, required for ignition.

Question for Reflection

1. List five (5) factors you consider before going into any relationship—be it business, platonic or love relationship. (Your answer may include; level of exposure; educational level; differences in personal history, including past successes and failure; differences in culture; differences in religion, etc.)

    a. ....
    b. ....
    c. ....
    d. ....
    e. ....

These factors may not stop you from relating but they will guide you in the manner in which you approach the other party or in the manner of your self-comporting and enhance your acceptability.

12

The Law of Like Feather

To sustain relationship with a person, the person must become like you or you must become like the person.

Falacy	You can be intimate with people without being influenced by them.
Fact	People often get along on grounds that they are alike—Birds of same feathers flocks together.
Basic Truth	People will observe you from a distance but will not relate until they realize that they share several things in common with you. We are comfortable around people who are like us in many ways. When there are too many differences between a person and another, closeness will be virtually impossible between them. To relate with someone who value relationship, relate as family; to relate with someone who is generous, relate as a giver; to relate with an orphan, relate as someone who is all too familiar with grief and loss; to encourage someone who has trust issues, relate as someone whose trust has been betrayed but not afraid to take the

risk to trust and love people. We relate with people on the grounds on which we are alike.

For us to be a part of a group we value or be with the people we love, we may need to change or act differently. We must show the aspect of us that looks like the ones we value and work on strenghtening positive values that are alike. After which we can walk along, give up alittle of ourselves and become more like them; they will give up alittle of themselves and pick up alittle of ours. Little by little we become more and more alike, thereby enhancing better understanding of each other.

Required

To maintain closeness to those you value or love, relate on grounds on which you are alike.

Question for Reflection

1. Mention three (3) instances when you have had problems with someone whose relationship you value, because you could not find a common ground with that person.

    a. ....
    b. ....
    c. ....

2. List three (3) ways you could have related differently to have ensured a smoother relationship. (Your answer may include; being more patient with him or her; do not make reference to past issues of differences when things go wrong; seek to understand

his or her point of view, and then take him or her on a journey to your point of view, etc.)

a. ....
b. ....
c. ....

13

The Law of Natural Effect

The hard way is not always the only way.

Falacy	If it is not difficult, it is not worth it.
Fact	There are people God has positioned to love us for who we are. All we need do is to reciprocate. The more of such people we are able to keep around us, the less difficult life will be for us.
Basic Truth	When it comes to true love, the hard way is not the only way, and more often, the hard is not the way at all. Most people often experience heart breaks because they set their heart on loving people who do not even know they exist. Only people who love you, will give you the emotional support required to create a suitable psychological environment you need to succeed in life. It is your responsibility to look for someone who will love you or at least generously reciprocate your love. If you like to always play it the hard way, you may never find love.
Required	Seek those who naturally love you and don't ever let them go.

Question for Reflection

1. Write down, at least, three (3) qualities you will find in people who value you. (Your answer may include; speak up for you in your absence; enjoy spending time with you; easily renders to help when you are in need, except when you have abused their usefulness, etc.)

   a. ....
   b. ....
   c. ....

14

The Law of Stability

Consistency commands respect.

Falacy

You can get into a relationship and break up at will. You have nothing to lose.

Fact

For every break up, you lose something. Sometimes, something so big that you may never want to relate again.

Basic Truth

Be careful before you get too intimate with a person or group. Check for a person's level of stability before you start relating freely with the person. People who are easily angered, love money, argue over trivial matters, enjoy undue competition, tell lies, are bossy, tribalistic or fanatical may be unstable in relationships.

We must understand, no man is born stable, and educational pursuits do not guarantee stability, either. Growth and stability is a deliberate achievement. You must take the initiative; stability comes with a great deal of personal effort. You must be tactful; listen to people, be patient and respond to them objectively. Avoid destructive attitudes. Seek to give people all the help they may need—be useful. Over look offences; forgive and forget.

Do these things long enough and people will consider you someone they can count on. Someone they trust enough to listen to, because stability commands respect and makes you a reliable person.

Required

Work on yourself daily, strive to be more understanding and your relationship with people will be more stable.

Question for Reflection

1. Express your feelings about your experience with the loss of a loved one or a broken relationship (with someone you still care about).

   ....
   ....
   ....
   ....
   ....
   ....

2. Write down five (5) factors to consider before going into or initiating a new relationship. (Check content for hints)

   a. ....
   b. ....
   c. ....
   d. ....
   e. ....

15

The Law of The Rough Road

There is no easy ride in any relationship.

Falacy	Good relationship is supposed to be without conflict.
Fact	Conflict is inevitable in any relationship. Conflict tests our resolve in a relationship.
Basic Truth	Frankly, we all want a peaceful and an understanding friend. One who condones our excesses and covers the gaps for our weaknesses. True friends may be that good but it does not stop conflict from emerging. There is no perfect relationship.

People are different. Our personal history, nature, ambition, passion and lifestyles differ. A very small difference between us and our friends, teams or spouses is enough to create a huge gap or misunderstanding. You cannot be like someone else and this difference may sometimes create conflict.

However, as human being we are a work in progress towards perfection and maintaining cordial relationship. When you are wrong be humble enough to admit it and apologize, but when your friend is wrong, show understanding, since it is established no man is perfect. You may even forgive him even before he renders any apology. Since conflict is inevitable in every relationship, patience is, therefore, key in achieving peace during rough times and relationship success.

Required

In conflict show understanding; when at an advantage, be merciful and ready to forgive.

Questions for Reflection

1. In every relationship, no matter how good, ... is inevitable.

2. Mention three (3) factors that may lead to conflict in relationship.

    a. ....
    b. ....
    c. ....

3. .... is key in achieving relationship success.

(Check content for the hints)

16

The Law of Symbiosis

Relationship benefits all.

Falacy	If you are too good people will always take advantage of you.
Fact	Whatever good thing you do for people, you do for youself.
Basic Truth	When you are determined to lead a successful life, being good to people must become your lifestyle. We only relate with people by what we share with or give to them but not what we hold back. Anything you hold back from a person for selfish reason, does not impact positively on your relationship with that person. If you hold back too many things from a person, your relationship with that person will suffer harm and die off.

However, it pays to be generous; it pays to relate well with people. For all we give to people are never lost but are investment for our own future gain.

Let me share this testimony of a young man called Tobi. Tobi was already an orphan |

in his first year in college. He had to go through college without financial support from his parents.

In his fourth and final year in college, it appeared Tobi will not graduate, because his academic and financial needs escalated. Fortunately, Mr. Badmus, who greatly benefited from the generosity of Tobi's mother, paid him a visit. At his departure he handed Tobi some money, without him making any demand. The money was enough to help him complete his registration and clearance, and was able to graduate with his course mates.

Relationship is the shield of the wise. Fools walk alone and suffer harm.

Required

Support people when they need help and appreciate generously when people show you kindness.

Questions for Reflection

1. .... must be a lifestyle when you are determined to live a successful life.

2. We relate with people by what we ....

3. State why it pays to relate well with people.

   ....
   ....
   ....

4. "Relationship is the shield of the wise." Those who reject this truth are ....

(Check content for the hints)

17

The Law of Relative Balance

People relate with you in the way you position yourself to relate with them.

Falacy	People are supposed to relate with you in the same manner.
Fact	People relate with you, in the manner you present yourself to them.
Basic Truth	We do not relate with people in the same way, but in the manner in which they present themselves to us. It, therefore, follows that if you present yourself in a different way to the same person, he will start relating with you differently.

People have some basic assumptions about you. Your actions, interactions and reactions validate or annul such assumptions. On 22nd January, 1916, the Chicago Tribune published an article which libeled Henry Ford as the enemy of the state and a man incapable of thought as to know the "ignominy of his performance".

Does this article have an effect on the

people? Yes, it does strongly; even though the truth was not authenticated, some people took it badly because Ford was a public figure. One Dr. J. M. Postle, after reading the attitude of Henry Ford as presented by the Tribune, took his Ford car to the blacksmith shop and pounded every trace of the name of Ford off his car.

On 23rd June, 1916, the Unity Press wrote an article in the defense of Ford. However, the attack on Ford's personality was so strong that it would require much more than a single article to redeem his public image. Ford sued the Chicago Tribune but it took three years before the case would receive a hearing and the court proceedings took more than two months.

In one of the court's proceedings the Tribune lawyer, Stevenson Elliot, cross-examined Ford to prove their claim was true. Ford was asked a range of questions, ranging from "Who was Benedict Arnold?" through to "How many soldiers did the British send over to America to put down the Rebellion of 1776?" His answers show complete ignorance of public knowledge.

Henry Ford's response as the questions get more and more outrageous and irritating demonstrated his ability to regroup. He pointed his finger at the lawyer who asked the questions, and spoke in a manner that floored the court and ended the hearing in an instant. "If I should really want to answer the foolish question you have just asked, or any of the other questions you have been asking me, let me remind you that I have a row of electric push-buttons on my desk, and by pushing the right button, I can summon to my aid men who can answer any question I desire to ask concerning the business to which I am devoting most of my efforts. Now, will you kindly tell me, why I should clutter up my mind with general knowledge, for the purpose of being able to answer questions, when I have men around me who can supply any knowledge I require?"

With this response he stopped the fun of the lawyer and silenced every one laughing him to scorn. There was silence in the court. Ford's response knocked the questioner cold and confused many of the jury.

That is the law of the relative balance in operation. When Henry Ford's responses lacked substance, the lawyer took the driver's seat, but when he replied soundly, gravity shifted in his favour. People relate with you as you are; when you change, you challenge them to relate with you differently.

Required

Present yourself to any man, in the manner you want the person to relate with you, it does not matter how you had related with him previously. It is never too late to change people's opinion of you.

Questions for Reflection

1. In what manner do we relate with people?

   ....
   ....
   ....

2. State what a man can do to change the way people relate with him.

   ....
   ....
   ....

3. You must present yourself to people in the manner in which you want them to ....

   (Check content for the hints)

18

The Law of the Coloured Glass

Love beautifies the way we see life.

Falacy: The days of love are long gone.

Fact: Love colours the way we see people and challenges us to make the sacrifices that improves our team and partners.

Basic Truth: You must have heard the saying that, "Love can never fail". This is very correct, because love colours the way we see people. When we are living the life of love, it challenges us to make sacrifices that improve our teams or partners. Love helps us to see the good in people and look beyond what we can get from them. It helps us to believe our little efforts are making a big difference in the life of someone.

The life of Apostle Paul and Mother Teresa, whose love for people create a wave of influence that outlasted their existence, made it clear that a life of love is a high quality life.

Love is indeed timeless. Live it and your life along with that of those around you, will be more beautiful.

| Required | Always make effort to put smiles on other people's face. |

Questions for Reflection

1. .... beautifies the way we see life.

2. Love helps us to belief our little effort is..

3. Why is love said to be "timeless"?

   ....
   ....
   (Check content for the hints)

19

The Law of Influence

Change is always under influence.

Falacy	We can get along fine with people without them changing us.
Fact	We are a product of our environment. This environment is made up of two categories of people: those with whom we spend most of our time and those we value.
Basic Truth	Unfortunately, when it comes to environmental influences, the strongest influence is often the negative. It is easier to carry on with a negative attitude than to adjust to positive.

When I was a boy, a certain woman brought her brother who she believed was a strong Christian to come live with them. She expected her brother to serve as a source of strong positive influence to her husband, who was a drunkard. It happened that her husband was a stronger influence than her brother. Consequently, the brother gave in to alcoholism and his life went down the hill worse than that of her husband. The brother eventually died of alcoholism.

Do not joke with the company of people with negative attitudes. They can turn you into what you do not want to be, and make everything good about you to become a thing of the past. The Bible warns, "Evil communication corrupts good manners". When you keep hanging around people with bad attitude, you are preparing yourself for a bad change. Not even Prophet Isaiah, in the Bible, was spared (Isaiah 6:5).

However, we have influence over those who hold us in high esteem. Those who value you are easily influenced by your actions. When you are in trouble, it is not wise to seek out new people for help but first consider people who are concerned about our wellbeing. Again, when you want to start up a new career, people who value you will give the platform to start and succeed. Therefore, relationship increases people's influence. The more you connect and relate with people the greater your ability to make them do things for you.

Required

Take a look around you. Evaluate the people whom you are constantly in contact with and make the decision to distant yourself from those who do not uplift your spirit, encourage you to be a better person or desire to mentor you to grow into your full potential.

Questions for Reflection

1. Mention two (2) people who can easily influence you.

   a. ....
   b. ....

2. List two (2) people you must avoid in life.

   a. ....
   b. ....

3. Mention three (3) positive influences you need in life for a desired change.

   a. ....
   b. ....
   c. ....
   (Check content for the hints)

20

The Law of Investment

When we love we invest; when we invest we tend to love.

Falacy	What we invest does not show how much we care.
Fact	"For where your treasure is, there will your heart be also" (Matthew 6:21, King James Version).
Basic Truth	Relationship is the greatest investment any man can ever have. This is because, it yields the greatest returns—Loyalty. When you continue to invest your time, money and emotions in relationship, eventually it (investing in relationship) becomes a part of you; you will be pleasantly shocked by what people will be willing to do for you. I was in church one day, the woman sitting next to me needed a pen, so I offered her mine and asked her not to bother returning it. She gave me something bigger, because she was moved by my willingness to invest. Investing in people may not always work that way, but it always yields the greatest returns.

Investing in people does not only affect how much they love us but it also increases our affection for them. The more you invest in a person the more you tend to love that person. I have heard people say that they have never fallen in love before. This is because they have not cultivated the habit of investing in people and relationship.

Why do you think most parents have great love for their children? They have invested so much in the relationship with their children. Investing in people triggers our emotional attachment towards them. The more you invest in a relationship, the more you become emotionally attached. To control your emotion towards a person, control your investment in the relationship with that person—To sever a relationship, stop investing in the relationship; so also, to improve relationship, increase your investment in that relationship.

When we are addicted to investing in people, where ever we turn, we will find people willing to follow us, or at least walk with us. Investing in people and relationship commands people's loyalty.

Note the following when you invest in a relationship:

- Investing in a relationship must be deliberate; not by mistake.
- Investing in a relationship must be continuous; do not stop.
- Investing in a relationship must be consistent; make it meaningful.

Required	– Investing in a relationship must be purposeful; have a target. – Investing in a relationship must be affectionate; how you do it matters. – Investing in a relationship must sometimes be sacrificial; it matters most when it hurts. Give your time, words, materials, money and yourself; give whatever it takes to make people you care about get better. Command loyalty!

Questions for Reflection

1. .... is the greatest investment anyone can ever have.

2. Investing in people does not only affect how much they love us, but it also ....

3. Why do you think most parents have great love for their children?

   ....
   ....

4. When we are addicted to investing in people, where ever we turn, we will find people willing to follow us, or at least walk with us. True/False

5. Mention five (5) things you must bear in mind (note) when relating with people.

   a. ....
   b. ....

c. ....
d. ....
e. ....
(Check content for answers)

21

The Law of Authority

God authorized you to love and express it.

Falacy	Only those that are favoured by life have the right to love.
Fact	Everyone can and has the right to love and show it.
Basic Truth	According to the scriptures, "He that loveth not knowth not God for God is love" (1 John 4:8, King James Version). This makes it clear that love is not only in your nature, as it is in God's nature, but that God expects you to express this love. Independent of your personal history, education or family culture, you can feel and express love. Moreover, just as you have the right to love and show it, you also have the right to be loved. Do not cage your destiny, love is your right. Live it!
Required	Remember, you have the right to live the highest quality of life possible—which is love. Dare to love!

Questions for Reflection

1. You are authorized by God to love and express it. True/False.

2. List three (3) factors limiting people from freely expressing love.

   a. ....
   b. ....
   c. ....
   (Check content for the hints)

22

The Law of Identity

Relationship defines people.

Falacy	You do not need people in your life; you just have to be yourself.
Fact	If you do not have people in your life, you cannot tell whether you are bad or good. In fact, it is most likely that you are bad.
Basic Truth	Relationship gives you identity. People are defined by how much they are valued by the members of the group they belong. Relationship is of great importance to us. It sometimes gives us reason to win, stand for what we belief and live. We want to know and understand ourselves, and relationship helps in accomplishing that. We are positive identity loving creatures. We want to be a strong force; and may sometimes not accept anything that will make us feel anything less. Actually, we want to feel good about ourselves, and when we find ourselves in the company of those who are not interested in relating with us or who do not value us we feel terrible, because our identity is challenged.

Staying around people, who love or value us, strengthens our identity. It gives us courage to face our fears; it raises our spirits to take risks and helps us to be our very best. Unfortunately, sometimes people who love us may hurt us if we are trailing the wrong path. However, if a person loves or truly values you, he will encourage you to take the right steps and give some incentive to help you achieve this.

Required

Stay in the company of people who value you and define you positively.

Questions for Reflection

1. People define themselves by how much they are valued by ....
   ....

2. In what situation is a person's identity said to be challenged?

   ....
   ....

3. Mention one (1) thing which, certainly, strengthens our identity.

   ....
   ....

   (Check content for the hints)

23

The Law of Flexibility

No relationship can work if people involved are unwilling to grow.

Falacy	People, who love you, will continue to show you love, no matter what.
Fact	To make people continue to show you love, you must respond creatively in being lovable. Always think of different ways to show or appreciate love.
Basic Truth	You desire a spouse or a good friend, wishing the person will come along and make you a better person, as you often see in movies. Therefore, you package yourself well. Someone comes around because you look attractive. Unfortunately, the attitude is out of place. You nag at every mistake, and expect the person to forgive all your inadequacy simply because you said, "I'm sorry". You are selfish but you expect the person to be selfless—in the name of love. The person gets tired and leaves. This happens with one, then another and then another. You conclude that you would never find love, because it does not exist. That is the situation of many.

To be loved, you must be lovable; demonstrate understanding and flexibility. You must make it easy to be loved. You have to be willing to get better with a relationship; anything that will not help the relationship to grow, has to go if you want the relationship to work. Adopt what is good about the other person and make yourself better for the relationship. Encourage the other person to improve for the sake of the relationship. If they are not willing to, walk away and seek love somewhere else.

The good news is, if you are flexible (that is, growing), you will not only find love, but also good people who will help you succeed in life. However, if you are rigid (that is, unwilling to change or get better), even bad people will not be comfortable around you, because even they are on the lookout for the good guys.

Required

In the pursuit of successful relationships, we must be willing to learn, and learning cannot be achieved without being flexible. This flexibility helps us to be open to new knowledge and more creative way of showing and reciprocating love.

Questions for Reflection

1. To make people continue to show you love, you must respond

....

2. To find good people who will help you succeed in life, you must

   ....

3. Mention one (1) thing that brings even a good relationship to an end, while the people relating still live.

   ....
   ....
   (Check content for the hints)

24

The Law of Sanity

You cannot be sane if you maintain unhealthy relationship.

Falacy Hanging around dangerous people will protect me from harm.

Fact Harmful people are selfish and often hurt people closest to them.

Basic Truth Keeping relationship with unhealthy or harmful people is unhealthy. More so, not all relationship involving good people are healthy.

The following may give rise to unhealthy relationship:

- When the person occupying a position that influences the lives of others in an organization is unstable, the relationship within the system will be unhealthy.
- When you are not getting along well with someone determined to be intimate with you, even though they appear to be good, the relationship will be unhealthy.

- When it is obvious your partner is a negative or bad person, the result is unhealthy relationship, no matter how hard you try.
- When the person you consider your friend, does not believe in you or your vision, the relationship cannot be healthy.
- When people you count on change for the worse and become unreliable, the relationship will become unhealthy.

All unhealthy relationships affect our psychological being. If you stay too long under the influence of an unhealthy relationship, your sanity will be affected.

Required **Avoid unhealthy relationships.**

Questions for Reflection

1. All unhealthy relationships affect our ....

2. Your sanity will be affected if you stay too long under the influence of ....

3. List four (4) instances that may give rise to unhealthy relationship.

   ....
   ....
   ....
   ....

   (Check content for the hints)

The Laws of Relationship • 59

25

The Law of Intimacy

People in intimate relationship share and keep secrets.

Falacy	It does not take more than ten minutes to know a person.
Fact	It may take quite a long time and high level of intimacy to understand and know a person.
Basic Truth	People have deep secrets they cannot share with anyone except people intimate with them. Intimacy is not cheap. It comes at a very high price. The prices are time and respect we invest into the relationship with people. Until you pay these prices consistently over time, people are not going to let down their guards.

Sometimes, a man may die with the burden they bear or the treasure at their disposal, because they cannot find someone willing to pay the price for intimacy.

Elisha, the great prophet, carried the anointing transferred to him by his master Elijah, at Elijah's departure, because he paid the price for intimacy. However, Elisha died with the burden of not having anyone willing to be intimate enough to receive the anointing. It was quite unfortunate that Gehazi, the closest person to him, chose the benefits of the anointing over intimate relationship with his master. His greed got the better of him and brought leprosy upon him and his generation.

Required

Give everything to stay close not only to those you value, but also to those who value you.

Questions for Reflection

1. List two (2) prices you must pay to achieve intimacy with a person you value.

   ....
   ....

2. State a condition, in relation to intimacy, when a person will not mind to die with the burden he or she is bearing.

   ....

3. It takes a .... and high level of .... to understand and know a person.

   (Check content for the hints)

26

The Law of the Open Door

Close the door to your past before it consumes or destroys you.

Falacy	Old ways of life and relationship fade away with time.
Fact	If you keep the door opened to past relationship and ways of life, you are leaving an in-road to the old life, thereby putting your present and future relationship at risk.
Basic Truth	Most people handle relationship carelessly. Our relationship with people do not always end when we say so, but when there is a mutual agreement or understanding by all parties involved to bring it to an end. Thinking we have autonomy to relate freely, make us end relationship without considering the pains it causes to the other person(s).

Sometimes people are badly hurt when their feelings are toiled with. When this happens, people dissatisfied try to get even by being vengeful and may seek the slightest opportunity to wreak havoc.

Moreover, each door we leave open affects

us emotionally. With each door left opened, a person's emotional state is disturbed and with too many doors opened to past relationships, a person may change from good to bad. If these doors stay opened for far too long, everything good about a person might be destroyed.

Imagine how you will feel when someone calls off a good business deal or love relationship—it hurts! Many problems may come from not closing doors to past relationships.

For your own good, it is wise you forgive people who hurt you. However, do not expect people to forgive you without making effort to close the door to a past relationship, appropriately.

The question is; how do I close the door?

Whether it is business or love relationship, the requirement is the same. Allow relationship to linger on for some time, while reducing commitment gradually until the other party reduces his emotional investment. Then you can apologize most sincerely and may also give gifts or a sum of money as compensation. Compensatory business may also help.

He that makes the move to end a relationship closes the door.

Required Kill interest before you walk away. Ensure that every closed door remains shut.

Questions for Reflection

1. People are careless with the way they handle relationship because of the wrong assumption that

   ....

2. List three (3) practical steps to take in order to close the door to past relationship.

   ....
   ....
   ....

   (Check content for hints)

27

The Law of Reconciliation

A once beautiful but battered relationship can be rebuilt.

Falacy	If a person truly loves me, he must be ready to forgive me whether I ask for forgiveness or not—Things always smoothen up themselves.
Fact	When you make a good relationship become sour, do not assume that the relationship will smoothen itself out, reconcile.
Basic Truth	Every relationship that has gone sour can be sweetened again, if one reconciles appropriately. Peter denied Jesus three times but reconciled and was forgiven. The prodigal son returned home after he had squandered his portion of his parent's asset, fell to his father's feet and asked to only be a servant, since he had abused his position as a son. On seeing his sincerity, his father forgave him and restored him, as a son. Judas Iscariot, on the other hand, betrayed Jesus, but failed to reconcile, rather he went and committed suicide.

To reconcile is to put things in order with the aim of recovering or sustaining a relationship.

We are not perfect. We make mistakes in relationships, but we can get back our relationships by making appreciable effort. Yet many people neglect this great opportunity to make their relationship as beautiful as they once were. It is not a bad thing for the person who loves more to make the first move, but it is the responsibility of the one who has done the harm to reconcile. To reconcile, you must forgive yourself, swallow your pride and ask for forgiveness. There is every chance that you will be forgiven and the relationship will be great again, if you ask in humility and sincerity.

Required

If a sour relationship was once beautiful, it can be beautiful again—reconcile.

Questions for Reflection

1. When a person loves you, he or she will always be willing to forgive you whether you do the right thing or not. True/False

2. List three (3) steps involved in reconciliation.

   ....
   ....
   ....
   (Check content for the hints)

28

The Law of Persistence

Love never gives up.

Falacy	Once things are tough, pull out.
Fact	When the hard way becomes the only way, resilience becomes the most required virtue.
Basic Truth	Sometimes things may not go as planned and winning the heart of the people we need may become tough. Then our resilience is tested. How strong our desire is, will be revealed by the extent to which we are persistent. Most things you desire will not come to you until your resolve is tested.

Teju was of age to marry, and she had hopes to marry a man who truly loves her. However, she had six suitors proposing marriage to her at the time. Judging by their actions and words, Teju was convinced that all suitors were serious and determined, this made her confused. To clear her confusion, she sought counsel from the Pastor of her church. The pastor gave her a simple suggestion, "Tell them that you intend to do your Master's Degree and then, your Doctorate before you will be prepared to settle down". She took the advice seriously. Told the six men what the pastor said she should tell them. They all disappeared, and this gave room for the real man to come along later on. Persistence in relationship is a strong demonstration of love.

Your persistence can make any man alter his resolve, whether in business or love relationship. You can make any man change his mind, if you hold out long enough.

> "Saying, There was in a city a judge, which feared not God, neither regarded man: And there was a widow in that city; and she came unto him, saying, Avenge me of mine adversary. And he would not for a while: but afterward he said within himself, Though I fear not God, nor regard man; Yet because this widow troubleth me, I will avenge her, lest by her continual coming she weary me" (Luke 18:2-5, King James Version).

Required To show your desire is sincere, you must persist.

Questions for Reflection

1. What is the most required virtue when the hard way becomes the only way?

2. You must .... to show your desire is sincere.

3. Recall how persistence has once helped you achieve something you desire. Briefly narrate the story.

....
....
....
....

Apply this principle to your relationship.
(Check content for hints)

29

The Law of Affinity Between Opposite Sexes

The opposite sex attracts and can easily appeal to a person's emotion.

Falacy — We relate in the same way with all sexes.

Fact — Relating to the same sex appeals more to our reasoning, but relating to the opposite sex appeals more to our emotions.

Basic Truth — Although, it is true that some people prefer dealing with the same sex as themselves, it is easier for the opposite sex to trigger a person's emotion. Some companies have been able to seal more business deals by applying this law. They simply allow the opposite sex to deal with the client.

People have gotten unexpected job offers and gained unimaginable favour simply by appealing to the emotion of the opposite sex. For instance, if a lady tells a man that he is handsome, the man tend to feel good about himself and may even be temporarily thrown off balance. The same thing goes from a man to a lady.

Affinity with the opposite sex also account for why people often do well when they take up a career dominated by the opposite sex.

Three elements play crucial role in affinity with the opposite sex: appearance (neatness), tone of voice and content of words. If the mix is right affinity is sure, but if not the opposite is inevitable.

However, if affinity with the opposite sex is not well managed, it may lead to immoral relationship.

Required

To gain advantage in relationship with the opposite sex, compliment them. Seek to strike the cord of emotion.

Questions for Reflection

1. Mention five (5) good things about your spouse.

   ....
   ....
   ....
   ....
   ....

   (Always let them know you see these things in them.
   You may also do the same to your good friends or client.)

30

The Law of Emergency

Everyman for himself; God for us all.
—Joy Chia

Falacy	Friends must depend on each other in all situations.
Fact	When a man depends on another in the same emergency situation as himself; catastrophe always compound.
Basic Truth	In an emergency situation the problem is the same but the approach must be individualistic.

    John and Rock are good friends working in the same organization. It happened that the organization was downsizing and they were both affected. The issue was an emergency for these friends. Rock knew one of the members of the Board of Trustees who can reverse management decision in his favour. He informed John, his friend, about his decision to see someone who can help him. On hearing this, John caught a glim of hope and intends to seize the opportunity to retain his job and so, he pleaded with his friend that he may go with him.

They both went to see this influential man in his office. He welcomed them both and offer them seat. Rock tabled his problem and entreated that he and his friend be reinstated. In disappointment, the man replied, "If it had been only you that required my help that would have been easy, but now that you are not the only one involved there is nothing I can do about it."

Wisdom did not avail Rock to solve his problem before offering to help his friend. Although, he had influence big enough to solve his problem, he allowed his friend to ruin his chance. It is good to be good, but when in an emergency situation, wisdom require that you look out for yourself before attempting to help another.

Required

In an emergency, everyone affected must depend on their individual influence to solve their problems. If you have none, depend on God—for there is no influence bigger than God.

Questions for Reflection

1. Have you ever been in an emergency situation before? Yes/No.

2. If you are in an emergency situation and you have no one to turn to or anyone with an influence big enough to solve your problem, who can you turn to

(Check content for hints)

31

The Law of the Boundary

Knowing your place, with God and men, relating within its confinement and navigating to the greatest height of acceptability, is wisdom.

Falacy	With intimate friends, there are no boundaries.
Fact	Boundaries exist and are the distinguishing elements in relationship. Relating within acceptable boundaries show respect for one another.
Basic Truth	In every relationship there are boundaries. People have dos and don'ts. The dos of a person are what he expects from others – what is acceptable by him – and the don'ts are boundaries that must not be crossed. A person's ability to adjust his boundaries and accommodate different people from different walks of life at various levels, allows him to assume certain social niche, at the same time. The way a man relates with one person, differs from the way he relates with another. These relationships can range from relating as an employee, with another a pastor, with another a son, with

another a brother, with another a friend, with another a husband and with another a father. The man occupies different places in the lives of these people and he is required to play different role and relate differently with each of them. If he acts contrary to what is expected of him, he has crossed the line.

When we cross the line too often, we lose the respect people have for us. If you learn to relate within defined or acceptable boundaries people will hold you in high esteem or at least relate with you respectfully.

A number of factors guide our boundaries with people:

Our Nature

Our personality make-ups are very important in guiding our relationship and determining our boundaries with people. These personalities define the type and number of people with which we can relate or be intimate and the amount of time we like to spend alone.

Our Experience

As we grow older, while relating with people, we discover that we are compatible with fewer and fewer. Usually we expect older people to be wise, but experiences don't always come with age, rather with exposure. These exposures might be personal encounters or experiences of others.

Past Encounter

When you cross a boundary with a person, there may be no going back. If a person doesn't want you to cross a boundary, don't force it; it is possible that someone else has occupied the position you desire or that the person is not psychologically prepared to open up new relationships.

In addition, there are people who consider themselves too good to be intimate with you; you will do yourself good to avoid them, because they will always make effort to deflate yourself-confidence.

On the whole, consider this:-

- Everyman has his place,
- Everyman must know his place,
- Everyman must stay in his place,
- Everyman has to pay a higher price to be qualified for a higher place,
- It is your responsibility to define and occupy your place per time.

Required

Always define your boundary with people.

Questions for Reflection

1. List five of your don'ts

   ....
   ....
   ....
   ....
   ....

   When you relate with people remember they
   have their don'ts. Please, respect that.

32

The Law of Perpetuity

Excessive attachment always ends in pains.

Falacy	If he is mine, he will always be mine.
Fact	No mortal being will last forever, not even time which defines mortality.
Basic Truth	When you share mutual love or respect with another person, you want that relationship to last forever. Unfortunately, no mortal relationship will last forever.

Since nothing lasts forever, here are my advices on matters of relationship:

- **Don't wait till tomorrow:** If you love someone, express your love now. If you intend to give a gift, give it now. If you intend to render help, do it now even with your limited resources. If you want to spend time with the person(s) you love, do your best to make it happen as soon as possible (possibly make the visit right away). Waiting till tomorrow may just ruin that golden

opportunity to be happy or strengthen your relationship.
- **Enjoy the moment:** Give your heart and complete commitment to those you value. Live the day as if you have no access to another. In that way, when you are separated, for whatever reason, the cherished moment will be of great comfort, because you held nothing back.
- **Create events and activities with lasting effects:** When you share moments with those you cherished, do things that create lasting memories. Take time out to go to beautiful places, take snap shots and keep the pictures. Seek out opportunities to render valuable assistance and support. Make yourself available and valuable.
- **Accept reality:** Nothing lasts forever. Be ready to let go when the time is up. Don't stop your daughter or son from getting married. Don't resist your friend from going to college because you dread separation. Don't stop the people you value from seizing opportunity that will change their lives forever.

More often than not, separation offers some blessings, in that it can lead us to a beautiful path. It gives us the chance to progress to the next phase of our lives. So when the people you value are gone, be open to new relationship. Make new friends and acquaintances, for

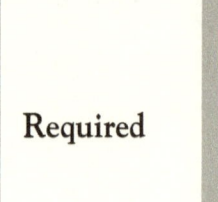

Required

it is a new phase of your life, providing you with the chance to grow stronger and wiser.

Always remember this: - You own no man and no man owns you. All souls belong to God.

Questions for Reflection

1. Since no mortal relationship will lasts forever, list at least four factors that must guide your every relationship.

   ....
   ....
   ....
   ....

   (Check content for hints)

33

The Law of Integrity

You cannot build a solid relationship on a faulty foundation.

Falacy	If you cannot tell lies, people won't love you.
Fact	Every relationship will be tested; only a true relationship will stand.
Basic Truth	We sometimes weaken our relationship with those we love by telling what we consider to be, "white lies". These lies seem harmless because, we mean well for those we love or we intend to cover our flaws in order to keep close to us those we value, but we have no control over their consequences.
	Telling lies to those we love does not strengthen the relationship for two reasons. The first is that you lie to those you love for selfish reasons. A lie protects self not the relationship, and as such weakens the relationship. Love rejoices in the truth but not in falsehood. Isaac lied to protect himself from being killed, even though the lie appeared necessary, it could have cost him his marriage (Genesis 26:7-10).

Secondly, you may lie to those you love to cover your flaws. This is often as a result of low self-esteem. When you want to be blameless, outstanding or appear perfect but fail to make corresponding effort to invest in yourself in order to grow up to such height. People who are attracted by this false personality get to know the truth when they get close and discover everything is a lie. These lies often hurt the person you love deeply and cause immediate termination of relationship.

Some people lie about their job to appear more important. They despise their little beginning in order to impress people. Some lie about their status in order to be accepted. Some black people get their skin toned to look like whites. In the end, they lose what is most important about them, their uniqueness or originality and becomes fake. All forms of falsehood are lack of integrity. Falsehood saps your inner strength; you will be nothing more than a surface personality and makes your relationship with people superficial.

There is no future for relationships built on falsehood—uphold your integrity.

Required

Questions for Reflection

1. There is no future for ....

2. Mention two (2) key reasons people tell lies.

   ....
   ....
   (Check content for the hints)

34

The Law of Legacy

You will be long remembered by what you handover to other generations.

Falacy

Once you are good and kind, many generations will remember you.

Fact

Whether good or bad, just or wicked, you will be forgotten as soon as the evidence of your existence is gone. Only your legacy will stand and live beyond generations.

Basic Truth

The people you have read about and all the stories of the great men you have ever heard are not the only most impactful people that ever lived, but the people who built an enduring legacy.

How were these people able to build a lasting legacy? They excelled at a field, handed a furnished structure to their protégés or family and put in place a system to ensure continuity of what they have built. Men and women who built lasting legacy first built up the idea and then the people, unified the people by common goals and motivate them by teaching them productive activities that will perpetuate the legacy as well as profit the person(s). Productive and profitable activities set men on fire.

Jesus is a perfect example of a person who built a lasting legacy. He first came with the ministry, commission twelve people, whom He called Apostles. These men knew Him, and understood what He stood for and represented. He invested in them individually.

He guided and sharpened the perspective of His Apostles. For instance, when they rejoiced that demons bow to the name of Jesus, he told them that they should rather rejoice that their names were written in the Book of Life.

After Jesus built his disciples, he united them. It is easy for a man to lose focus, but a group of people with common goals often inspire one another to stay on course.

Jesus sets his disciples on fire by guiding them through productive activities. He taught them to pray, depend on the Holy Spirit, share the Holy Communion, fellowship together, look out for one another and do several other productive activities, which are necessary to keep their faith alive.

Jesus ensured that his activities were documented for generations to come. He had us in mind when he did these. Written documents are more lasting legacy than spoken words. We never saw Jesus or any of His disciples but we got His messages, because they were written (John 20:31).

Required

To be long remembered build a lasting legacy.

Questions for Reflection

1. People are remembered because they ....

2. List five (5) steps Jesus took to build a lasting legacy.

   ....
   ....
   ....
   ....
   ....

   (Check content for hints)

35

The Law of Dignity

Honour is the pillar of marriage.

Falacy	If my spouse behaves well, then I will also behave well.
Fact	Marriage is a high-risk venture. There is every chance that it will not work if you solely depend on your spouse's honour.
Basic Truth	The success of any marriage depends on the honour of both parties involved; not only on the honour of either of them. This is why the marriage vow reads:

> ...for better for worse, in sickness and in health, till death do us part.

It is, therefore, obvious that any side of the coin is possible; things may get better or worse. If you depend on your spouse's honour only, your marriage will have more problems than it ordinarily would. You will give too much credence to frivolities and negative thoughts, which have the capacity to overwhelm you. And when these things happen, you will spend a lot of time and energy fighting to save your marriage or may give up and file for divorce.

The wife of Job left Job when he was very sick. She thought all would always be well, because Job was a godly man. But things did not turn out the way she expected. She asked Job to curse God and die. She walked out on her marriage and relationship with Job, when he needed her support the most. Honour makes you stick to your spouse, no matter the challenge. It validates your marriage. For without honour, marriage is hopeless.

Relationship has aura of dignity when the people involved uphold their individual honour.

Required

Always keep to your promises and uphold your vows; they dignify your relationship.

Questions for Reflection

1. On whose honour should your marriage depend?

   ....

2. .... validates your marriage.

3. State one (1) reason many marriages are not working today.

   ....

   (Check content for the hints)

36

The Law of Compatibility

Intimacy unveils our weaknesses.

Falacy	We can't be intimate, if we are not compatible.
Fact	Our distinct differences and non-compatibility always unearth what is lacking in our spouses.
Basic Truth	Non-compatibility is a normal phenomenon in very intimate relationships. One of such relationship is marriage. Marriages only work when people relate with understanding and put their differences aside—change for the sake of the marriage in order to build a good home.

People start having problems in their marriages when intimacy uncovers their weaknesses and that of their partners'. The marriage relationship continuum moves from intimacy through non-compatibility to compatibility. If people are willing to make positive changes, their marriage relationship moves from non-compatibility to compatibility, and then forging of a strong family bond. But, if people are unwilling to cross the hurdle of non-compatibility the relationship get sour, issues linger on until it finally collapses.

Everyone in a marriage relationship will at one time or another has to cross the hurdle of non-compatibility, if they are to forge a strong family bond.

The Marriage Continuum

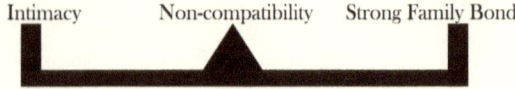

Reasons We Must Overcome Non-compatibility in Our Marriages

- **The society depends on the family:** The family plays a very big role in societal building. Parents must invest quality time in their children. Tell your children, your success stories and failures; share with them principles you have learnt from life. If you invest correctly and adequately your time in your children, individually and collectively, they will give you peace and you will provide the society valuable individuals capable of provoking and sustaining positive societal changes.

  The problem is, we love our children but we don't make the effort to overcome the non-compatibility that exist between us and our spouses, which robs us of the joy and inner peace required to impact positively on our children. The consequences are broken homes and destroyed destinies. If parents fail to overcome non-compatibility, their children will suffer setbacks in life or completely ruined destinies.

- **Our spouse and children are a great source of joy:** There is no better group with whom to spend wonderful moments other than our families. If we overcome the challenge of non-compatibility, we will build good homes that will be a source of great joy and inspiration, invariably the place to be.
- **Our families are our most reliable friends:** Most times, it is easier to get help from a family member than other people. If parents develop love at home, every member of the family becomes a reliable ally; someone that can be called upon in times of need. "A friend loves at all times, and a brother is born to share trouble." (Proverbs 17:17, God's Word Translation).

How to Overcome Non-compatibility in Marriage

- **Sacrifice:** One of the blessings of non-compatibility is that sacrifices are obvious. You and your spouse differ in many things like types of food you enjoy, activities you like to participate in, certain values, language, culture and many more. There is definitely something you like that your spouse doesn't like. So, if he or she goes out of her way to give you that thing special to you, respond in like manner —don't just say thank you, give something special in return.

- **Reward positive action:** You may have been seriously offended or deeply wounded but having a loving family is worth more than any pain you can ever bear. You may not get excited over a simple positive act from your spouse but for the sake of building your home, you have to respond positively. Nothing makes life more colourful than a loving family.
- **Be selfless:** According to John C. Maxwell, the root cause of bad attitude is selfishness. Selfishness places self ahead of others. It makes you desire happiness even if it will bring sorrow to another. There is hardly a home that can survive in a hostile environment controlled by selfishness. Spouses must do everything possible to avoid appearing selfish at any time.
- **Be patient:** We are human; we make mistakes, and therefore not perfect, and we are never going to be perfect. We must be ready to forgive and be patient with one and another, especially that someone committed to spending and investing their time in us. Always be kind with words— Show understanding, and remember, a gentle tongue can break the bone.
- **Give irresistible gifts:** There is a part of us that is childish. We can never grow out of certain habits or hobbies; hence there are certain gifts we never resist. It may be jewelries, parties, craving for attention, (men) teaming up with your spouse to do house chores, going out together to watch movies and so on. Learn how to trigger the

childish nature in your spouse and spice up your relationship.
- **Embrace the larger picture:** The world does not revolve around you. Sociologists tell us the most introverted of people will influence 10,000 others in an average lifetime. Think of the effect of your actions on your spouse and children and what type of influence they will have on people as a result of what you invest in your family.
- **Seek help:** When your marriage relationship is troubled you may need to seek the help of a marriage counselor. Your pastor, parents or a friend gifted with the ability to give sound counsel, can suffice in the absence of a counsellor.
- **Eliminate alternative(s):** Nothing fuels non-compatibility in marriage like alternatives. As long as you are seeing someone else or have eyes for someone other than your spouse, your marriage will not receive the attention and resources it deserves. Most conflicts between spouses arise when a person compares his or her spouse with another. If you really want the most peaceful life and home, you must take your eyes off other people, except your spouse. Be a one-man or one-woman person. Be determined to live your life with only your spouse and children.
- **Pray always:** Mr. and Mrs. Oliver's marriage had been going through turbulent times and something had to be done quickly to prevent it from hitting the rock.

Required

By a striking fortune, she stumbled across a story of a woman, who non-compatibility got the better of her marriage. Who, being short of options combated it in prayer. After about thirty days of consistent prayers, things changed and peace was restored to her home. Her faith was triggered by this testimony; she tendered her case before God in prayer and peace was restored in her home. If you have tried all and nothing worked, try this and you will see result. Demonstrating faith through prayer and fasting to God may be all you need to get back your life and marriage. As long as you are a praying family, you will be a united family. If God is in charge of your home, peace is a sure factor.

If other people's marriages are working yours can also work. You must be determined to overcome non-compatibility and forge a strong family bond.

Questions for Reflection

1. When do people start having problems in their marriages?

   ....

2. What hurdle must be crossed in order to forge a strong family bond in marriages?

   ....
   (Check content for hints)

37

The Law of Consistency

*The society can change, but the values that hold
a family together remains the same.*

Falacy	What once was, no longer is, even for the family.
Fact	Family values can never change—they are ageless.
Basic Truth	In the society, leaders can say one thing and do the direct opposite. Those who want to be good will be good. In the family it is not so. Parents must say and do the right things. Their words and deeds must be in synchrony. This is because their words and acts determine, largely, what children learn, their believe system and become in life. Parents must model love, hard work, truthfulness, courage (actions showing hope), integrity and faith in God. They must stand for what they believe, not only for their own good but also for the good of their children. Parents are not to just watch their children succeed, but also guide

Required

and push them to. They must encourage what they want to see in their children, in words and deeds.

When parents choose to be inconsistent, the family will be in disarray. When there are clear disparities between what parents say and do, the family will be divided. Each member of the family will seek his own value and patterns from an already decayed societal system.

When the family lays the foundation for strong and lasting relationship life, it infuses into the society people who can make positive fundamental changes. If the family fails to build up its members, the society is hopeless.

"Train up a child in the way he should go: and when he is old, he will not depart from it" **(Proverbs 22:6, King James Version).**

Questions for Reflection

1. Family values are ....

2. List five (5) family values.

   ....
   ....
   ....
   ....
   ....
   (Check content for hints)

38

Operating and Suspending Natural Laws

Obeying or breaking natural laws attract consequences that cannot be manipulated.

The laws of relationship are natural laws; they are not put in place by man. So also are the consequences; they cannot be manipulated by man. Laws exist in nature. Almost every existing law can be suspended by the operation of another law. In reality the law is not broken, but only temporarily suspended by putting in operation another law. However, if you suspend a law for far too long by the excessive operation of another law, the law in operation loses its effect on the law suspended and the law suspended is broken. Airplanes, for instance, may suspend the law of gravity by operating the law of aerodynamics, but this suspension is temporary, has it cannot stay air-borne forever without responding to the law of gravity, at some point in time. One of the dangers of breaking natural laws is that, they are followed by natural penalties, which may not seem immediately apparent until the situation is almost irredeemable. We must therefore understand and operate various laws, giving them their due places.

Breaking the Laws of Relationship have its Consequences

Moses (Exodus 2-3; Exodus 32:12-14; Deutronomy 1:13-14; Numbers 20:8-12)

Moses, one of the greatest leaders that ever lived, continuously suspends the law of clarity by operating the law of common language. The bible describes him has the meekest man on earth, in his days. Moses always finds a common ground with his people and was able to lead them all the way out of Egypt. However, Moses' suspension of the law clarity for far too long took its toll on him—he always waits until he can no longer bear things and then explode angrily—it cost him the Promised Land.

Lot (Genesis 12:4-5, 18:32-33; 19:12, 13, 24, 25 & 26)

Lot, Abraham's nephew, suspended the law of influence by operating the law of relative balance for far too long. The result is disastrous. He was certainly the most God fearing man in Sodom and Gomorrah. When the land experienced God's wrath due to the great height of wickedness of the people of the land, his righteousness only spared him, but he lost everything he had, even the most special person to him—his wife.

Samson (Judges 16)

Samson, like lot, took for granted the law of influence, compensating himself for his good work with Delilah, a harlot and arch enemy. Operating the law of sacrifice and responsibility towards his people, makes him felt so secured as to allow any kind of person into his life without him being influenced. Samson thought himself untouchable. But he was wrong; he had to pay with his life. You must choose with care the people around you. Do not cleave to or hang around people, who can add no value to you—people who don't add value to you, will make you less valuable.

We all have excessively suspended different laws and have carelessly broken others. We have suffered the consequences of our actions, and bore the pains of things and opportunities we have lost that can never be regained. It is time to start relating right and to start building lasting relationships and achieving worthwhile goals.

39

Remember the Golden Rule

Do unto others what you expect them to do unto you.

> *"Therefore all things whatsoever ye would that men should do to you, do ye even so to them: for this is the law and the prophets."* (Matthew 7:12, KJV).

Abraham Lincoln was a man from a humble background but with a great vision. One day, he walked 40 miles to listen to one of the best lawyers, known for his great oratory, who was to defend a client charged with murder. When the lawyer was done and on his way out, Lincoln met the lawyer, stretched out his hand and said, "I walked forty miles to hear you, and if I were to do it over, I would walk a hundred". Unfortunately for Lincoln, the man was too arrogant to consider him someone deserving his attention—the lawyer walked out on Lincoln without speaking a word.

When Lincoln became the president of the United States, this same great lawyer came to petition the president on behalf of a man condemned to death. Lincoln listened to what the lawyer had to say, after which he reminded the lawyer of his unwelcoming act at their first meeting before he signed the pardon. The lawyer was broken that he could only mutter a brief apology.

You must do unto others what you want others to do unto you. The Lawyer looked down on young Lincoln, but he had no power over the future. When Lincoln had the power to repay the Lawyer, he chose to forgive. The president, Abraham Lincoln, seized the opportunity to do things right. He simply did what he expected the lawyer to do to him, had roles been switched.

Be to others how you expect them to be in relating with you and do to them what you will expect them to do to you.

There are, at least, five ways you want others to treat you:

- You want others to encourage you;
- You want others to appreciate you;
- You want others to forgive you;
- You want others to listen to you;
- You want others to be patient and make the effort to understand you.

Go and do likewise.

Strive to apply the golden rule to your relationship and in the end, you will be satisfied that you led a fulfilled life and like Jesus, you can take a deep breath and say, "It is finished", or like Apostle Paul, "I have fought a good fight…"

> *"If you really keep the royal law stated in Scripture, "Love your neighbor as yourself," you are doing well."* (James 2:8, King James Version).

About the Author

An educationist, theologian, and most importantly, good student of relationship, Eric O. Enejoh is endowed with the unique ability to equip people and help them find their places in life. He is based in Nigeria with his wife, Favour, and two children.

www.ingramcontent.com/pod-product-compliance
Lightning Source LLC
Chambersburg PA
CBHW031924240526
45464CB00022B/788